A Cultural-Historical Approach towards Pedagogical Transitions

Transitions in Childhood and Youth

Series Editors: Marilyn Fleer, Mariane Hedegaard and Megan Adams

The series brings together books that present and explore empirical research and theoretical discussion on the themes of childhood and youth transitions. Special attention is directed to conceptualizing transitions holistically so that societal, institutional and personal perspectives are featured within and across books. Key to the series is presenting the processes of transitions between practices or activities and their relationship to the person, in contexts such as intergenerational family practices, the processes of care, a person's development, the learning of individuals, groups and systems, personal health, labour and birthing and ageing. All books take a broad cultural-historical approach of transitions across a range of contexts and countries and when brought together in one place make an important contribution to better understanding transitions globally. Books in the Transitions in Childhood and Youth series offer an excellent resource for postgraduate students, researchers, policy writers and academics.

Advisory Board:
Anne Edwards (University of Oxford, UK)
Fernando Gonzalez-Rey (University Center of Brasília, Brazil)
Jennifer Vadeboncoeur (University of British Columbia, Canada)
Anna Stetsenko (City University of New York, USA)

Also available in the series:
Children's Transitions in Everyday Life and Institutions, edited by Mariane Hedegaard and Marilyn Fleer
Developmental Dynamics and Transitions in High School, Sofie Pedersen
Qualitative Studies of Exploration in Childhood Education: Cultures of Play and Learning in Transition, edited by Marilyn Fleer, Mariane Hedegaard, Elin Eriksen Ødegaard and Hanne Værum Sørensen
Supporting Difficult Transitions: Children, Young People and Their Carers, edited by Mariane Hedegaard and Anne Edwards

Forthcoming in the series:
Exploring Young Children's Agency in Everyday Transitions, Pernille Juhl

A Cultural-Historical Approach towards Pedagogical Transitions

Transitions in Post-Apartheid South Africa

Joanne Hardman

BLOOMSBURY ACADEMIC
LONDON • NEW YORK • OXFORD • NEW DELHI • SYDNEY

BLOOMSBURY ACADEMIC
Bloomsbury Publishing Plc
50 Bedford Square, London, WC1B 3DP, UK
1385 Broadway, New York, NY 10018, USA
29 Earlsfort Terrace, Dublin 2, Ireland

BLOOMSBURY, BLOOMSBURY ACADEMIC and the Diana logo are trademarks of Bloomsbury Publishing Plc

First published in Great Britain 2023
Paperback edition published 2024

Copyright © Joanne Hardman, 2023

Joanne Hardman has asserted her right under the Copyright, Designs and Patents Act, 1988, to be identified as Author of this work.

For legal purposes the Acknowledgements on pp. xiii–xiv constitute an extension of this copyright page.

Series Design by Joshua Fanning
Cover image: © subman/ Getty Images

All rights reserved. No part of this publication may be reproduced or transmitted in any form or by any means, electronic or mechanical, including photocopying, recording, or any information storage or retrieval system, without prior permission in writing from the publishers.

Bloomsbury Publishing Plc does not have any control over, or responsibility for, any third-party websites referred to or in this book. All internet addresses given in this book were correct at the time of going to press. The author and publisher regret any inconvenience caused if addresses have changed or sites have ceased to exist, but can accept no responsibility for any such changes.

A catalogue record for this book is available from the British Library.

A catalog record for this book is available from the Library of Congress.

ISBN:	HB:	978-1-3501-6470-3
	PB:	978-1-3502-2695-1
	ePDF:	978-1-3501-6471-0
	eBook:	978-1-3501-6472-7

Series: Transitions in Childhood and Youth

Typeset by Integra Software Services Pvt. Ltd.

To find out more about our authors and books visit www.bloomsbury.com and sign up for our newsletters.

For my mother Valerie-Anne, my father Peter and my daughter Bella, with deep love and gratitude.

Contents

List of Figures	viii
List of Tables	ix
Preface	x
Series Editors' Foreword	xii
Acknowledgements	xiii

1 Introduction   1

Part 1   Context

2 Vygotsky's Pedagogical Legacy in the Twenty-first Century   7
3 Curriculum Transitions: 1994–2019   37
4 Pedagogical Transitions: 1994–2019   57

Part 2   Cultural Historical Approaches to Pedagogy

5 School Science for Eight-year-olds: A Cultural Historical Analysis   77
6 Hedegaard's 'Double-Move' in Teaching in Grade 2   97

Part 3   Towards a Pedagogy of Inclusion

7 New Technology, New Pedagogy? Investigating Shifts in Pedagogy in Disadvantaged Grade 6 Mathematics Classrooms   115
8 The Transition from Face-to-face to Computer-based Pedagogy   133
9 Conclusion: The Case for Hedegaard's Radical Local Model of Pedagogy   155

Appendix A	170
Appendix B	180
Appendix C	187
Notes	191
References	196
Index	214

Figures

2.1	Concept development	18
4.1	A change from fundamental to progressive pedagogy	67
5.1	Analytic indicators: 'Wild animals'	88
6.1	Pedagogy in practice	106
7.1	An activity system	117
9.1	Hardman's conceptual figure	158
9.2	The double-move in pedagogy	160
9.3	Decolonial inclusive pedagogical model	167
A.B1	Hardman's conceptual figure	181
A.B2	The double-move in pedagogy	183
A.B3	Diagram: The mediating interaction	183

Tables

5.1	Attributes of a simple scientific concept	84
5.2	Rating scale for simple scientific concepts	87
5.3	Farm animals: Old MacDonald and his domesticated animals	89
5.4	Wild animals	92
5.5	Beginning knowledge in CAPS: Wild and Farm animals	93
5.6	Wild animals in the CAPS documents	94
6.1	Coding framework	102
6.2	Comparison between two teachers' talk when teaching science in grade 2	103
7.1	Linguistic tools: Mathematical questions	122
7.2	Comparison of types of episodes across the schools: Face-to-face and computer lessons	130
8.1	Categorical framework for conceptual acquisition	140
8.2	NVIVO and coding Analysis – Talk time and concepts overall	143
8.3	Student talk	145

Preface

The twenty-first century has ushered in a renewed desire to refine education in schools to produce students who are critical thinkers, capable of making significant changes in our world. The need for creative thinkers capable of dealing with the significant crises we have in the twenty-first century (such as climate change) has led some scholars to suggest that we need a new pedagogical model that can develop the kinds of 'heads' that can solve the complex problems facing humanity's future. This book arises as a response to the call both for a new pedagogical model for the twenty-first century and the call for new knowledge to be taught in schools. Drawing on cultural-historical work that finds its foundations in the work of the Soviet psychology of Lev Vygotsky, I present an argument in this book for the development of a novel pedagogical model that draws on cultural-historical work as well as the work of Freire and Feuerstein and is based in dialectical rather than binary logic. This book is primarily concerned with pedagogical transitions over time. What conditions allow for the production of novel pedagogies, and how does pedagogy shift in times of change? The focus on transitions situates this book with a South African context because it is in this context that pedagogical transitions in the twentieth and twenty-first centuries have, arguably, been most obvious. It is in times of crisis and upheaval that the contradictions leading to transformation become visible. South Africa's emergence from an apartheid regime in the late twentieth century sets the stage for transforming teaching and learning. As we shall see in this book, change, when it comes, is not without significant challenges. It is my interest in change, especially in relation to schooling and the product of schooling (young 'heads'), that underpins this book.

Although this book took three months to write, my journey towards this book has been one undertaken over two decades. My fascination with pedagogy began as a master's student in psychology when I tutored first-year students. It was at this juncture of my education that I was first introduced to the work of Lev Vygotsky by Jill Bradbury. Having been trained very specifically in the individualistic stance of Western psychology that locates pathology in an individual, my reading of the book *Mind in Society* fundamentally altered how I began to approach psychological questions, not the least of which was why I was faced with such extreme differences in the performance of the first-year students I was tutoring. Rather than locating this under-performance as a deficit of a student, I began to look to the social context in which the individual is formed to understand different performance levels. At this time, I found Vygotsky's assertion that scientific and everyday concepts need to be linked in a pedagogical setting incredibly interesting, but exactly how to achieve this eluded me for many years. It was when I read the work of Marianne Hedegaard and Feuerstein that I began to see the potential for linking these concepts in real classrooms. It is this understanding that has led to the current book, where I outline a model of pedagogy that I believe can truly alter children and their environments, which is surely what education must be about.

A caveat though: pedagogy is political. This is clearest in my own country where apartheid politicians sought to control what kind of knowledge people of different race groups would be allowed to acquire. This was such a powerful political weapon that even the arrival of a democratic state has, unfortunately, not yet been able to dismantle the huge inequalities set up in South Africa's education system. Change is difficult, traumatic even, when we are challenged about our ways of knowing. The inclusion of more voices in our curriculum, a move, if you will, to decolonizing education, is necessary if we hope to develop children. But this is, I note, a challenge. Decolonial education and its pedagogical praxis is not well developed in the literature. It remains a hollow signifier. This book attempts to address this with real examples of teaching in schools. Ultimately, my hope is that this book provides readers with a model for changing pedagogy in such a way that the status quo that currently exists in education in South Africa shifts to becoming inclusive of all.

Series Editors' Foreword

In this book series we have chosen to focus on transitions through the lens of cultural-historical theory. Specifically, transition is conceptualized to encompass the changes in daily activity settings, the changes in everyday moves between different institutional practices and the changes on entering new practice through life course trajectories, such as going to school, leaving school, entering the work force or entering into parenthood. Through transition into new practices, children and young people meet new challenges and demands that may give them possibility for development.

Important for a cultural-historical conception of transition is the person's agency or intentions, which can be used as analytical tools for gaining the person's perspective during microgenetic transitions between activity settings within an institution, such as indoor play, lunch and outdoor activities in kindergarten, in daily moves between home and kindergarten, school or work, and during macro-transitions that involve new practices. As the person or people take forward their intention within the daily transitions or the new institutions that they attend, a dynamic interplay between the person and the institution can be observed. Cultural-historical studies of transitions across a range of contexts and countries are brought together in this book series, where they can make an important contribution to better understanding transitions globally.

Acknowledgements

Books don't write themselves; more's the pity. This book would not have come about without the direct input of three amazing female professors: Jill Bradbury, Anne Edwards and Marilyn Fleer. All three have influenced me academically in different ways. Without Jill, who supervised my master's research, I doubt that I would have become an academic. Thanks Jill, for believing in me. Anne is one of the most generous academics I have ever had the privilege to meet. She has shared many powerful thoughts with me and has influenced my own work in many ways. Marilyn's work in science has always fascinated me, and it's thanks to her that this book owes its actual existence. Thanks, Marilyn, for asking me to write a book in your *Transitions* series. Much of my better academic thinking owes its foundation to Harry Daniels, who co-supervised my PhD years ago. He is one of the most intellectually generous academics I have ever met. Paula Ensor supervised my PhD many years ago, and she taught me to think in ways that I had never done before. I am not someone who can usually generate diagrams to illustrate my thinking; thanks Paula for showing me how useful this could be. Seth Chaiklin and Marianne Hedegaard's work has had a profound impact on my own thinking. Thanks, Seth, for engaging me in conversation along the way in relation to some of the ideas expressed in this book around radical-local pedagogy. Janet Condy and Carolyn McKinney have both opened my thinking in relation to language and how it is and can be used in classrooms.

Crain Soudien took a chance on me twenty years ago, when I joined his department. I have come to appreciate his intelligence and wisdom more and more as I navigate academic life. I have been very lucky to work with an amazing head of department, Azeem Badroodien, who has kept me motivated through this process. My friend, colleague, wing man, Warren Lilley, has helped me immensely with diagrams and reading some of my chapters. Aslam Fataar, Viv Bozalek and Warren Lilley offered useful insights into Chapter 2, which is really the foundation of the book. Viv has challenged me to go beyond the confines of my own thinking, and I thank her for that. My critical reader Lance Stringer deserves a huge vote of thanks for reading through some of the theoretical issues I pose and offering seriously interesting insights that I feel have added to the book. Thanks Lance, you are not only one of the best critical readers I have ever had, but you are also probably the most humorous. Nina Allchurch and I went to school together, and now I find myself relying on her excellence in English to refine my own use of the language in the book. Any linguistic mistakes in the book are mine, not hers! Derek Ballantyne has come to my rescue with technical assistance. Many thanks Derek. Morgan Mocke and Rose-Anne Reynolds have always been my cheerleaders. Every tribe needs two women like these. Thanks both for the cake and breakfasts along the way. My parents Peter and Valerie-Anne have always had my back. My mother is the best teacher I have ever met, and it's largely thanks to her that I am fascinated by teaching and learning. Thanks, you two. Finally, and most significantly, my partner Ian has cooked many a meal and done many a school run; he has put up with bouts of writer's block and many a day spent alone. Thanks for all. Thanks, beyond words, to my delightful daughter Bella; the world is so much nicer with you in it.

1

Introduction

There are several significant books that have been written about the Russian psychologist Lev Vygotsky and his impact on education and pedagogy. Why write a new book in this field? The decision to write a book on Vygotsky and his potential as a decolonial pedagogue became clear to me following the student protests that brought academia in South Africa to a standstill in 2015. For me, education is necessarily a social justice issue. The recognition of the importance of education as a transformative good is contained too in the Freedom Charter (1955) laid out by the African National Congress (ANC) and its allies. For them, the doors of education and learning should be open to all. How exactly one achieves this, however, is where the story stalls. Previous curriculum changes and longed for consequent pedagogical changes have done little to enable children in South Africa to access learning in a transformative manner. While many more children are attending school in a democratic South Africa, few manage to achieve the learning outcomes required for navigating the twenty-first century. Access to schooling, without a subsequent pedagogy that enables development, cannot lead to attainment. The fact that South Africa continues to lag significantly behind the rest of the world on benchmarking tests such as Progress in International Reading Literacy Study (PIRLS) and Trends in International Mathematics and Science Study (TIMSS) is indicative of a schooling system in crisis. While many authors point to teachers' lack of content knowledge (Venkat & Spaull, 2015) and schools' lack of human and material resources, there is a dearth of research on what exactly pedagogy should look like to enable students to meaningfully construct knowledge in school. The student protests of 2015 and, indeed, renewed protests of 2021 led to a call for decolonized education across the board, not only at Higher Educational Institutions. What exactly is meant by 'decolonial' education was not well articulated however, and the debates have yet to produce a coherent pedagogy that can decolonize education. It is in this context of upheaval and protest that the current book situates itself and develops a view of a decolonial pedagogy capable of including all students' voices in the teaching/learning scenario. Rather than looking for a novel technology, as many authors call for in the twenty-first century, this book looks backwards to the work of Vygotsky and, more currently, Neo-Vygotskians to illustrate how a decolonial, inclusive pedagogy, based on a dialectical rather than dualist epistemology, is found in Vygotsky's work.

There is no reason to attempt to develop new pedagogies to develop the core competencies required for the twenty-first century, I will argue in this book, because these principles are to be found in Vygotsky's work. The five core competencies of the Fourth Industrial Revolution being the need to collaborate, communicate, develop computational thinking, to be creative and, finally, to think critically are all found in Vygotsky's work. The crises of the twenty-first century such as climate change, racism, poverty, homelessness and pandemics force educators to look critically at the current curricula in schools. What content knowledge do students need to change themselves and the world? In this time of the Anthropocene, what kind of pedagogy and curricula will develop both students and transform the world? These are the questions that have led me to this book.

I want to understand what kind of pedagogy can lead to learning in such a way that the child's mental functions grow and change. I also want to understand how, in the most unequal country in the world, we can give access to marginalized voices in our classrooms to create new knowledge that is meaningful to all, not just to a few. It is this central question of 'how' that drives this book coupled with a deep desire to see change in my own society. What follows is my attempt to answer the 'how' of decolonial pedagogy in a manner that is coherent and clear; but more than that, in a manner that can translate into action. Moving away from the Western fixation on the individual, I want to propose a pedagogical model that is situated in collective activity. I am acutely aware that the term 'decolonialism' has no fixed, agreed upon definition. At worst, this leaves the theoretical space of decolonialism susceptible to a relativist philosophy where all knowledge is equal, and no disciplines can claim more epistemic weight than others. Moreover, for some people at least (this is illustrated in Chapter 1 of the book), decolonialism refutes all Western knowledge in a bid for an Afrocentric worldview. This is not how I view decolonial education. Specifically, for me, a decolonial pedagogy is based in dialectical logic, where contradictions between the Western canon and other cannons of knowledge give rise to new knowledge. While I draw on the African philosophy of ubuntu, I do not do this in a desire to 'Africanize' pedagogy; certainly, I do not think that there is something unique about 'African-ness' that necessitates a special model of pedagogy reserved only for Africa (see Long, 2018, for an elegant argument about the pitfalls here). This kind of logic is what underpinned apartheid's segregationist sentiments. What I do think, though, is that the collective care implied in ubuntu should underpin education if it is to include the voices of children. It is in the sense of including previously marginalized voices that I feel decolonial pedagogy can pave the way for a more socially just society. This view of pedagogy sees the teacher as a mediator a canon of specialized knowledge, agreed upon by the disciplines it is drawn from (such as mathematics or science for example). The child's voice is included in the construction of knowledge in the classroom in so far as their everyday concepts are linked to the abstractions taught in schools. It is in this way, as Zippin (2017) has shown, that local knowledge can be used together with scientific knowledge. Local knowledge, on its own, has little epistemic weight; it gains this through its linking to abstract, general principles. It is in the sense of linking abstraction with everyday concepts that I understand the content that needs to be taught in schools using a decolonial pedagogy. I adopt neither a postcolonial nor postmodern basis in my work. We are not 'post' colonial influence, and the decolonial turn must be seen, I would argue, as a critique of colonialism and as adding to the knowledge of the Western canon, rather than erasing it.

This book also avoids a postmodern approach to child development. I find that postmodernism lacks an ethics and can too easily slip into relativism and ultimately nihilism. What follows in this book is a critique of modernism and a call for something else; not for a 'post' modernism but rather for a decolonial epistemological turn that values marginalized voices against the background of an understanding that a person becomes who they are only through interaction with other people. Clearly, this is not a call to return to a pre-modern world; a critique of modernism doesn't equate with a desire to revert to horse-drawn carts and ploughing of fields by hand. Rather, as I detail in this book, a critique of modernism stands in opposition to the 'progress at all costs' and colonialism that is intricately intertwined with modernism.

While Chapter 1 has set the context for the book, Chapter 2 sets the theoretical foundation for the book and Chapter 3 journeys into curriculum transitions from apartheid to a democratic government, illustrating how crises in education have manifest as contradictions, which have led to curricula change. Although content and pedagogy should not be separated, Chapter 4 builds on Chapter 3 by outlining how different curricula have called for different pedagogies in South African schools. The theoretical and historical grounding of this book are covered in Chapters 1–4, whereafter the book turns to empirical studies to illustrate how the theoretical framework speaks to pedagogical transitions in actual classrooms in South Africa. Chapter 5 deals with the content of what is taught in schools with an empirical focus on analysing a portion of science as it is outlined in textbooks students and teachers use, while Chapter 6 illustrates how teachers' pedagogy differs when they are taught to use the double-move to teach science in grade 2. The third and final section of the book utilizes the theoretical framework outlined in Chapter 2 to analyse data from grade 6 mathematics lessons in relation to the use of technology as a tool (Chapters 7 and 8). The focus in these chapters is on the transitions in pedagogy that occur in the presence of novel technology. Chapter 9 provides a detailed conclusion of the book that links the theory and empirical work together to support my argument that Vygotsky's work can serve as a foundation for the development of a decolonial, inclusive pedagogy in both developing and developed countries.

Part One

Context

2

Vygotsky's Pedagogical Legacy in the Twenty-first Century

Introduction: Charting the Theoretical Framework for Pedagogy in the Twenty-first Century

It has been nearly three decades since the first non-racial democratic elections in South Africa brought an end to the system of apartheid, which had purposively under-resourced the education of children who were not 'white' and which had imposed a curriculum that sought to indoctrinate school children with a view of history and culture that the apartheid regime believed would undergird its claim to legitimacy. While the school curriculum has undergone significant changes since the elections, schools continue to grapple with both the legacy of a uniquely unfair distribution of wealth and knowledge production under apartheid and a curriculum that many still consider insufficiently inclusive and free from colonialist influence. This book seeks to contribute to this imperative by exploring what inclusivity and decolonialization might mean for the further reform of pedagogy within South African schools and what such a pedagogical framework might look like. Our starting point, necessarily, is to contextualize the discussion, and in this introductory chapter I chart a theoretical course for developing a model of decolonial pedagogy by tracking pedagogical transitions in South Africa.

The Case for Focusing on Pedagogy in South Africa

One might well ask, why focus narrowly on one context, namely South Africa? South Africa has, over the past three decades, witnessed significant transformation in its education system. Unlike education systems in relative stasis, periods of such transition and transformation offer the researcher the opportunity to 'capture' and analyse the underlying dynamic of the change. It is in times of upheaval and transition that contradictions become available as analytical sites, where one can chart the disjunctions that give rise to new practices. For this reason, South Africa's move from an apartheid education system to a democratic one offers a unique space for the researcher to 'see' change as it unfolds. While neither novel nor unique to South Africa, the discussion of the decolonialization of education has attracted increasingly serious discussion since 2015, particularly after students, beginning at the University of Cape Town, under the #FEESMUSTFALL movement, brought the entire higher education system of South Africa to a complete standstill (Chikoko, 2021; Cini, 2019; Francis & Hardman, 2018). There is no precedent for this in the twenty-first century in any other country espousing a focus on decolonizing education. The study of pedagogy in transition requires a theoretical framework and this book brings to bear the cultural-historical theory, first articulated in the early twentieth century, of Russian psychologist, Lev Vygotsky (1978; 1986). Cultural-historical theory arose out of Vygotsky's desire for a more cohesive, less individualistic focus on cognitive development of the child within society. We begin our journey by briefly outlining Vygotsky's work.

Obuchenie: Teaching/Learning

For Vygotsky (1986), one cannot teach without learning nor can one learn without being taught. He utilizes the word *obuchenie* to describe this dialectical process of teaching and learning. There is no direct English translation for this word, but it means something akin to teaching/learning; that is, one coin with two sides. The notion that teaching and learning are inextricably linked is now well established, but when Vygotsky's work was in its infancy, the predominant understanding was that teaching involved transferring knowledge to a child, where the passive recipient of this knowledge 'learnt' through rote repetition of what was taught. The novelty of *obuchenie* in Western epistemology meant that this notion was not taken up much before the early 1980s in the West. While Western countries such as Denmark, Sweden and Finland had access to and studied Vygotsky's work as early as the 1960s, his work really only gained momentum with the English publication of his 1978 book, *Mind in Society*. Since 1978, the appeal of Vygotsky's theoretical articulation of teaching/learning and cognitive development has been taken up in the West as socio-cultural theory. For Sameroff (2010), dialectical education, which Vygotsky proposed, moves forward through conflicts and contradictions.

This understanding of dialectics in education allows us to conceive of teaching/learning as involving cognitive dissonance, which is resolved through access to mediational means and taught through a co-construction of the meaning of the object under study. *Obuchenie* becomes further animated by Vygotsky's concept of *perezhivanie*, a cultural historical concept Vygotsky uses to indicate that emotion and thinking are unified (Fleer & Hammer, 2013). One is struck by the Vygotskian joining of emotion and thinking in the teaching/learning space as it echoes the decolonial sentiment that academic knowledge cannot be separated from emotions. Practically, these understandings inform one of Vygotsky's most well-known concepts: *mediation*. For Vygotsky, mediation refers to the guidance of a culturally more experienced other, who, together with the student, opens a social/psychological space, or Zone of Proximal Development (ZPD), in which teaching/learning leads to cognitive development. While mediation can take the form of gestures or actions, for Vygotsky, it is language that is the primary tool for cognitive development in the growing child. Vygotsky proposed a General Genetic Law that stated:

> Every function in the child's cultural development appears twice: first, on the social level, and later on the individual level; first, between people (inter-psychological), and then inside the child (intra-psychological). This applies equally to voluntary attention, to logical memory, and to the formulation of concepts. All the higher functions originate as actual relations between human individuals.
>
> (Vygotsky, 1978: 57)

Something as fundamental to schooling, then, such as voluntary attention, needs to be mediated to the child. This general genetic law overcomes the binaries of mind/society and of theory/praxis by indicating that there is a dialectical relationship between mind and society and between theory and praxis; the social is transformed as the mind is transformed in much the same way that practice shifts with theory and theory shifts depending on practice. This law then overcomes the Cartesian dualism that underpins the Enlightenment project in favour of a dialectical logic. The binary logic emerging from dualism has, in many ways, informed the epistemologies underpinning coloniality. The very ability to challenge and create dissonance implied in a dialectical logic can surely enable the decolonial educational project to challenge modernity and the colonialism it arrives through. The mechanism for doing so can be found in Vygotsky's notion of mediation.

As mentioned above, mediation happens in a unique social space, the ZPD, opened between the child and the culturally more competent other. This concept has gained much traction in educational research and is often used to describe *any* assistance given to a child during an activity. In fact, this is not what the ZPD *is*. It is a cognitive developmental space geared towards the development of Higher Cognitive Functions (HCF). For Vygotsky, the ZPD

> is the distance between the actual developmental level as determined by independent problem solving and the level of potential development as determined through problem solving under adult guidance or in collaboration with more capable peers ... the actual developmental level characterizes mental development retrospectively, while the zone of proximal development characterizes mental development prospectively.
>
> (Vygotsky, 1978: 86–7)

What we can see from this quote is that the ZPD requires intersubjectivity or shared meaning, not unlike Taylor's (1989) notion of 'horizons of significance'. It is not just the child who develops and moves within this space, but the teacher as well. If we conceive of education as a social justice project in which the voice of the marginalized gains traction, it is to the ZPD that we can look to articulate how this process can happen (Chaiklin, 2003; Cole & Engeström, 1993; Daniels, 2001; Hasan, 1992; Hedegaard, 1998; Mercer, 2000a; Moll & Greenberg, 1990; Smagorinsky, 1995; Tharp, 1993; Tharp & Gallimore, 1990; Wells, 1999). Here I will focus my discussion on those aspects of the concept that are germane to the main theme of this book.

For Vygotsky (1978, 1986), the ZPD represents the gap between what a student can accomplish with assistance and what that student can accomplish on his/her own. The zone is clearly social, highlighting the 'interdependence of the process of child development and the socially provided resources for that development' (Valsiner, 1988: 145). The ZPD represents a move in Vygotskian theory from focusing on sign-mediated actions to socially mediated actions (Moll & Greenberg, 1990). This 'move' into socially mediated activity should be viewed in conjunction with the significance of tool and sign mediation, adding a broader social dimension to Vygotsky's (1978) developing theoretical system, providing an essential 'space' for educational intervention (Hedegaard, 1998). This focus on the social basis of learning is important in that it highlights the fundamental role teachers' play in the classroom.

Much post-Vygotskian research into the ZPD (Diaz, Neal & Amaya-Williams, 1993; Gallimore and Tharp, 1990; Moll & Greenberg, 1990; Myhill & Dunkin, 2005; Myhill & Warren, 2005; Tharp & Gallimore, 1988) deals with the notion of collaboration/assisted performance as central to the ZPD. While this is, of course, one of the necessary features of the concept, it is not sufficient to explain how children come to learn (and therefore, how one should go about teaching them) within this zone. To fully appreciate and indeed operationalize the ZPD, one needs to clarify Vygotsky's use of the notion of imitation as an indicator of the child's ability to engage with more competent peers. It is in the notion of imitation that one finds an explanation of how one can potentially assess the ZPD. The notion of imitation enables us to understand how a child can benefit from assistance and, consequently, how the ZPD is formed between the child and the assistor. 'The child can enter into imitation through intellectual actions more or less far beyond what he is capable of in independent mental and purposeful actions or intellectual operations' (Vygotsky, 1998b: 201). So:

> If I am not able to play chess, I will not be able to play a match even if a chess master shows me how. If I know arithmetic but run into difficulty with the solution of a complex problem, a demonstration will immediately lead to my own resolution of the problem. On the other hand, if I do not know higher mathematics, a demonstration of the resolution of a differential equation will not move my own thought in that direction by a single step. To imitate, there must be some possibility of moving from what I can do to what I cannot.
>
> (Vygotsky, 1987: 209)

The above quote indicates the centrality of imitation for understanding the ZPD and that there is 'a strict genetic pattern between what a child is able to imitate and his mental development' (Vygotsky, 1987: 202). By focusing on imitation, one can ascertain the beginning points of the ZPD. Importantly, the notion of imitation indicates that there are ceilings to the ZPD; one cannot teach a child something that a child is unable to imitate. For Vygotsky, imitation refers to 'everything that the child cannot do independently, but which he can be taught or which he can do with direction or cooperation or with the help of leading questions' (1998b: 202). Imitation is possible, then, because the child's maturing functions are not yet able to support independent performance but have developed sufficiently for the child to benefit from using the collaborative actions of another person to solve the problem at hand (Chaiklin, 2003; Van der Veer & Valsiner, 1993; Vygotsky, 1986, 1998b). The ZPD then represents a socially constructed space in which imitation forms the basis of coming to know new concepts through mediation. It is in this space, too, that abstract concepts can be acquired by the novice through social interaction and dialogue with the culturally more competent other. Cultural competence here refers to the person who is instructing having more cultural embedding or more knowledge of the meanings of the concepts being taught. This is because the meanings of abstract concepts are culturally constructed and often have little relation to concrete, empirical reality. Think here of the instance of the written word 'dog'. When a child comes to learn this word, there is nothing in the letters d-o-g that tell the child what it references in the real world. The sounds of the letters and the meaning of the word are culturally constructed and agreed upon in that cultural context. This needs to be learnt through instruction and cannot be empirically derived from interactions with the actual furry, four-legged animal that is a dog.

The ZPD is most often understood solely as a principle around collaborative learning, with the more knowledgeable peer/teacher assisting the child to solve a problem outside of his/her current level of independent performance, as outlined in the following quote:

> It is the difference between the actual developmental level as determined by independent problem solving and the level of potential development as determined through problem solving under adult guidance or in collaboration with more capable peers.
>
> (Vygotsky, 1978: 86)

This understanding has been enthusiastically interpreted, particularly in educational settings, as being related to task-specific interaction. Hence, we have a picture of two people (one more competent than the next) interacting together to complete a task (see, for example, Wink & Putney, 2002). As Chaiklin elegantly points out in his 2003 paper, this common conception of the ZPD leads to the following general, but questionable, assumptions: (1) the generality assumption (which assumes that learning as collaborative interaction in the ZPD is applicable to learning different subject matter), (2) that learning is dependent on the assistance of a more competent peer and (3) that 'potential' is a property of the individual learner.

The generality assumption is perhaps easiest to deal with as it very clearly seems to suggest that the ZPD is task-specific; one works on particular tasks in a collaborative manner in order to achieve completion of the said task (Chaiklin, 2003). This leads to the assertion that 'for any domain of skill, a ZPD can be created' (Tharp & Gallimore, 1990: 56). The point to be made here is simply this: Vygotsky refers to the zone of proximal *development*, not the zone of proximal learning. His concern is not with the development of skills on tasks but, rather, with development in general (Chaiklin, 2003). Here he is quite clear: 'No one has ever argued that teaching someone to ride a bicycle, or to swim, or play golf has any significant influence on the general development of the child's mind' (Vygotsky, 1986: 167).

This critique is not to suggest that we disregard the commonly accepted view of the ZPD as related to the development of task-specific knowledge but that we appreciate this understanding as a recontextualization of Vygotsky's work, rather than as a faithful reproduction of his work. While I agree with Chaiklin's (2003) critique of this assumption, I am inclined to view the generality assumption as based on an understanding of the *subjective* ZPD, rather than on an understanding of the general ZPD concept, which contains both an *objective* and *subjective* element. Understood as a reading of the subjective ZPD, the research cited above begins to make more sense in a Vygotskian worldview. While Chaiklin (2003: 48–50) does indeed outline the difference between the objective and subjective notions of the ZPD, he does not indicate that the generality assumption is based on a reading of the subjective ZPD. This, then, is a reading *I* derive from my understanding of Vygotsky's (1986) and Chaiklin's (2003) work. It is probably more accurate to think of the generality assumption as deriving more fully from the works of Bruner (1985) (who acknowledges his debt to Vygotsky) and Wood, Bruner and Ross's (1976) notion of scaffolding. For Bruner (1985), the ZPD is conceptualized as follows:

> I have puzzled about this matter (zone of proximal development) for many years, and I think that I understand what Vygotsky may have meant. Or at least I understand the matter as follows ... If the child is enabled to advance by being under the tutelage of an adult or more competent peer, then the tutor or the aiding peer serves the learner as a vicarious form of consciousness and control. When the child achieves that conscious control over a new function of conceptual system, it is then that he is able to use it as a tool. Up to that point, the tutor in effect performs the critical function of 'scaffolding' the learning task to make it possible for the child, in Vygotsky's word, to internalise external knowledge and convert it into a tool for conscious control.
>
> (215)

The second common assumption, relating to the role of the more competent peer, is also present in Bruner's quote. While Vygotsky (1978) undoubtedly stressed the importance of a more competent partner in achieving developmental milestones, he indicates in his later work (*Thought and Language* published in a retranslation in 1986) that any collaboration is developmentally significant; that is, the child can complete difficult tasks with assistance far more easily than he/she would be able to do independently. The point is not in the superior competence of the mediator, per se, but in the 'meaning of that assistance in relation to a child's learning and development' (Chaiklin, 2003: 43). This leads directly on to the final common assumption made in relation to the ZPD, which locates it as a property of an individual child. This zone is not something a child possesses, but rather, it is an indication of certain maturing functions. The zone is a social process, if you like, not an individual property. The source of the zone lies in the social situation, then, rather than in the individual child.[1] Note, however, that this does not suggest that the social situation dictates development directly. Rather, the social environment's effects are indirect, only impacting on development through the active child's participation in 'shared and culturally shaped social collaboration' (Stetsenko, 2006: 509). One can create a subjective ZPD between oneself and a child by ascertaining the extent to which the child can *imitate* your problem-solving actions.

The ZPD in Vygotsky's Developmental Theory: Subjective and Objective Zones

Chaiklin (2003) indicates that it is possible to understand the ZPD in two ways: as an objective[2] zone that outlines certain psychological functions that all children in a particular culture/historical period need to form during given age periods and as a subjective zone that indicates the extent to which an individual child has reached the developmental milestones that form the objective zone. The objective zone can essentially be seen as normative in that it reflects certain developmental expectations that have developed historically in societal practices. So, for example, it is understood that school going children must be able to reason in specific ways manipulating academic concepts as tools to solve problems. Individual children who are unable to reason in these ways are said to differ intellectually from most school-age children.

The subjective zone, that is the individual child's development, can be ascertained in relation to this objective zone. So, one talks about the subjective zone in terms of the development of an individual child in relation 'to the objective, historically formed period of next development' (Chaiklin, 2003: 50). The ZPD then refers both to the functions that are developing ontogenetically for a given age period (objective) and to the extent to which the child's current development in relation to the functions that ideally need to be achieved (subjective) develop. When dealing with students in a classroom, it is primarily the subjective zone that teachers focus on in developing learning tasks. It is, however, almost impossible to think of individual development outside of the objective zone which, in a sense, sets the developmental parameters that need to be achieved. In this book, when I refer to the ZPD it is in relation to the subjective zone that teachers' aim to develop over the year by what they teach an individual child. The objective zone forms the background for understanding what kinds of functions students are required to develop during school; in schools in South Africa the objective zone is highlighted by the Revised National Curriculum Statement (DoE, 2002) and includes the ability to manipulate subject content knowledge (scientific concepts) creating a 'lifelong learner who is confident and independent, literate, numerate, multi-skilled, compassionate, with respect to the environment and (who has) the ability to participate in society as a critical and active citizen' (DoE, 2002: 3). For Vygotsky,

> In a problem involving scientific concepts, [the child] must be able to do in collaboration with the teacher something that [s/he] has never done spontaneously ... we know that the child can do more in collaboration than he can do independently.
>
> (Vygotsky, 1987: 168, 9; 216)

In this quote, it is clear that a scientific concept arises in the relationship between the teacher and student in the ZPD. Instruction, then, is central to the development of scientific concepts. This understanding of learning as dependent on guided instruction (or mediation) differs from the constructivist notions of Piaget (1970) and Dewey (1902), which held that a child could gain access to scientific concepts through exploring their world, thereby 'discovering' knowledge. This clearly is not what Vygotsky has in mind considering the above quote (1987).

While the scientific concept differs from the everyday concept, Vygotsky indicates that both are necessary for the development of HCF.

> The formation of concepts develops simultaneously from two directions: the direction of the general and the particular ... the development of a scientific concept begins with the verbal definition. As part of an organised system, this verbal definition descends to concrete; it descends to phenomena which the concept represents. In contrast, the everyday concept tends to develop outside any definite system; it tends to move upwards toward abstractions and generalisation ... the weakness of the everyday concepts lies in its incapacity for abstractions, in the child's incapacity to operate on it in a voluntary manner ... the weakness of the scientific concepts lies in its verbalism, in its

insufficient saturation with the concrete ... we are more concerned to show that systematicity and consciousness do not come from outside, displacing the child's spontaneous concepts, but that, on the contrary, they presuppose the existence of rich and relatively mature representations. Without the latter, the child would have nothing to systematize. Systematic reasoning, being initially acquired in the sphere of scientific concepts, later transfers its structural organisation into spontaneous concepts, remodelling them 'from above'.

(Vygotsky, 1986; 187: 163, 168, 169; 172)

These quotes, drawn from chapter 5 in *Thought and Language*, indicate to us how one might go about teaching scientific concepts; if a child is to grasp the scientific in a meaningful way, it must be linked to everyday concepts. Similarly, everyday concepts come more readily under voluntary control when the child begins to manipulate scientific concepts (Wardekker, 1998). While everyday concepts have empirical referents in the child's environment, scientific concepts' relation to the empirical is mediated through other concepts so that 'The inception of a spontaneous concept can usually be traced to a face-to-face meeting with a concrete situation, while a scientific concept involves from the first a "mediated" attitude toward its object' (Vygotsky, 1986: 193–4). This is an important distinction; the empirical, practical nature of everyday concepts means that they can all too often result in misunderstandings. Hence, the importance of the fact is that everyday concepts undergo development when they encounter scientific concepts. The process of concept development is described below.

Everyday/Spontaneous Concepts and Scientific Abstract Concepts

Vygotsky makes a distinction between everyday concepts (also called spontaneous concepts) and abstract concepts (also called scientific or true concepts). For Vygotsky, everyday concepts are those concepts that the child acquires through empirical interaction with the world. They do not need to be taught and are learnt spontaneously by the child as s/he transacts with the environment. Scientific concepts, on the other hand, are abstract and necessarily taught. Generalization and systematization are the essential features of a scientific concept. According to Vygotsky, 'the *absence of a system* is the cardinal psychological difference distinguishing spontaneous from scientific concepts'

(Vygotsky, 1962: 116). A fully formed scientific concept develops over time; moving from being, initially, a complex then to being a pseudo-concept, until it is finally formed into a full-blown scientific concept (Smagorinsky et al., 2003).

The Development of Concepts

As noted earlier in this chapter, Vygotsky (1987) distinguishes between everyday concepts and scientific (abstract) concepts by illustrating that everyday concepts are grounded in empirical, everyday interaction with the world while scientific concepts must necessarily be taught in school.[3] However, scientific concepts develop slowly over time and begin not as fully formed concepts but rather as complexes, before becoming pseudo-concepts and then, finally, developing into full abstract concepts.[4] Complexes describe the thinking of very young children who associate various objects with each other based often on empirical means, rather than on any systematic, essential characteristic that is shared. A child who has a cat at home, faced with another four-legged animal, will label this a cat because it has four legs, just like her domesticated cat (Smagorinsky et al. 2003).

An example animates this: When my daughter was three years old, her grandfather took her to see wild animals on an animal farm. She had a dog at home and confidently called her dog 'woof'. However, faced with a giraffe, she labelled this a 'woof' too. Pseudo-concepts, developing from complexes, appear to unify individual elements. However, again, there are no essential features that characterize the grouping of individual elements together. So faced with any canine-like creature, it would be expected that my daughter would call this a 'woof'; that is, liken say, a jackal, to a dog. In a fully formed concept, however, individual elements are linked because they share an essential feature(s). This development of a concept is illustrated in Figure 2.1.

Scientific concepts are distinct from everyday concepts because of their systematicity and generalizability, as indicated in the quote below:

> If consciousness means generalization, generalization in turn means the formation of a superordinate concept that includes the given concept as a particular case. A superordinate concept implies the existence of a series of subordinate concepts, and it also presupposes a hierarchy of concepts of different levels of generality. Thus, the given concept is placed within a system of relationships of generality.
>
> (Vygotsky, 1962: 92)

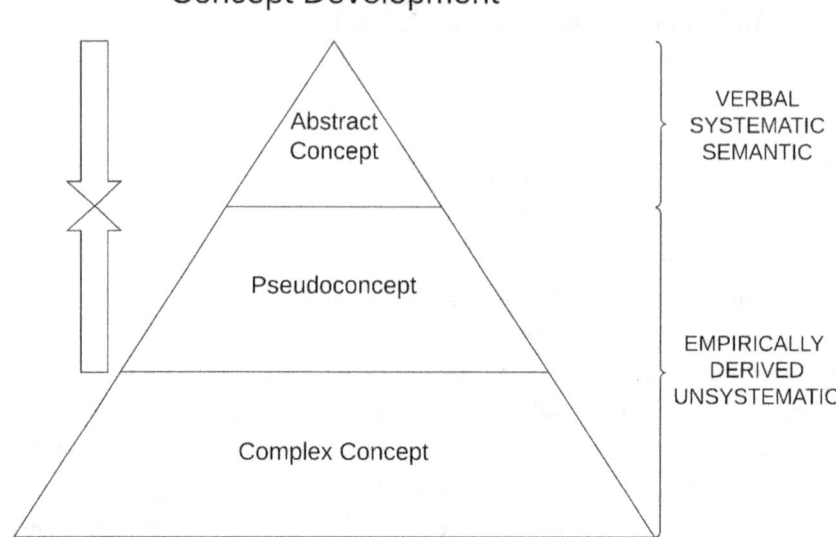

Figure 2.1 Concept development.

A scientific concept then implies all individual elements are unified by a single idea. For Davydov:

> A combination of two, three, or more abstract and general attributes which is formed by the significance of a certain word (most often by means of a definition) is usually called a concept. Generalization and abstraction are indispensable conditions for forming it. The group of generalized attributes of an object is the content of the concept.
>
> (Davydov, 1990: 7)

The above quote indicates that concepts have essential and non-essential attributes. It is the essential attributes that make the concept what it is. Davydov illustrates the notion of essence with reference to a triangle. Essential to the concept 'triangle' is three sides and three angles; non-essential attributes like colour can vary, but if the lines alter or the angles alter, we no longer have a 'triangle'. Further, scientific concepts are systematically interrelated within hierarchical knowledge systems, indicating that they are mediated by other scientific concepts. Davydov (1990) developed Vygotsky's (1986) notion of scientific concepts to include content and procedural knowledge as constituting the concept. Procedural knowledge refers to knowing how to utilize the concept while the content of the concept relates to the schooled knowledge being taught. The aim of school science, according to Driver et al. (1994), is for children to be able to utilize these concepts to interact with their lived experience, understanding as they do so, what lies behind the concept. Clearly, a child in school cannot learn the entire body of scientific knowledge that informs a specific concept, say, for example 'democracy'. What a child can learn, however, is how to use this concept to understand the notion of voting. For Davydov:

> Mastering a concept means not only knowing the attributes of the objects and phenomena embraced by the given concept but also being able to apply the concept in practice, being able to operate with it.
>
> (Davydov, 1990: 1)

This quote indicates that without procedural knowledge, the concept cannot be animated in practice and indeed cannot serve a developmental purpose. Another extension of Vygotsky's notion of scientific concept relates to these concepts being taught in school. It is in the school setting that the context-dependent, everyday concepts can be developed and linked with scientific concepts throughout the child's development. As the child progresses through various levels of schooling, concepts become more developed and simpler concepts are recruited into ever more complex ones (Hedegaard, 1998).

From Scientific and Everyday Concepts to Theoretical and Empirical Learning

Davydov (1986) has shown how pedagogy must be structured to develop scientific concepts in students. His work and the work of his colleagues (Davydov, 1990; Talyzina, 1981) further indicate that a different kind of learning is required if one is to develop students' scientific concepts. Davydov refers to the kind of learning that results in the development of scientific concepts as 'theoretical learning' while that resulting in the acquisition of everyday concepts is 'empirical learning'. Empirical learning results from the child selecting the salient features of a group of objects or events and generalizing based on these features. So, for example, if asked to sort pictures of fish, cows and whales into the categories of fish and mammals, the child, utilizing everyday concepts, will sort whales and fish into one category and cows into another category. The child does this based on external salient features, in this case, fins. This strategy might of course work if the salient features do indeed represent the essential characteristics of the object that are common to all representatives of that class of object (the concept of the colour blue, for example can be learnt this way), but it can go horribly awry if this is not the case. This feature of empirical (or discovery-based) learning explains why it is that students develop misconceptions and why it is so difficult for teachers to shift these misconceptions. Theoretical learning, on the other hand, refers to the acquisition of methods for scientific analysis of objects across subject domains. In this scenario, the teacher teaches the methods of scientific analysis, which are internalized by the children and become cognitive tools that can mediate students' further problem-solving activity (Karpov, 2005). To acquire true scientific concepts, this knowledge must be directly taught to the students, as opposed to them being left to discover it on their own. Drawing on Davydov's work, Hedegaard (1998) refers to scientific concepts as 'school-based concepts', as they are most often taught in schools. Everyday and scientific concepts are, however, dialectically linked: without the everyday, the scientific has no personal meaning for the child; and without the scientific, the everyday cannot fully come into consciousness.

The notion of a scientific concept is not dissimilar to Freire's (1970) notion of the *word* that characterizes dialogue in learning/teaching spaces. Linking the word to praxis animates the word and helps it rise above mere *verbalism*. For Freire, 'There is no true word that is not at the same time praxis. Thus, to speak a true word is to transform the world' (1970: 68). Freire's work is the basis of most approaches to dialogical pedagogy, where true dialogue between partners shifts and transforms both. Here, we have a very clear picture of a challenge to the asymmetrical power of the colonial voice, through incorporating the voice of the child. I refer to this movement towards a co-constructed and shared meaning as *perceptions of intelligibility*.[5] In this hypothetical perception space, the teacher and the taught negotiate the meaning of the object being studied. Differing cultural and historical approaches (through everyday concepts) are linked, delinked and debated in relation to the cultural and historical meanings of the scientific abstractions being taught. The understanding of, say, schizophrenia can shift and change in the presence of an appreciation of ancestors who talk to the living through various things. In the South African context, a person prays to their ancestors, who can respond to them. Hence, hearing the voices of ancestors calling to you is not necessarily an incidence of schizophrenia in South Africa; it could be related to a strong bond with the ancestors. Similarly, in the West, it is not necessarily a cause of psychological concern when a Christian hears God speaking to them. The new meaning of the object under construction must be perceived by both parties and understood.

Of course, readers familiar with Vygotsky and how he has been domesticated, particularly in the West, will point out that scientific concepts echo Michael Young's (2014) notion of 'powerful knowledge', that is, knowledge gained through teaching that is specialized knowledge. Incidentally, Young (2012) sees everyday concepts as limiting the child to concrete, everyday experiences. My reading of Vygotsky does not see everyday concepts as limiting. Rather, they should be viewed as sense makers; that is, scientific and everyday concepts are so inextricably related that a child doesn't grasp the abstract in the absence of the everyday concept and moreover, the everyday concept changes, comes fully into consciousness, when linked to the abstract, scientific concept. One concept is not superior to the other; both are essential in the construction of meaning between teacher and student. In a decolonial curriculum, a scientific concept, such as democracy, draws on the everyday to become meaningful to the child. This new knowledge/meaning is aimed at violently dismantling the colonial understanding of democracy; the use of the word 'violence' here does not refer to physical violence but rather to the psychological trauma one feels when one's worldview is required to shift. An example animates this point.

As a young lecturer, I taught evolutionary psychology to first year students. Inevitably, someone in the class would break down and even drop the course, because the fact that the earth is millennia old does not sit with certain fundamentalist-Christian beliefs that the earth is only a few thousand years old. Think too of how someone with racist beliefs reacts to having the colonial mindset of us/them challenged. It is in this sense, then, that we can experience 'violence' when our world view is challenged and why learning of new knowledge can be so unsettling. It requires that we literally step out of what we know, into what is novel and still in the process of construction. This can be achieved through the mediation of scientific concepts and their active linkage to everyday concepts.

The Double-move: Radical Local Pedagogy

The linking between scientific and everyday concepts, as articulated by Vygotsky, is operationalized in the work of Hedegaard (1998) and Chaiklin and Hedegaard (2005) in what Hedegaard calls the 'double-move' in pedagogy. Hedegaard's work develops Vygotsky's notion of the importance of the link between the scientific and everyday concepts in her notion of a practical move in pedagogical settings that she calls the double-move. For Hedegaard,

> the teacher guides the learning activity both from the perspective of general concepts and from the perspective of engaging students in 'situated' problems that are meaningful in relation to their developmental stage and life situations.
>
> (Hedegaard, 1998: 120)

What we have here is an understanding that education must involve the development and change of both the child and *the child's context*. While education transforms the child, the child can use this education to transform their lived experience. It is through the double-move that one ascends from the abstract to the concrete; that is, one begins with the abstraction and works towards making sense of this for the child by linking it with the concrete, everyday concept (Hedegaard, 2020). One works from the germ cell, the underlying, foundational abstraction underpinning the concept, to linking this with the everyday concrete concept the child brings to the lesson.

Think here of how one could teach photosynthesis. Children in South Africa are given a bean to grow in grade 1. This is the first time they are introduced to both the notion of living things as well as the notion, indirectly, of photosynthesis as that process that enables a plant to grow. The process of photosynthesis is taught throughout years one to five. Unfortunately, in all the schools I have done research in, I have never seen a teacher take the concept of photosynthesis outside of the classroom to encourage the students to, say, grow their own food in their home environments. This transformation of the garden into a vegetable production site would represent the double-move nicely as it shows how the abstract concept changes not only the child, but also the child's environment. Equipping children with this kind of thinking has the benefit of making them better equipped to deal with the challenges the twenty-first century presents.

While providing an operationalization of the linking of abstract and everyday concepts in the double-move, Hedegaard does not explicitly outline specific mediational techniques that one can use in a lesson. If we are to develop a pedagogy for South Africa, and indeed, the wider world, the praxis, inextricably linked to the conceptual position outlined above, needs to be developed. Having briefly explored the linking of everyday and scientific concepts we can now turn to exploring more fully what mediation in the ZPD should look like in a real classroom.

Mediation in the ZPD: Feuerstein

In the late 1970s Wood, Bruner and Ross (1976) developed a structured form of teaching that they called scaffolding. Scaffolding is often, erroneously, confused with mediation in the West (see, for example, Wink & Putney (2002), whose work elides the two into one deceptively seamless process). For clarity's sake, it's worth noting that Vygotsky never used the word 'scaffolding' in his own writings and certainly his notion of mediation as a developmental process, that takes years, differs quite substantially from Wood et al (1976) conceptualization of scaffolding. While scaffolding aims to achieve problem-solving in relation to a specific task, mediation happens over a longer period and is geared towards the development of HCF, what we today call, executive functioning (that is, functions that control, inhibit and monitor physical and mental activity). Although Vygotsky proposed that it is only through mediation that a child comes to develop HCF, he died before elaborating exactly how mediation can or should be operationalized in the classroom. To develop a picture of what mediation could look like in classrooms I turn now to the work of Reuven Feuerstein, an Israeli psychologist who believed, as did Vygotsky, that cognition could be modified with mediation. While I draw on Feuerstein to animate Vygotsky's pedagogical concept of mediation, it is important to note that Feuerstein himself did not ever mention drawing on Vygotsky's work and developed his own theory independently of Vygotsky's work. Nevertheless, Feuerstein's work dovetails well with Vygotsky's and can fruitfully be drawn on in understanding how to operationalize mediation in the classroom.

Feuerstein and Mediated Learning Experiences

Feuerstein proposes that children develop cognitively if they are given the appropriate Mediated Learning Experiences (MLE) throughout development. MLE refers to a special kind of social relation between the child and the teacher/more capable other. As one can see, this is very similar to Vygotsky's notion of mediation in the ZPD, which leads to cognitive development. Our modern understanding of neuroplasticity, that cognition can be transformed through specific interventions, is no longer novel, but was when Feuerstein first proposed his programme for cognitive development. Cognitive ability was viewed as somewhat fixed and stable like IQ and Feuerstein's claim that cognitive ability was not set in stone but amenable to change was considered beyond the pale. Of interest to this book are the practical pedagogical strategies Feuerstein developed for changing cognitive ability. Vygotsky's general genetic law proposed that social relations were internalized by the child over time and Feuerstein's MLE provides a basis for understanding how internalization happens throughout development (Pressiesen & Kozulin, 1992).

Feuerstein outlines twelve parameters for MLE; the first three are universal and I deal with these here, namely, *mediation of intentionality and reciprocity*, *mediation of meaning* and *mediation of transcendence*. Mediation of intentionality underpin the teacher's desire to teach. It focuses the students on the object of learning. This is linked to reciprocity, which refers to the students' desire to learn and their receptiveness to the teacher's input. In this reciprocal learning/teaching space, meaning is constructed by students and teachers. In a decolonial classroom, reciprocity would be fostered through the teacher encouraging students to use their own voice and bring authentic problems to the class to solve. Together, intentionality and reciprocity create a space for meaning making, another universal characteristic of MLE.

Echoing Freire's notion of dialogical pedagogy as relating to authentic social contexts, the mediation of meaning requires that tasks are related to the child's lived experience. The teacher achieves this by openly sharing his/her aims with the class and eliciting students' understandings of the topics under discussion. Here, the teacher makes explicit what underlies his/her pedagogy, and students are encouraged to ask *why* and *how* questions. This requires that the teacher can interrogate his/her own assumptions about what they are teaching. In teaching about, for example, racism, the teacher must be able to reflect on and share their own biases and beliefs in this regard. The final universal characteristic of MLE is the mediation of transcendence, where the child can bridge ideas across contexts. These three universal aspects of MLE can be used easily by a teacher in a classroom to develop meaningful interactions that lead to knowledge that transcends the immediate classroom. Taken together with the foundations of Vygotsky's educational theory that learning precedes development and occurs in the ZPD, Feuerstein's MLE provides concrete pedagogical steps that can be taken to motivate students to develop creatively within a decolonized classroom.

The Decolonial Turn: #feesmustfall and the Rise of Social Justice in Education

In 2015 Chumani Maxwele threw excrement at the statue of Cecil John Rhodes, which had a prominent position at the University of Cape Town. His action brought into the open the widespread feelings of anger against the glorification of colonialists who had taken from Africa and yet, given little in return. The #Rhodesmustfall movement soon gained a following, which led to the removal of the offensive statue from the university (Francis & Hardman, 2018). It soon became clear, however, that merely removing statues does not go far enough in overcoming the legacy of colonialism. The #feesmustfall movement followed quickly behind and began to overtake the #Rhodesmustfall movement (Fataar, 2018; Ruznyak, Hlatshwayo, Fataar & Blackie., 2021). While calling for free education, the students also indicated what kind of education they were looking for: a decolonial education, free of inherently racist notions underpinning coloniality; an educational system that would speak to their needs; that included their voices and the voices of African people.

As with all terms that gain currency and become widely used, the notion of decolonial education has begun to lose coherence as people use the term in varying contexts. Long (2018) refers to the notion of 'decolonisation' as an 'empty signifier' (Long, 2018: 20); the challenge with an empty signifier is that everyone wants to populate it with their own ideas. Sokal's (1996) prank illustrates how dangerous is it to leave a term unpopulated with theoretical coherence.[6]

There are many questions about what decolonial education is (Hoadley & Galant, 2019). To stabilize this term for this book, I draw on the work of Fataar (2021) and my own work in this field (Hardman, 2021). First, decolonial education cannot be premised on a relativist endeavour to accept all knowledge as equal. I agree with Muller (2009) that disciplinary knowledge has epistemic weight. In a bid to decolonize disciplines we must not eradicate the boundaries between disciplines but, instead, add relevance to these disciplines by drawing on the work of authors that are not exclusively drawn from white and Western academics. In discussing this notion of epistemic weight, I draw from the work of Bernstein (1999) who distinguishes between vertical and horizontal discourses, where vertical discourse structures are decontextualized and abstract while horizontal discourses are closer to one's context and everyday lived experience. Importantly, and as we shall see throughout this book, this is in line with Vygotsky's (1978) notion of the distinction between everyday and scientific concepts. Second, I draw from Zipin's (2017) conceptualization of 'knowledge problematics', where he suggests that communal, local knowledge can interact with abstract, general knowledge. His example of water management in a flood shows how the scientific understanding of weather patterns can be linked to the community's everyday experiences of addressing flooding. Again, this echoes Vygotsky's notion of the importance of linking scientific and everyday concepts. It's important to note here that Zippin does not accord the local, community knowledge the same epistemic weight as scientific knowledge. As we shall see in Chapter 3, when this happens in schools a child cannot develop cognitively. Finally, I view decolonial education as a social justice project that includes the voices of previously marginalized people, in the case of this book, children's voices. In what follows and throughout the book, I develop a notion of what decolonial pedagogy can look like in the twenty-first century.

For clarity then, decolonial education cannot be about the summary removal of 'Western knowledge' from the cannon. It also cannot be about a slippery slide into relativism, where all knowledge is equally (or preferentially) valuable by virtue of some person or group holding that knowledge. I will try, in what follows, to offer my understanding of what decolonial education, specifically, decolonial pedagogy, can be. I do not pretend to have all the answers, but I develop a picture of an additive pedagogy that includes all voices. In this I acknowledge the work of Elizabeth Walton (2018) who develops an argument about inclusive education that, while based on a different theoretical foundation than mine, is interesting. Further, her move into the philosophy of *ubuntu* as underpinning an inclusive pedagogy resonates well with my own understanding of how one includes different voices in knowledge production. The question I ask below is: What can one mean by decolonial pedagogy and how does the work of Vygotsky help us to articulate this?

Decolonial Pedagogy: Ubuntu and Marx, Bridging the Divide

The concept of 'coloniality of power', first coined in 2000 by Quijano and Ennis, arose as a critique to the status quo built on modernity's promise of progress at all costs. The notion of a decolonial lens with which to view the world sought to liberate people from colonial epistemologies, allowing for 'a specific epistemic, political and ethical instrument for transforming the world by transforming how people see it, feel it and act in it' (Tlostanova & Mignolo, 2009: 21). For Tlostanova and Mignolo (2009), decolonial education has two facets: instruction (knowledge used to practically navigate the world) and nurturing (knowledge aimed at personal and collective well-being in the world, that is, knowledge that is not focused on the individual). One thing emerges from the literature on decoloniality: decolonial education (referring to both what is taught and how it is taught) must challenge colonial epistemologies and ways of being in the world (Mbembe, 2001; Mignolo, 2005). No longer can knowledge and subjectivity be controlled by the state/curriculum/ teacher. Decolonial education must necessarily de-centre modernist/colonial epistemologies and re-humanize the curriculum by including the voice of the 'other'. While there is a body of literature emerging on decolonialism, there is a paucity of published work on what a decolonial pedagogy might look like – although see, Fujino et al., 2018, for an argument for transformative pedagogy in a decolonial context (see also Fataar, 2018, for an argument about focusing on students in higher education settings when developing decolonial spaces for thinking, being and becoming). While interesting, no actual pedagogical practice is outlined. De Lissovoy (2010) does outline a pedagogy drawing solely on Freire's (1981) work and proposes a pedagogy of lovingness, which espouses a caring, place-based pedagogy.

A special issue of the journal Education Research for Social Change has two papers that deal with decolonial pedagogy. Waghid and Hibbert (2018) refer to a defamiliarization pedagogy, capable of contesting colonial knowledge. Based on the work of Shklovskij (1917/1965) this mode of defamiliarization pedagogy proposes engaging students in a critical, participatory way in the reading of say, an African text alongside a Western text, with the aim of using art to defamiliarize automated understandings of something we feel is familiar. Essentially, here, you are trying to find the 'strange' in the familiar. This is an interesting notion of pedagogy, but, for me, it lacks a coherent mechanism for cognitive development. Another paper from this special issue is by Noor David's who proposes using ideology critique to decolonize pedagogy. This approach recognizes the dialectical in its work but focuses more on Lefebvre's (1991) notion of space as productive, rather than on cognitive development. For me, pedagogy is necessarily geared towards cognitive development and, therefore, a decolonial pedagogy must be capable of producing this development. This is not merely a language game we are involved in when we discuss a decolonial pedagogical turn; we are dealing with real children and their development. High level concepts and slippery signifiers are not going to assist in a real-world setting. What is needed is a form of praxis that teachers will be able to follow to develop the thinking of children. It is against this rather small output of published papers outlining a decolonial pedagogy, that I argue that Vygotsky and the Neo-Vygotkians provide an elaborated, practical pedagogy for decolonial education through the notion of mediation of scientific concepts in the ZPD.

If we return to the notion of the ZPD, this 'space' should be viewed as a jointly constructed, social space; indeed, a truly dialogical space where both the teacher and the taught move towards new understandings of culturally embedded concepts. In this sense, the ZPD provides for a pedagogical foundation that aims at social justice and inclusion. One can go further, in fact, and claim that the ZPD allows for a pedagogy that moves from the colonial picture of pedagogy as transmission to a decolonial notion of pedagogy as dialogically constructed between participants. The General Genetic law that forms the theoretical basis of the ZPD resonates with current moves in African psychology (Ratele, 2019) that seek to undo the harm caused to marginalized identities by colonialism. For Ratele (2019) we can only study psychological phenomena in their cultural, historical and social context using the voices of the people who we study, rather than imposing a Western psychological, often deficit model onto the people studied. Underpinned by Marx's notion of *consciousness*, Vygotsky's General Genetic law echoes the African notion of *ubuntu*, a Nguni word roughly translated as 'I am because we are' and derived from the Zulu phrase 'Umuntu ngumuntu ngabantu', meaning that a person becomes a person through other people. Compare this with Marx's understanding that 'it is not the consciousness of men that determines their existence, but, on the contrary, their social existence that determines their consciousness' (1923: 143) and one can see the foundation of Vygotsky's psychology as a social justice project. Hedegaard's operationalization of the link between everyday and scientific concepts as animated in the double-move in the classroom coupled with Feuerstein's elaboration of what mediation could look like in a classroom provides a researcher with the tools one needs to study pedagogy in a classroom as well as the conceptual tools to design what kind of content should be taught in the twenty-first century. Underpinned by an ethics of care,[7] articulated as ubuntu, this pedagogical stance enables us to dismantle the binary logic imposed by colonialism in favour of a dialectical logic, that is capable to involving multiple voices and, through contradictions and conflicts, transform single-voiced, dominant and/or unjustifiably privileged colonial epistemologies.

Of course, readers familiar with Vygotsky's (1978, 1986) work will undoubtedly point to the fact that his work is modernist and therefore intricately attached to coloniality, as modernity cannot exist without its ugly sister, coloniality. Indeed, Vygotsky saw himself as moving humanity forward through a socialist modernity; progress from the individual to the collective, if you will. Historically, when Vygotsky was producing his work, the notion of progress as good and achievable was in vogue. The dialectical logic, however, underpinning Vygotsky's work, speaks to ruptures and contradictions as sites of dynamic change, which could lead to progress, but need not necessarily do so. Unlike Cartesian ego-psychology, Vygotsky gives us a view of development that is collective and not inevitably progressive. What is remarkable and useful in Vygotsky's work is that he gives us tools, based in dialectical logic, to address 'modernity' and 'colonialism' as in need of rupture. Dialectics looks for the contradiction, for the rupture and dissonance, that speaks to the beginning of dynamic change. It is in this revolutionary sense, then, that Vygotsky talks to the twenty-first-century pedagogue.

Pedagogy for the Twenty-first Century: Back to the Future?

Scholars have called for new core competencies for humanity to navigate the twenty-first century and its challenges, not least the advance of technological capability as summarized in the notion of the so-called fourth IR (Lee et al. 2018). Five core competencies have been identified for successfully engaging with the fourth IR, which are, creativity, communication, collaboration, computational thinking and critical thinking (Shahroom & Hussin, 2018). The development of these competencies, it is claimed, would require a novel pedagogy. However, an extensive search of PubMed and Scopus revealed few articles that explicitly outline what this novel pedagogy should look like. While Eleyyan (2021) suggests an entire overhaul of the education system, little practical detail is given regarding what exactly pedagogy should or could look like given increasing digitalization, aside from a rather bleak view of teaching/learning entailing less face-to-face interaction between teacher and taught and a vague hope that technology would improve learning by giving students' access to larger volumes of data. What is missing here is an idea of what exactly pedagogy should look like if students are going to acquire these core competencies. Practically, in the actual classroom, what must teachers and taught do for these core competencies to develop?

While I appreciate the novelty the current century presents, I argue that we do not need a novel pedagogy to develop students' core competencies as just such a pedagogical model already exists. If we return to the original work of Vygotsky, who himself was writing in turbulent, fast changing contexts, we can see in his pedagogical model a practical method for developing the sought core competencies. In his notion of mediation, Vygotsky captures the essence of learning and creating through collaboration and communication. The ZPD is that collaborative, social space in which communication, in dialogue, leads to the creative co-construction of meaning in the classroom. Empirical data indicating how this can happen is provided later in the current book; for now, I note that the core competencies of creativity, communication and collaboration are contained in Vygotsky's notion of mediation. What of computational thinking and critical thinking? Answering this question depends very much on what you think critical thinking and computational thinking are.

As with many terms that gain currency, the meaning of 'critical thinking' has become somewhat opaque. For some authors, critical thinking is defined as the ability to reason (Moodley, 2021). This meaning, however, is surely tautologous as critical thinking and reasoning are synonymous in some published work (Ennis, 1996; Huitt, 1998; Tama, 1989). What then is critical thinking? In the first instance, critical thinking, in this book, has its foundation in the Vygotskian notion of scientific concepts; that is, abstract ideas. But this is insufficient to understand what is, in fact, a complex process that unfolds over years and developmental phases. The ability to think critically relies on the person being able to evaluate and analyse a situation using the following cognitive skills: systematic thinking (that is, in a Vygotskian sense, the ability to mobilize scientific concepts in understanding a situation); the ability to weigh up evidence and to change your mind if novel evidence refutes your current thinking (not unlike Piagetian (1976) accommodation, in the sense that the novelty clashes with what is known by you, and therefore, requires cognitive change); the identification of logical fallacies which can then be discarded; selecting relevant over irrelevant knowledge; the ability to notice biases and avoid them and finally, the ability to look beyond the obvious (Huitt, 1998). This definition of critical thinking clearly fits well with a Vygotskian notion of the development of HCF. In fact, acquiring scientific concepts and linking them to spontaneous concepts to solve problems in the world, is surely what critical thinking is. But what about computational thinking; can that be accommodated in a Vygotskian framework?

Contrary to its name (which appears to imply the use of computing), computational thinking does not require the use of computers and is not novel to the twenty-first century. This kind of thinking requires abstraction (formulate the problem), automation (model the solution) and analyses (execute and evaluate the solution). This way of thinking is based in a constructivist view of pedagogy, which views students as active cognizing agents as opposed to behaviourism's view of students as vessels that needed to be filled by more knowledgeable teachers (Papert, 1980). A brief caveat is in order; the term 'constructivism', as with many popular terms, has become rhetorically hollow. This is especially true in relation to work done by researchers in the field of ICTs and teaching/learning (Li & Ma, 2010; Rosen & Salomon, 2007). For this book, constructivism aligns with Piaget's (1976) notion of cognitive constructivism, where a child transacts with their world to acquire knowledge, and with Vygotsky's notion of cultural historical theory, where HCFs are mediated through interaction between child and (m)other. Significantly, 'constructivism' in this book recognizes that learning is active, collaborative and geared towards the acquisition of abstract concepts. As we shall see in Chapter 3, the notion that a teacher can transmit knowledge directly into the child's head, is flawed.

If we look at the thinking processes required for computational thinking, it becomes clear the Vygotskian and Neo-Vygotskian approaches to teaching/learning certainly meet the criteria for developing computational thinking. The move from the abstract to the concrete implied in computational thinking is precisely what Vygotsky captures in his notion of mediation in the ZPD. In fact, collaboration, higher order thinking skills, real world problems, all of these find their genesis in Vygotsky's early theorizing. Why then, do we need a new of teaching/learning for the twenty-first century when the work of Vygotsky and the Neo-Vygotskians provide decades worth of research to show that their pedagogical theory is not only developmentally sound but that it meets the needs of teaching twenty-first-century competencies.

Pedagogical Content in the Twenty-first Century

Plant trees,
Save the seas,
Punch Nazis and
Decolonise epistemologies
(Graffiti on a wall in Cape Town city central).

Above I have discussed what pedagogy can look like in the twenty-first century and now I turn to what is actually taught in the classroom. What content do children need to acquire in this new century? It is in this challenging space that the work of Hedegaard (1998) and Chaiklin & Hedegaard (2005) equips us with the tools to teach for transformation, not only of the individual child, but of the child's lived experience, their social context.

Hedegaard's double-move, discussed earlier in the chapter, provides a concrete pedagogical mechanism for linking scientific and everyday concepts in such a way that the child changes and is also equipped with the cognitive functions to change his/her immediate environment. In this pedagogical strategy the teacher moves from abstract to concrete and back again, developing the child's cognitive functions throughout in the ZPD. What is of significance for this book is the fact that the double-move seeks to equip students with cognitive functions to alter their environment. If we look at the graffiti quote that begins this section of the introduction, we can see what kind of knowledge many believe we should be aiming to teach in the twenty-first century. For example, teaching children the fundamentals of climate change and how to stop it must surely be a key curriculum item. This is not to suggest that the content of schooling today is entirely out of touch with the needs of this century. Indeed, a child learning about photosynthesis at school is, in effect, learning about how to alleviate climate change if the child is shown how to grow trees, for example. That is, teaching photosynthesis merely for the sake of children acquiring this content in a static manner that they can reproduce on an assessment, is not making use of the double-move in pedagogy. However, if one teaches a child about photosynthesis and makes the growing of trees, plants and vegetables an outcome of the acquisition of this concept, then the curriculum content can truly lead to both individual and societal change. I would argue too, that it's insufficient to merely teach content in the absence of an ethics of care underpinning the curriculum, where collective well-being takes precedence over the individual ego.

For most of its history, Western psychology has focused its analytical gaze on psychological dysfunction, rather than on defining mental health in terms of the presence of positive attributes, sometimes referred to as positive psychology (Ryff, 2014; Seligman, 2002). This is not unusual as Western psychology was borne out of the need to understand psychological illness, rather than wellness. However, African psychologies focus very much on the collective, rather than on the individual, critiquing the social and institutional systems that perpetuate oppression, particularly of Black people, by highlighting how poverty, for example, leads to pathology. That is, African psychology is premised on a dialectical logic that views the individual and social as inextricably intertwined. Pathology then, for African psychology, is located in the social and institutional systems that perpetuate inequality, rather than in a single individual (Ratele, 2019). The epistemic foundation of this collective focus is captured in the African notion of 'ubuntu', mentioned earlier in the chapter. For Magumbate and Cherengi:

> [ubuntu] refers to a collection of values and practices that black people of Africa or of African origin view as making people authentic human beings. While the nuances of these values and practices vary across different ethnic groups, they all point to one thing – an authentic individual human being is part of a larger and more significant relational, communal, societal, environmental and spiritual world.
>
> (2020; vi)

As one can see, the philosophical notion of ubuntu takes account of the collective as well as the social and environmental world students inhabit. A curriculum premised on this notion, then, can achieve what Hedegaard outlines in the double-move as well as the notion of consciousness as developing in and through social interaction, as is echoed in Vygotsky's psychology. I would argue that this epistemic base calls for an ethics of care, which focuses on the collective experience of being human within the natural world and eschews an individualistic stance towards human development in favour of describing care as relational (Bozalek, Zembylas & Tronto, 2020). We might even say that decolonial, African psychologies, founded as they are on dialectical logic, are necessarily underpinned by an ethics of care that goes beyond caring for a single individual alone.

In this chapter, I have briefly outlined the theory of this book focusing on coloniality to argue for how Vygotsky and the Neo-Vygotskians provide concepts for a decolonial pedagogy. The need to challenge the colonial status quo in education caught fire in South Africa in 2015, with students at UCT calling for Rhodes to fall. This decolonial 'moment' quickly spread across the globe, even surfacing in Oxford University, perhaps the very foundation of a colonial epistemology. There is no suggestion here that Vygotsky or the Neo-Vygotskians referenced would see themselves as decolonial thinkers. What I have attempted to do in this chapter is to develop a more radical view of Vygotsky by returning to his actual work, rather than the more domesticated manner in which he is used in some contexts in Western literature (Roth & Jornet, 2017; Stetsenko, 2021). In this domesticated guise we find, for example, mention of the ZPD as a scaffolding tool, linked to specific tasks, when, in fact, this is not what the ZPD is for Vygotsky and this narrowing of the concept loses that sense of social justice and transformation that inheres in Vygotsky's original framing of the concept. In fact, the ZPD is precisely that space where the voice of the marginalized is heard and developed throughout cognitive development. That is, it is a space for social justice and decolonial thinking.

This requires that scholars in this field return to these concepts in a critical manner, reflecting on how they enable us to approach the inequality in schooling through social justice initiatives. The dialogical work articulated by Freire and indeed a cornerstone of Vygotsky's own thinking provides such a basis for pushing at the boundaries of colonial, Western, traditional views of schooling through viewing 'the word' in praxis. It is here too that Hedegaard's (1998) work challenges the status quo in schools by mobilizing the double-move in pedagogy to link scientific concepts with culturally embedded everyday concepts; viewing these as dialectically entailed, with neither concept viewed as superior to the other in meaning making. This is of particular use in an African, and indeed, South African context, where calls for decolonizing the curriculum (Francis & Hardman, 2018) need to be met with practical pedagogical mechanisms for achieving this in a socially just manner.

By marrying the work of Vygotsky, Freire, Hedegaard and Feuerstein, this chapter develops a view of twenty-first-century pedagogy that moves away from using Vygotsky's work in a domesticated fashion, which maintains the status quo, to a view of pedagogy as capable of transforming children's trajectories and using education to reduce inequality by including the voice of the marginalized and challenging colonial epistemologies. Can this proposed pedagogy work in practice? I believe the argument together with the empirical data presented in the rest of the book indicates that this pedagogy can work. However, it is contra the ego-epistemology of the Cartesian kind that focuses on the individual and it seriously challenges modernity and coloniality. It requires of us more than a leap of faith; it requires a severing of ties with the knowledge we have held as 'true' in the past. It requires an epistemology of collective well-being, an ethics of care and an ability to reflect critically on current epistemologies. I return to the work of Ratele (2019) and his notion of identity as collective, situated historically and culturally, to an understanding of the African epistemology of Ubuntu. Some critics may say that an 'attack' on modernity requires that we return to the dark ages; this is un-founded. Critiquing modernity does not suggest that we return to the pre-modern world and relinquish the knowledge accumulated over centuries. It requires that we are sensitive to voices other than Western ones.

Another critique may well suggest that this kind of pedagogy relies on a relativist approach to knowledge, a la Rorty (1991, 1996). Relativism has no ethics of care or collective well-being and represents, in my opinion, a slippery slope into nihilism. This is not the case in the current argument; the linking of scientific and everyday concepts theorized by Vygotsky and operationalized in Hedegaard's work illustrates that knowledge acquired in schools must be useful in transforming not only the child, but the world. We see the movement away from modernist colonial thinking emerging in South Africa. Out of the ashes of the 1976 student movement, African psychology has begun to finally take root in South Africa, challenging the traditional, colonial, Western view of psychopathology as located not solely in the individual but rather in the social, cultural and historical context of that person's development (Ratele, 2019). In closing this chapter, I suggest the following definition of decolonial pedagogy as:

a structured process whereby a culturally more experienced peer or teacher uses cultural tools to mediate or guide a novice into established, relatively stable ways of knowing and being through the co-construction of meaning, within an institutional context, in such a way that the knowledge and skills the novice acquires lead new ways of acting and new relations with the world.

Conclusion

This chapter sets out the theoretical principles that underpin this book, by outlining a foundation for understanding pedagogical practice as it shifts over time and context. The transitions in pedagogy from apartheid to a democratic South Africa form the remainder of the book, where shifts in curricula impact shifts in praxis.

3

Curriculum Transitions: 1994–2019

Ambushed by History: Curriculum Changes, 1948–2008

In 1948 the Nationalist Government of D.F. Malan came to power in South Africa, advocating for the segregation of white and Black people. The policy of apartheid called for distinct schooling for Black and white children, in large part because the Nationalists realized, through the work of Dr Verwoerd, what power education has in limiting personal growth and maintaining inequality through the systematic under-education of most of the population. The Eiselen commission of 1951 pointed out the importance of using education as an institution 'for the transmission and development of black cultural heritage' (Christie & Collins 1982: 59). Consequently, a Bantu Education Act was introduced in 1953 that set out to centralize Bantu education under the powers of the, then, Minister of Native Affairs, Dr Verwoerd, and which set about systematically closing the missionary schools where Black children had received an education closely aligned with that given to white children. While previously missionary schools had strived to mould Black children into the Christian, Western ideals they espoused, Bantu education now sought to deny Black children access to the kind of knowledge 'reserved' for white children. Of course, in the twenty-first century, one can only be critical of the missionary zeal to effectively eradicate 'Blackness' through education that aimed at producing black children who, as Fanon might refer to, wore white masks. Indeed, the idea that missionaries knew what was best for Black children's education is largely unpalatable to us today but was well in keeping with the colonial mindset of the time. As problematic as the missionary education system was, there is a sense at least, in which the missionaries' provided equitable education, however misguided by their desire to produce a Western, Christian 'human'. Bantu Education would seek to undo any gains of missionary education by producing a curriculum and, consequently, pedagogical praxis, that effectively narrowed the scope of what Black people were allowed to learn in South Africa. In 1959 the Promotion of Bantu Self-Government Act designated certain areas of South Africa as Black homelands that would be governed by separate Black governments, which ultimately were beholden to the white National government for funding. Coupled with Bantu Education, this Act clearly had in mind the production of workers for the South African economy as evidenced in the following quote:

> I am in thorough agreement with the view that we should so conduct our schools that the native who attends those schools will know that to a great extent he must be the labourer in the country.
>
> (Eiselen, 1951)

To this end, Bantu education was poorly funded in comparison to the funding of white schooling, with students receiving instruction in basic numeracy, literacy and basic communication together with a strong religious and moral training aspect to the curriculum. The effect of apartheid on the education of the Black South African, then, was the establishment of central control over Black education, with a curriculum tailored to producing manual labourers, in general, rather than highly skilled citizens and creative thinkers. The centrally controlled Bantu education system provided for lower-primary (grade 1–4) and higher-primary (grades 5–8) schools and, for a few selected students, some post-primary school. Progression was automatic and after the first four years of basic schooling, students would sit a test to determine who would benefit from furthering their education. Students going on to higher primary education would continue to learn basic subjects such as gardening and agriculture, as opposed to, for example, mathematics.

Those children selected for post-primary school were chosen because they were deemed capable of taking up a role in 'Bantu society' (Christie & Collins, 1982: 70). White teachers were gradually phased out of Black schools and female teachers were selected over male teachers to cut costs in these schools. To meet the growing need for teachers in Black schools, teachers were accepted with a three-year post form 1 certificate and a three-year post form 3 certificate, lowering the educational level required to teach Black students. As a result, quality education was difficult to acquire in these schools. The impact of systematic under education for Black children would continue to be felt well into South Africa's democracy, indicating the powerful effect pedagogy and curriculum can have on development.

Curriculum as Developmental Tool

The opening quote, that education is always political, is especially clear when one turns to analysing curricula. Central to Vygotsky's thesis is the notion that the individual's interaction with objects in the world is mediated by cultural artefacts: signs, symbols and practical tools. Artefacts carry with them a history of use and are themselves altered, shaped and transformed when used in activities. From a Vygotskian perspective, tools alter our external world and signs (which Vygotsky denotes as 'psychological tools') alter our internal, mental world. Signs *'... are directed toward the mastery of control of behavioural processes- someone else's or one's own – just as technical means are directed toward the control of processes of nature'* (Vygotsky, 1978: 137) whereas, tools have a specific external direction: *'The tool's function is to serve as the conductor of human influence on the object of activity; it is externally oriented; it must lead to changes in objects'* (Vygotsky, 1978; 55). While Vygotsky distinguishes between signs and tools, it is useful to think of a curriculum as both sign and tool; tool, because it aims to alter the larger environment in its production of specific types of thinkers and sign in that it aims to develop cognitive functioning. While it is tempting to think of a curriculum as devoid of anything more than specific content, for example, mathematics, when one really looks at a curriculum, it's clear that it is not simply a mechanism for delivering content. Certain knowledge is presented, other knowledge not and it is here, in what is presented and what is left out, that one sees the hand of those with power, controlling what can and cannot be taught.

For the Black child, 'Bantu education' sought to develop, in the main, manual labourers to drive the South African economy and the curriculum served as a tool to systematically under educate these children. For the white child, Christian National Education (an education system), based on Calvinistic principles,[1] rolled out a curriculum that was heavily focused on performance[2] and a transmission mode of pedagogy. The firm religious basis on which Christian National Education was founded had a direct impact not only on what was taught in schools but also, on how it was taught and on who was considered 'worthy' of being taught.

For white children, this provided a model of curriculum that was based on behaviourist premises that saw children as empty vessels waiting to be filled with knowledge from the teacher. Fundamental pedagogics in the apartheid State aimed to separate mental from manual work, with white children being taught science and mathematics while Black children were taught about, for example, agriculture. The focus of fundamental pedagogics is on the performance of the child that is, what is produced on a summative examination, rather than on the competence a child brings to a task. This distinction is in line with Vygotsky's (1986) understanding of the difference between what a child can perform on their own, which is indicative of what they already know, and what the child has the potential (or competence) to achieve, given the requisite mediated engagement. Thus, individual problem solving is indicative of performance whilst problem solving with a culturally more knowledgeable other is indicative of developing the students' competence. The sociologist of education, Basil Bernstein (1996), sees the distinction between performance and competencies in relation to the curriculum, not to learning as Vygotsky does. For Bernstein, a performance model is teacher-centred and asymmetrical[3] while a competence model of curriculum is learner-centred and geared towards developing students' understanding rather than simply their performance on a test. Competence models are further divided into progressive competence models, populist models and radical models of the curriculum. A competence model focuses on cognitive empowerment, while the populist mode is geared towards cultural empowerment and the radical mode forms the basis for political empowerment. As we shall see, the South African curriculum that was rolled out after apartheid, contains features of all three models of curriculum identified by Bernstein (1996; Taylor, 1999). These are, of course, ideal types and one may find these models interacting together in any given school. A key distinction between the types of curricula is to be found in the pedagogy that is enacted in the classroom.

For Taylor (1999) performance models favour a pedagogy that is teacher-centred while competence models are learner centred, where 'learner-centred' requires that '... learners take control of their own learning: they are active, creative, and self-regulatory. Direct interventions by the teacher are seen as suspect and as interfering in a natural process'[4] (Taylor, 1999: 256). I find this distinction between teacher- versus learner-centred pedagogy highly problematic.

The terms 'teacher-centred' and 'learner-centred' are, I suggest, rhetorically hollow but are used here because they appear in policy documents. Embedded as I am in the dialectical logic of cultural historical theory, I cannot see how pedagogy can be anything but centred on the learner, that is, on learning. Surely the very act of teaching implies learning, and hence a learner. If teaching is viewed solely as reinforcing a canon of knowledge through instruction, without requiring the development of higher cognitive concepts, then one can conceive of it as being teacher-centred and perhaps it is in relation to this understanding of schooling that one can speak of teacher- versus learner-centred pedagogy. Any familiarity with the work of Vygotsky (1986) or Piaget (1976) must, however, seriously call into question the notion that a learner directs their own learning of abstract concepts in the absence of strong, structured teaching, which I would call mediation. If, as Taylor (1999) indicates above, learning is the result of a 'natural process' that a teacher must not intervene in, then I would argue that the only concept that a child learns in this instance is an everyday, empirical concept, that is, not an abstract concept. As discussed in Chapter 2, abstract concepts are necessarily taught. Everyday concepts are essential to higher cognitive development, but only when they are linked to abstract concepts. Similarly, abstraction only makes sense to a child if they can link it to their everyday concepts. It makes more sense, I suggest, to think of the performance-based model in terms of a transmission-based mode of pedagogy as distinct from a progressive acquisition mode of pedagogy. A transmission mode focuses on content at the expense, often, of cognitive development, with the teacher viewed as expert and the students viewed as passive recipients of the 'Truth'. Knowledge is not up for debate in this scenario and meaning is fixed by the teacher without recourse to students' own understandings. An acquisition mode of pedagogy, on the other hand, is geared towards the student acquiring new knowledge, through transacting with the world and other culturally more expert peers/teachers. This active, cognizing agent, the student, co-constructs knowledge with the more expert 'other', making sense of abstraction in relation to what they already know and developing higher cognitive functions through the linking of scientific (abstract) concepts and everyday concepts. The skill, if you like, of the teacher is to link these two concepts in such a manner that the student can move from a place of not knowing, to a place of knowing. This type of pedagogy, sometimes referred as 'constructivist' pedagogy, is difficult and requires that teachers have access to resources to aid them in defining the abstract concepts and linking these to everyday concepts. The textbooks that a teacher uses, for example, must contain explicit elaboration of abstract concepts and provide mechanisms for linking these concepts to the child's everyday concepts. As we shall see in Part 3 of this book, this is not what some textbooks, at least, are like in South Africa.

The dangers then, of progressive pedagogy, lie in how it plays out in a classroom, which depends heavily on the material and cognitive resources that the teacher has access to. In my own research I have seen teachers use inappropriate metaphors when trying to link abstract knowledge to everyday concepts (Hardman & Techsmacher, 2019). I have also seen teachers draw entirely on the everyday, without linking this to any abstract concept or point to real world examples of something that don't, in fact, relate to the abstraction being discussed (Hardman & Set, 2021). Behind this lies a lack of teacher training and material and cognitive resources, for both teachers and taught (Gumede & Biyase, 2016; Spaul, 2013). As we shall see in Chapters 5 and 7, how knowledge is presented in textbooks impacts directly on how a teacher teaches. Failure to provide a teacher with deep, elaborated knowledge about concepts hinders their ability to teach these concepts. This point regarding progressive pedagogy (located in a progressive curriculum model) and its potential pitfalls will become important as we discuss the post-apartheid move to a democratic, progressive curriculum in South Africa.

The Rise of a Democratic Discourse in Education: South Africa Mid-1980s to 1990s

The mid-1980s marked a move away from the rigidity of Christian National Education due, in part, to the governments' realization that they needed to modernize apartheid educational policies to make them more palatable to their opponents and, in part, to the democratic movement's realization that the end of apartheid was inevitable (Cross et al., 2002; Harley & Vedekind, 2004; Jansen 1999). It had now become necessary to think about alternative policies aimed at building a new South Africa. By the end of the 1980s and the beginning of the 1990s, the Department of National Education (DNE) formulated a Curriculum Model for South Africa (CUMSA). CUMSA was underpinned by the socio-historical positioning of the two bodies who constructed it: namely the Human Sciences Research Council (HSRC) and Afrikaans educationalists.

CUMSA therefore embodied the elitist, technocratic ideals underpinning research in these circles (Cross et al., 2002). The government sought to address labour market concerns by strengthening the vocational component of the curriculum through the Educational Renewal Strategy (ERS), which sought to 'renew and restructure the South African education system in order to improve existing deficiencies, … and training opportunities for an ever-growing population' (Department of National Education, 1995: 5). This curriculum (the latest version was issued in July 1994) sought to modernize the apartheid education system while strengthening the vocational component to meet the growing economic needs of globalization. The ERS was soon eclipsed by the National Education Policy Investigation (NEPI) reports that were written on the request of the liberation movement. These twelve reports highlighted the need to reconceptualize the education system in terms that were non-racist and non-sexist and that promoted democracy, equity and social justice. The NEPI reports where critiqued for their 'impoverished notion of policy implementation' (Cross et al., 2002). Sehoole (2000), for example, refers to these reports as lacking 'policy literacy', by which he means, the understanding of the complexities involved in developing, negotiating, adopting and implementing policies within particular contexts. After NEPI, the ANC's Head of Education constituted an independent policy research agency, the Centre for Education Policy Development (CEPD), which, working closely with academics, trade unions, NGO's and mass-based movements, CEPD, provided the foundation for the 1994 ANC Policy for Education and Training. Unfortunately, the visionary and symbolic nature of these policies did not factor in the challenges that implementing such policies would have in a country where government resources are limited, and a large segment of the population has been systematically under-educated.

Curriculum Reform in Post-apartheid South Africa: From Fundamental to Progressive Pedagogy

March 1997 saw the launch of Curriculum 2005 (C2005), marking a departure from content to outcomes-based education (OBE) and a progressive response to apartheid's performance curriculum model (Spreen & Vally, 2010). While OBE was certainly influenced by competency-based debates in New Zealand, Scotland, Canada and Australia, it is an oversimplification to suggest that OBE has merely been transplanted into South Africa (which Kallaway, 1997, for example, suggests would be another form of cultural imperialism) (Cross et al., 2002). In fact, OBE owes some of its substance to the National Training Board (NTB) and Congress of South African Trade Unions (COSATU; at the time South Africa's largest labour union), who together produced the National Training Strategy Initiative policy document, which provided the foundation for the national training strategy that was later developed (Jansen, 1999b).

The NTB recognized the need for a technologically literate labour force, capable of using maths and science, that could facilitate South Africa's economic growth. One of the key issues for COSATU was that workers could gain recognition for what they could do. This focus on competency-based education began to dominate the National Qualifications Framework debates and gained expression in the development of C2005. If one appreciates OBE's genesis in the labour movement, one can begin to understand one of the key critiques facing

OBE today; namely that teaching in South African schools today serves a skills acquisition, rather than a development, function. Of interest, however, was OBE's promise of a break with the past and a move from fundamental pedagogics to progressive pedagogy underpinned by a learner[5]-centred approach to teaching and learning. The need to move away from a curriculum that separated mental and manual work or academic and vocational training was recognized in the curriculum's focus on the integration of education and training. The ideological thrust behind C2005 is outlined in the White Paper on Education and Training (1995) and the South African Schools Act (1996), emphasizing the social justice imperative to provide quality education for all through developing democratic citizens capable of participating in the knowledge economy of the twenty-first century. Past inequities were to be redressed through the provision of new pedagogical strategies enabling flexible delivery of services across diverse learning contexts through equitable distribution of technological resources. The move to OBE in C2005 looked to completely transform the curriculum with the policy stating that:

> No thought is given to the existing curriculum. Instead, schools (or local districts) are told they can choose any content and use a wide range of teaching methods as long as these develop citizens who display the agreed-upon critical outcomes.
>
> (South African Department of Education, 2000b: 19)

The focus on assessment, then, was geared towards outcomes. The above quote, however, is extremely troubling when one is dealing with an unequal country. We have noted how poorly Black teachers were trained under apartheid, and yet, this quote indicates that teachers will not only select the methods they favour for teaching, but also (and most worryingly) they will decide on the content to be covered if they meet the entirely vague 'agreed upon critical outcomes'. Teaching is a challenging job when one is well prepared to do it and one has a structured plan to follow. When one is not trained and has been given no structure to follow, the outcome appears obvious: failure of the new curriculum. Of course, the political motive for the transformation in the curriculum is important and the quote below illustrates this:

> An integrated approach implies a view of learning which rejects the rigid division between 'academic' and 'applied', 'theory' and 'practice', 'knowledge' and 'skills', 'head' and 'hand'. Such divisions have characterised the organisation of curricula and the distribution of educational opportunity in many countries of the world, including South Africa. They have grown out of, and helped to reproduce, very

old occupational and social class distinctions. In South Africa such distinctions in curriculum and career choice have also been closely associated in the past with the ethnic structure of economic opportunity and power.

(South African Department of Education, 1995: 15)

This quote indicates the desire to break down the boundaries that existed under National Christian Education and fundamental pedagogics and can be read through Vygotsky's dialectical logic as attempting to overcome a binary logic that separates things that are, in fact, dialectically entailed: such as theory and practice. There is no theory without practice and no practice without theory. These are admirable sentiments and are, I would argue, entirely correct for developing sound pedagogy that can lead to the development of cognitive functions. However, this depends *entirely* on how the curriculum is rolled out and the level of training teachers are given, so that the intricate intertwining of, for example, knowledge and skills is understood.

Fundamental pedagogics has favoured binary logic since the Enlightenment, with the Cartesian ego as the centre of knowledge. How a teacher who is not thoroughly trained in dialectical logic will be able to move from this Cartesian logic, without great difficulty, is not immediately obvious. Jansen (1999) warned of the potential failure of C2005 because he understood, and had worked in, the unequal schooling terrain in South Africa. Unfortunately, Jansen was right; C2005, although admirable in its quest for social justice, resulted in a radical form of learner-centredness that soon appeared to disadvantage the very students it was meant to promote, namely, poor second language students in under-resourced schools with poorly prepared teachers (Harley & Vedekind, 1999; Muller, 2000). The government had failed to 'read the room'. In a country with the highest Gini co-efficient in the world, the one size fits all, underspecified curriculum presented as C2005 had little chance of succeeding in the absence of serious training for teachers.

The focus on 'learner-centred' pedagogy led many teachers to a view of learning as based in group work (Harley & Vedekind, 2004). While there is nothing inherently wrong with working in groups (it can be an effective mechanism for learning where students are at different developmental levels), the success of learning in a group depends on how the group is designed. If one assumes, drawing from Vygotsky (1986), that a child can learn more through mediation with a culturally more competent other (this could be a peer), group work makes a lot of sense as a mechanism for promoting learning. However, this is not how group work was carried out in schools using C2005. Students were broken into random groups, often the groups they sat with, and given roles such as 'scribe' or 'time-keeper'. A group promoting learning should have partners that are at different developmental levels and are, therefore, able to assist each other to develop. Moreover, the task that one assigns a group to solve should be one that is ill-structured (Strohm-Kitchener, 1981), that is, a problem with many competing viewpoints, not with a single, simple answer. Cutting up a poem into various sections and getting each group to report on each different stanza is not what group work is about. And yet, I have seen this type of group work more than once in my career. With this type of 'group work' serving as an indicator (for teachers) of a learner-centred pedagogy, there were bound to be issues with what children could learn under C2005 (Brodie, 2000; Ensor, 2001). Pedagogy aside, C2005 failed due to its complexity, lack of teacher training and uneven roll-out (Vally & Spreen, 1998).

For many (see, for example, Jansen, 1999), OBE had failed to achieve its emancipatory goal of educating all South African school children. Indeed, the failure of OBE was predicted before it was rolled out (Chisholm, 2005; Muller, 2000). Two years after implementation, the C2005 was reviewed given the challenges that had arisen. The Review Committee into Curriculum 2005 Report (Chisholm et al., 2003) consequently found that C2005 was over-designed and under-stipulated. In its attempt to pursue a policy of integrating subjects and real-world material, C2005 rendered the sequence, pacing and progression requirements, of especially the gateway subjects of language, mathematics and science, invisible to teachers and students alike (Muller, 2000). The result was staggeringly poor learner progression. One main lesson of the Review was thus that explicitness of the learning and evaluation requirements could not, under present South African conditions of learning, be sacrificed in the name of learner-centredness without impairing learning. This lesson is now embedded in the National Curriculum Statement (NCS) for grades 1 to 9, that was rolled out in 2009. While this critique is valid, it is useful to understand why OBE was doomed to fail in C2005. I would argue that it is not the focus on the student (what OBE refers to as learner-centred pedagogy) and on the harnessing students' everyday knowledge to teach, that lies at the heart of OBE's failure; rather, it is the context in which this pedagogical model was rolled out that essentially doomed it to fail, coupled with a very vague understanding of what everyday concepts are.

In post-apartheid South Africa, most teachers who worked in the 'Bantu Education' system were extremely poorly trained. Even teachers working in more well-resourced schools, it has transpired, have poor content knowledge, especially in core areas such as science and mathematics (Hoadley, 2011;

Spaull, 2013). Presenting these teachers with a curriculum and consequent pedagogical praxis that was not well specified, and which appeared to focus most heavily on everyday concepts, left the abstraction that needed to be taught firmly in the hands of the teacher. Where a teacher lacked the requisite knowledge to develop a link between the everyday and abstract concepts in the school, the curriculum was mute on how to bridge this. This led teachers, whose knowledge of abstraction was weak to begin with, to rely more heavily on the local, contextual everyday concepts in their teaching. As noted in Chapter 2, a focus on everyday concepts in the absence of linking these to scientific/abstract concepts cannot lead to development. Rather, it leads to, and perpetuates, misconceptions by the learner.

If constructivism, which underpins OBE, has any real meaning, its meaning is underpinned predominantly by the work of Piaget (1976) and Vygotsky (1978; 1986). Especially in relation to the development of higher cognitive functions, there is no way that a child can develop these in the absence of explicit instruction in abstract concepts that are linked with everyday concepts. One cannot privilege everyday concepts over the abstract, nor vice versa. Both are necessary for the development of thinking. Where you have a situation of under-resourced schools and teachers who lack content knowledge, the ability to link abstract concepts to the everyday becomes near impossible in the absence of either teacher training or, at the very least, textbooks that elaborate the abstract concepts in depth. As we shall see in Chapter 5, even with the revised curriculum and the new Curriculum and Assessment Policy (CAPS), textbooks remain largely silent in relation to abstract concept owing, I would suggest, to the continued focus on pedagogy as largely outcomes based. This is clear in the following quote which purports to give outline of what teaching is supposed to look like in a South African context:

- the active learner and ideas of uniqueness and difference the active teacher who, rather than following a prescriptive syllabus,
- makes decisions about what to teach and how to teach it
- the relative importance of activity and skills as a basis for knowing and knowledge
- the relative importance of induction over deduction. (South African Department of Education 2000a: 47)

Whilst these points are all crucial in developmental teaching, nothing stated above is self-evident and each point requires a deep understanding, on the teacher's behalf, of both content knowledge and of developmental principles underpinning learning. An 'active learner' is not simply a child engaged in a hands-on activity. Thinking is active. Therefore, teachers need to be taught that simply doing something, or moving about, is not the only way a child can be active. The ability to select content for students is key to teaching, and yet, we have already discussed the fact that teachers' content knowledge in South Africa is poor (Hoadley, 2011). The final bullet point above is, I suggest, the most troubling. Teaching/learning is surely *both* inductive and deductive? A focus solely on inductive teaching/learning will lead to empirical knowledge; that is, knowledge that stays at the level of the everyday concept and is, therefore, contextually bound, and devoid of abstraction. More problematically, however, is the fact that a focus solely on inductive teaching/learning can lead to misconceptions. So, while I agree with the spirit of the points above, there is much to be done in teacher training before this can become a reality in South African classrooms. I am a proponent of progressive pedagogy, but there is a need to understand where this pedagogical model comes from.

It is clear, to this author at least, that progressive pedagogy is based on the theoretical foundations of Piaget and Vygotsky, one a cognitive constructivist and the other a cultural-historical theorist. In its implementation in C2005 and OBE, however, this foundation was recontextualized to mean something akin to discovery-based learning (see, for example, Botha, 2016). As a pedagogical practice, discovery-based learning is fraught with challenges and is not based on the work of either Piaget or Vygotsky in any coherent fashion. The problem with discovery-based learning is that, left to their own devices, children will 'discover' incorrect information. This is especially so if one assumes that discovery-based learning can lead to the acquisition of abstract concepts (Karpov, 2005). An example illustrates the difficulties here: a child who sees a dolphin and a shark will assume, by looking at them and 'discovering' their apparent similarities, that both are, apparently, fish. They both have fins, live in the ocean and are carnivorous. A dolphin, however, is more closely related, genetically, to a cow than it is to a shark. There is nothing in the empirical realm that will help a child to discover the differences between mammals and sharks. It is at this juncture, faced with this information from a child, that a teacher can begin to link to the everyday concept with actual abstract concepts such as mammals. A further example of how one can link the everyday concept to abstraction in science relates to an activity that children are familiar with: taking a bath. When the child gets into the bath, the water 'magically' rises and when the child gets out of the bath, the water sinks to the previous level. This is a perfect time for a culturally more expert other to introduce the notion of Archimedes law.

The 'Post' Progressive Turn: The Problem with Progressivism in Practice in South Africa

We briefly highlighted the problems with the implementation of a progressive curriculum model in South Africa, such as the C2005 and the development of the NCS. The NCS was rolled out in schools in South Africa in 2002 and by 2009 this curriculum was again under scrutiny for its focus on OBE and painfully low attainment in students' outcomes. The NCS Review Report put a focus on what is to be learnt, rather than on vague outcomes, suggesting that 'clear content, concept and skill standards and clear and concise assessment requirements' should replace the notion of outcomes (South African Department of Education 2009: 45). Based on the work of Basil Bernstein in large part, the review of the NCS pointed again to the importance of a knowledge-based curriculum and offered a detailed critique of OBE. This review was taken on board ostensibly with the minister of Education saying in parliament that she 'had signed OBE's death certificate' (Motshekga, 2009).

Revisions to the NCS did not specify a constructivist pedagogy, although the understanding that children are active in constructing knowledge was accepted. Following the NCS review report a new Curriculum Assessment Policy Statement (CAPS) was introduced that focused more on specifying knowledge and assessment standards. It might be, though, that the pendulum has swung too far back to a more traditional pedagogy, as CAPS is very administration, content and assessment heavy, leaving little time for teachers to engage in developing deep understandings of knowledge (Du Plessis, 2015). Moreover, teachers have once again received very little training in how to deliver CAPS and how to effectively teach in a constructivist manner that aims to develop children cognitively. The failure of a constructivist approach to teaching through OBE has led many to turn away from this as a model of pedagogy. However, if one reads the work of Piaget and Vygotsky, upon which the notion of constructivism is built, one comes to see that this work has been recontextualized rather badly and has ended up with an understanding of constructivist teaching/learning as 'discovery-based'. As discussed earlier, discovery-based learning is highly problematic as it leads to misconceptions in that it fails to link the everyday with the subject's abstract concepts. With CAPS, teachers have so much content to cover and so many assessments to deliver, that the very idea of tailoring the content to, for example, the students' space (as one would in a constructivist classroom) cannot be carried out. There simply is not enough time to develop understanding when the load is so heavy. What we see emerging in classrooms is a contradiction between content coverage versus developing understanding of the content (Hardman, 2016). Heavily mired in assessments, with children as young as eight being formally assessed on summative tests, little time is given to ensuring that children understand core concepts (Hardman, 2020).

Goetze (2016) indicates that the impact of CAPS on children is an increase in anxiety amongst ever younger children, due to the content heavy curriculum, over assessment, the rigidity of the curriculum and the excessively fast pacing needed to cover such a content dense curriculum. With CAPS, it seems, we have thrown the baby out with the bathwater. Viewing curriculum change in South Africa through a dialectical lens, we must appreciate that CAPS has produced a contradiction in the object of the activity of schooling: curriculum coverage versus understanding. What we have is children who are over assessed and, in some instances at least, this has led to teachers teaching to the test, rather than developing students' understanding of concepts. Moreover, the actual content that students learn has changed very little over time, and there is little difference in the content of what is taught in the twenty-first century to what was taught in the twentieth century. This is surely problematic as the world our children face today is not the world of the previous century.

The Decolonial Turn: Whose Knowledge and Who Decides What Counts as Knowledge?

> 'Science as a whole is a product of western modernity and the whole thing should be scratched off. Especially in Africa,' she says. 'I have a question for all the science people. There is a place in KwaZulu-Natal called Umhlab'uyalingana. They believe that through the magic, you call it black magic, they call it witchcraft, you are able to send lightening to strike someone. Can you explain that scientifically because it's something that happens?'
>
> (Henderson, Business Live, 17 October 2016)

The newspaper excerpt above comes from the context of the #feesmustfall movement in 2016. Here a young woman, registered in a university faculty of Humanities, indicates that her idea of a decolonial curriculum requires that science should be 'scratched off'. She goes on to explain that science in Africa is unable to explain how witchcraft can be used to kill someone using lightening. This might sound strange to an international audience, but the idea that someone can be struck by lightning due to witchcraft is not unfamiliar to me.

When I was a child growing up in Botswana, a man was killed by lightening. This was attributed by some people to the malevolent intervention of an old woman residing on the outskirts of his cattle post who was envious of his lifestyle. While this young woman, quoted above, believes that science has no place in Africa, this, surely, cannot be what a decolonial curriculum or its contents looks like? In what follows, I puzzle through some of my own and others' arguments about what can be taught in a decolonial curriculum.

In Chapter 2 I spoke about the difficulties of defining decolonial education, specifically, decolonial pedagogy. The call to decolonise education is not novel, but it certainly has gained traction in the twenty-first century, especially in South Africa where the #feesmustfall movement managed to close all South African universities until some of the protestors' terms had been met. The students were adamant that one of the core issues that needed to be addressed was a decolonizing of the curriculum at universities. Jansen (2017) has elaborated what a decolonial curriculum could look like and outlines six ideas of what decolonizing knowledge entails. In the first instance, the decentring of Western epistemologies and the replacing of Western voices with previously marginalized ones. Second, he discusses an additive or inclusive curriculum. This is not unlike what I discussed in Chapter 2 of this book. Here, decolonial knowledge adds substance to the established canon. Third, the entire Western canon is replaced by an Afro-centric canon. Fourth, regarding pedagogy, a decolonial curriculum requires a critical engagement with established knowledge. This is not unlike David's (2018) suggestion of a pedagogy of critique. Fifth, an engagement with how the knowledge of the colonized and colonizer are intertwined and entangled. And, finally, using a decolonial position to repatriate knowledge that has been occupied by the Western canon. These are useful points, but they don't enable us to answer the question that heads this section of the chapter – whose knowledge is it and who decides on what counts as 'useful' or 'good' knowledge?

Davydov (1990) argues that two distinct knowledge forms arise from the differences between these scientific and everyday concepts: empirical and theoretical knowledge. Empirical knowledge we know spontaneously through our engagement with the world. These are not mediated, and their meaning is local, and context bound. On the other hand, theoretical knowledge needs to be explicitly taught to the developing child. Abstract concepts cannot be learnt through an empirical engagement with the world because their meaning is culturally and historically constructed in a specific context. These are decontextualized concepts whose meaning needs to be mediated to the developing child. The distinction between empirical and theoretical knowledge seems to be a good place to begin a conversation about what kind of knowledge needs to be in the curriculum and therefore, explicitly taught by a culturally more competent other. However, and this is where we can harness indigenous knowledge, there is a necessary link between everyday and scientific concepts. One cannot understand the scientific without the everyday and the everyday only rises fully to consciousness in the presence of the scientific. Schooling, I would argue, requires the mediation of theoretical knowledge, but this cannot be achieved in the absence of empirical knowledge. If we accept, then, that theoretical knowledge must be taught in school (because empirical knowledge can be learnt anywhere), then the next question becomes, what kind of content do we want our children to learn? And who will select this content knowledge?

The kind of knowledge children need for schooling today must reflect the kind of world we find ourselves in. For example, climate change is very real and yet children are not explicitly taught in school how to address this issue. This is a large body of knowledge that can be taught across all the different subjects, because it requires that children are literate, numerate, have scientific knowledge (for example, how to desalinate sea water), biological, geographical and historical knowledge. Constructing a curriculum to meet the needs of the twenty-first century will require various stakeholders. Educators, of course, need to be involved in this endeavour, but so too do scientists as well as those within our communities who are the keepers of traditional knowledge and wisdom. And here I am aware that this is not a novel solution. In fact, I am open to critique precisely because I am stating an obvious solution to content in schools, one that many, if not most, educators would have thought of before. So where is the novelty in my suggestion?

To address this, I turn to the work of Basil Bernstein, the British educational sociologist who describes, rather elegantly, how disciplinary knowledge becomes recontextualized in schools through something he calls the 'pedagogic device' (Hoadley & Gallant, 2019). I take this step into sociology to illustrate how what is learnt in schools, what counts as knowledge and who determines this, lies in the evaluation criteria that are agreed upon by members of disciplinary subjects; that is, those criteria that are selected to determine what counts as knowledge in, say, a test. What is the difference, if you will, between an answer that obtains 80 per cent and one that fails? What criteria determine this and who selects these criteria?

Bernstein (1977; 1996) views curriculum in terms of power. He describes two core concepts in relation to the curriculum and pedagogy: classification, which refers to the strength of boundaries between disciplines and framing, which refers to pedagogic control over pacing, sequencing, selection and evaluation criteria. Classification (operating at the level of the curriculum) is strong where very strict boundaries are maintained between disciplines and knowledge is viewed as very specialized, and weak when boundaries are more porous. Framing (operating in relation to control over pedagogical praxis) too is described in terms of whether it is strong, with the teacher entirely in control or weak, with students' controlling sequencing, selection, pacing and the evaluative criteria in a classroom (Bernstein, 1977; Daniels, 2004; Hoadley & Gallant, 2019; Vinjevold and Taylor, 1999). In this chapter we would view fundamental pedagogics as strongly classified and framed; that is, strong boundaries between disciplinary knowledge and very strong teacher control over rules of pacing, sequencing, selection and evaluative criteria. OBE, on the other hand, as a form of progressive pedagogy, is more weakly classified and pedagogy is controlled more by students (in theory), weakening the framing/control the teacher has in the classroom. For Bernstein (1996), evaluation 'condenses into itself the pedagogic code and its classification and framing procedures, and the relationships of power and control that have produced these procedures' (1996: p.18). Evaluation, then, provides us with a window into the teacher's epistemic assumptions regarding what the subject content is. It provides a window through which to view pedagogical practice. Evaluative rules are those rules that transmit the criteria to produce legitimate texts, behaviour and relations. In a sense, these rules are psychological tools that the teacher provides to the children (Karpov, 2003). These rules are 'framed' to greater or lesser degrees depending on the amount of control exercised by the teacher. In relation to evaluation criteria, where framing is strong, one expects to see the teacher making visible the rules for successful engagement with the task. Conversely, where framing is weaker, rules become less visible and the criteria for generating a legitimate text become more opaque to the student (Morais et al., 2004). Framing refers, then, to relations within boundaries. When the student oversteps or challenges these often-tacit boundaries the teacher is forced to re-assert the boundary, making visible the previously invisible rules of engagement.

If we were to think about this in cultural historical terms, we could say that *'evaluative criteria communicate the object'* to be constructed by illuminating how one arrives at a legitimate text (Hardman, 2019: 91). In his 'pedagogic device', Bernstein (1996; 39) illustrates how knowledge obtained through scholarly research is recontextualized into school content knowledge through classification and framing. Curriculum, then, amounts to a recontextualization of disciplinary knowledge that is transformed into content that children acquire in school (Hoadley & Gallant, 2018). At the level of the classroom, control over the pace, sequence, selection and, crucially, how evaluative criteria are transmitted and acquired, and it is here, in the classroom that 'what counts as knowledge' is ultimately decided (Hoadley & Gallant, 2018). It is at the level of the classroom that the rules for producing a legitimate text/answer are made explicit or kept implicit.

Turning back to the question posed at the beginning of this section, whose knowledge is it and who decides what counts as knowledge, I suggest that 'whose' knowledge it is, is to be found in our understanding of the link between the everyday and the scientific concept. The child makes sense of the abstraction taught in the class by reference to their everyday concepts. The knowledge constructed in the classroom is our knowledge: the knowledge of both the individual child and the teacher (embedded in the curriculum content, recontextualized from disciplinary knowledge). The devil, it seems, is in the detail. If we think of everyday concepts as referring to everything the child encounters in their empirical world, we are mistaken about our understanding of concepts. A concept is an idea; an everyday concept is an idea developed through empirically interacting with the world and it can, therefore, be incorrect. When we speak about the everyday as essential in the child making sense of the scientific concept, we need to remember that they could have misconceptions and it is through the act of teaching and co-constructing meaning that we will overcome these misconceptions. The meaning of the scientific concept is not idiosyncratic; it is a recontextualization of disciplinary knowledge, packaged for schooling. Who decides what counts as knowledge then is the disciplinary experts who can articulate what the meaning of say, photosynthesis is, and how understanding this can, for example, help us understand climate change and how it might be combatted? The abstract knowledge is shared by a cultural community (in this instance, biologists and scientists, botanists, and conservation biologists) and making sense of this knowledge is part of the job of the everyday concept that the child brings to the classroom.

Conclusion

This chapter tracked curriculum change from apartheid's rigid National Christian Education to democratic South Africa's new CAPS. Curriculum change is a tricky thing, especially in a country like South Africa with its oppressive past and legacy of skewed access to resources and wealth. C2005, introduced post-apartheid, was a political rather than a pedagogical reform. The subsequent failure of OBE was to be expected. With little training and heavily under-resourced, teachers appeared to understand learner-centred education as requiring that they took on the role of guide on the side, rather than as an expert in subject matter. Group work, that ever-present token of learner-centred education, became more about activity, defined, not as thinking, but as doing, such as cutting and pasting, colouring in and generally accomplishing non-academic tasks. Teachers were (and in many instances still are) not well prepared enough to teach abstract concepts in the absence of a well-defined, structured curriculum. The revision of the curriculum and the establishment of CAPS brought with it the hope that students would be able to access more tightly defined abstract knowledge. However, CAPS is content, assessment and administratively heavy. How can any single curriculum cater to the needs of the least-resourced together with the most-resourced? My response to this is that no curriculum should be a one size fits all curriculum. Currently in South Africa, the same curriculum faces you whether you attend a school under a tree or whether you attend a school with your own iPad, in an air conditioned classroom. Something is clearly wrong with this picture. I am not a curriculum expert and cannot claim to have the answers to re-working the curriculum. However, teaching/learning is my field, and I believe that it is here, at the coal face, that the teacher can adapt the curriculum to meet the needs of individual students, through a specific type of pedagogy, what I am calling a decolonial pedagogy, based in the work of Vygotsky, Chaiklin and Hedegaard, Freire and Feuerstein. The objective of the current chapter was to illustrate, in broad brush strokes, the socio-historical conditions that have given rise to the possibility of a new pedagogy within a developing country such as South Africa. The rest of this book aims to illustrate how this is possible.

4

Pedagogical Transitions: 1994–2019

Pedagogical Transitions from Apartheid to Democracy

While education, defined as, learning new knowledge through a more experienced other, has a long history, schooling as we know it today is a relatively new invention, begun in the nineteenth century primarily to educate males to become civil servants. By the twentieth century, both girls and boys were attending schools, which gradually became compulsory. Schooling, then, is perhaps the biggest social experiment of the last 150 years, and there is still much to be learnt about how exactly children learn, although neuroscience and educational psychology is making inroads here. While research on schooling is ongoing and shifting all the time, one of the things we do know about schooling is that children need to be engaged with someone who can guide them to new knowledge, a teacher. Pedagogy is essential to schooling; children do not only learn the body of knowledge contained in a school on their own, but they also need to be guided in learning new cognitive skills, such as learning to read.

In this book I draw on my own definition of pedagogy as: *a structured process whereby a culturally more experienced peer or teacher uses cultural tools to mediate or guide a novice into established, relatively stable ways of knowing and being within a particular, institutional context, in such a way that the knowledge and skills the novice acquires lead to relatively lasting changes in the novice's activity; that is, learning* (Hardman, 2019: 5). Broadly speaking, there are two poles of pedagogical practice; on the one end is the understanding that passive children learn through facts that are transmitted by the expert teacher and one the other end is the notion that children are active cognizing agents who learn through acquiring knowledge through interaction with a more expert teacher. The former understanding is 'transmission' pedagogy while the latter is 'acquisition' pedagogy; also referred to as teacher-centred versus learner-centred pedagogy. South Africa, since 1994, has experienced both types of pedagogy.

In this chapter, we investigate the pedagogical shift from apartheid's teacher-centred pedagogy to democracy's learner-centred pedagogy. A brief caveat, as mentioned in Chapter 3: the terms teacher- and learner-centred are problematic from a cultural historical viewpoint because all teaching necessarily centres on both learner and teacher. However, as these terms are widely used in literature on teaching and learning we will use their widely used meaning. It is probably more accurate, though, to refer to teacher-led pedagogy and learner-led pedagogy.

Fundamental Pedagogics: Apartheid Education

Referred to in most literature as traditional pedagogy, fundamental pedagogics accepts the student as a passive recipient of knowledge transmitted from the knowledgeable teacher to the student. Education, here, is thought of as a body of (static) knowledge transmitted to the student, who must then be able to reproduce this knowledge, generally in a summative assessment. For Dewey 'the traditional scheme is, in essence, one of imposition from above and outside' (1963: 17). Essentially, here education is seen as the reproduction of a known body of knowledge and the school going child's cognition changes quantitatively over the schooling period, but not qualitatively. That is, the child has more content in their head, but new cognitive structures are not formed, nor indeed, are they necessarily desired. Pedagogy in a lesson, therefore, has the teacher leading the classroom, generating closed questions that elicit known content answers from students. Open questions that promote dialogue are not encouraged as the body of knowledge being transmitted is already known to the teacher and no debate or dialogical interaction is required to develop novel knowledge. The pace of the lesson is driven by the teacher who selects the sequence in which the work is transmitted. Little control over the teaching and learning space is in the children's hands and power relations are asymmetrical, with the teacher holding the power over both the knowledge being transmitted and the sequence and pace at which this knowledge is transmitted. A traditional Initiate, Respond, Evaluate (IRE) sequence is generally followed with the teacher asking questions and eliciting known answer responses (Coulthard & Sinclair, 1975). In the apartheid classroom, rote learning and corporal punishment were favoured above the development of a critical citizenry that could grow up to interrogate apartheid. National Christian Education[1] favoured fundamental pedagogy because the object of education for white children was the reproduction of a body of knowledge and, for Black children vocational knowledge; neither of which were up for debate. There was no focus on developing children's personality either in the Bantu education system or in the National Christian education system.

Fundamental pedagogy could only be considered a sensible approach to education if knowledge never shifted or changed, or children were born blank slates. But this does not reflect reality. Bodies of knowledge are always shifting. Even fundamental laws of physics shift or are refined over time. The physical law that nothing can travel faster than c, the speed of light, remains unchanged, but has shifted over time as someone has more accurately measured c in terms of meters per second. While c remains the upper bound, this knowledge has shifted. Even our understanding of humans is subject to change over time. Well into the twentieth century, Spencer's (1895) notion that women were incapable of abstract thought and were best suited to caring, was widely accepted, excluding women from, for example, voting (Beeghly, 1983). This body of knowledge has been entirely discredited in the twenty-first century, however. The fact that knowledge is not static is not the only flaw underpinning fundamental pedagogics. The idea that a child is a passive recipient of knowledge is also problematic, despite the work of Behaviourists developing this hypothesis, which in many ways, echoes the view of the child taught using fundamental pedagogics

Behaviourism: The Passive, Blank Slate

'But to give the pupil new concepts deliberately … is, I am convinced, as impossible and futile as teaching a child to walk by the laws of equilibrium' (Tolstoy, 1903: 143)

Post-Second World War, Behaviourism provided a theoretical rebuttal of eugenics, which had gained traction especially in Germany in its desire to eradicate 'lesser' humans. Basing itself firmly on the understanding that humans could be 'bred' to reproduce desirable genetic traits, eugenics was largely discredited after the Holocaust (King & Hansen, 1999). Behaviourism, with its focus on studying observable behaviour, as opposed to either genetics or cognition, offered a way to understand learning as conditioned by the environment (Hardman, 2012). It also represented a response to Freudian psychoanalysis that indicated that human development was largely beyond conscious control and was predicated on the unconscious (Hardman, 2012). In response to both eugenics and psychoanalysis, Watson[2]'s Behaviourism set out to study only that which could be observed, behaviour. This is not to suggest that behaviourists denied the existence of a mind, or brain. Rather, they decided they could not study it as it could not be observed and their desire to make the relatively new field of psychology empirically robust, led to their focus on observable behaviour, at the expense of a focus on cognition.

For behaviourists such as Watson, it was the environment that led to child development, rather than any innate, natural capacity that a child was born with. This notion of a 'tabula rasa' or blank slate had a serious impact on pedagogy in the mid-twentieth century, with children viewed as empty vessels into which knowledge could be transferred by a teacher (Hardman, 2012). It is against this theoretical background that fundamental pedagogics found its theoretical impetus. For behaviourists, stimuli in the environment elicit responses in behaviour and through conditioning, the child learns new behaviours. Hence fundamental pedagogics focus on providing stimuli, in the form of a body of static knowledge, that a child must learn. The behaviourist desire to study only what can be observed, controlled and predicted was developed further in Skinner's (1948) radical behaviourism, which accepted the existence of an internal mind but suggested that this could not be analysed through observable behaviours. While behaviourist theories can account for what Bateson (1972) refers to as 'Learning 1', the acquisition of appropriate responses in a specific context, these theories are not able to account for how a child internalizes knowledge. Further, the role they assign to teaching is very much limited to a stimulus-response approach, where the teacher transmits knowledge to the child mono-directionally. This passive view of learning denies the fact that children actively bring different experiences to bear on the classroom setting, constructing different world views as they do so. A behaviourist model of learning and development sees these processes as synonymous (Daniels, 2001). Meeting the challenge of explaining learning as an active process, Piaget (1970, 1977) illustrated how children progress through various stages, constructing stage-specific knowledge as they do so.

Outcomes Based Education and Progressive Pedagogy

'The doors of learning and culture shall be opened' – Freedom Charter

Apartheid's demise saw the need to correct the systematic under-education of Black children for decades. Not only would the curriculum change from a static body of knowledge to be transmitted to a developing body of knowledge to be acquired, but pedagogy was also to change from fundamental to progressive (Department of Basic Education, 2001). Progressive pedagogy insists that children are active in their learning and that they construct meaning through acting with and in the world. Rather than summative assessments, Outcomes Based Education (OBE) suggested that assessment should be formative and developmental, focusing on outcomes rather than content. Anyone who spends their time studying teaching and learning will know that all education must be outcomes based in the sense of producing the kinds of 'heads' required to navigate society successfully.

As far back as the ancient Greeks, Aristotle made claims about the *telos* of education being the development of the child – as an oak tree represents the *telos*, or final cause, of an acorn. However, what the Greeks appeared to know, and we seem to have forgotten, is that education *as development* requires the development of novel cognitive structures academically,[3] and of a personal identity, emotionally.[4] This requires a very specific kind of curriculum and society. To meet this need, I would argue that a society must in the first place, be equal, with children having equal access to the kind of knowledge they need to acquire. Even a cursory look at current South Africa (more than twenty-five years into democracy) will disabuse one of the ideas that this society is equal. With the highest Gini co-efficient in the world, it is fair to ask how OBE could ever have succeeded, given that children would unrealistically, yet necessarily need access to fairly similar, or at least fairly equal, opportunities to learn (Spreen & Vally, 2009).

The need for equal access to material and physical resources implied in OBE lies in the outcomes that it proposes to reach: the development of the child both academically and emotionally. The fact that OBE was rolled out in South African schools that were unequal and ill-equipped, should have been a red light for policy makers (Jansen, 1999). Added to this vast inequality of material and human resources across South African schools was the addition of continuous assessments that would serve as markers of students' progress through the year, rather than a single summative assessment after each term. That is, teachers' workloads expanded exponentially (Jansen, 1999) with no concomitant salary increases, to add further burden to the scenario. Further impacting on the possible success of OBE is that there is evidence that since its inception in 1997, it had not in fact been rolled out properly even as late as 2009 (Spleen & Valley, 2009). Many of the elegant theoretical underpinnings of OBE were not sufficiently engaged with and in-service teacher training did not serve to assist the teachers' in defining what OBE pedagogy practice could look like in an actual class. The notion of 'learner-centred', for example, is meaningless unless one is shown how, in praxis, a student can control pace and sequence in a lesson, in a manner that doesn't deviate from the content covered. How does a teacher relinquish control, even slightly, to students without feeling himself/herself under threat of challenge? Teachers were not trained pedagogically how to deal with a vastly different classroom that OBE proposed from the top down, heavily asymmetrical, teaching under apartheid.

OBE requires that knowledge is co-constructed; that meaning comes from both the teacher and the taught. This is in direct opposition to the fundamental pedagogics under apartheid. The failure of OBE, however regretful, was bound to happen given the constraints of an unjust and unequal society, which in 1997, South Africa was (and still is). The failure of OBE to produce the kinds of students that the new South Africa wanted, led to serious attacks on the notion of OBE and calls for a new curriculum statement and different pedagogy (Hoadley, 2017; Jansen, 1999; Muller, 2000; Taylor & Vinjevold, 1999). From the teachers' perspective, an article written in 2010 on the agreed dissolution of the OBE curriculum reflected that 'The SA Democratic Teachers' Union general secretary ... said teachers have complained about a lack of training and the work overload. We have always pointed out our concerns around lack of training, work overload and the poor quality of textbooks being used in classrooms.'[5]

This is unfortunate, as, used as it should be used, within a strong theoretical foundation, OBE is surely the way to produce a socially just educational system. It is, I would argue, the failure to adequately address and embed the theoretical foundations of OBE that were part of the reason it failed.

OBE, theoretically, finds its home in a 'constructivist' theory of education, where knowledge is actively acquired by the child rather than passively transmitted by the teacher. The word 'constructivism' has been so widely used in so many different contexts and spaces, that its real meaning has become quite slippery and there are even some 'constructivist' thinkers who suggest that all knowledge is a construction (von Glaserfeld, 1984). The problem with the logical outcome of this thought is that it leads us right back to behaviourism with its notion that the child brings nothing to the transaction s/he has with the world. For clarity, in this book, constructivism is understood as developing in the West from the genetic epistemology of Piaget (1970) and in the East, from the cultural-historical work of Vygotsky (1978, 1986). Fundamental to the notion of 'constructivism' is the acceptance that a child is an active cognizing agent who constructs meaning through transactions in the world.

Arguably, the most famous Western educational psychologist, Piaget's (1970) claim that children learn through actively transacting with objects in their environment has had a lasting impact on education. While Piaget was not the first to suggest that learning required active cognizing agents (Dewey (1963) for example was a proponent of progressive education), his theory has had possibly the greatest impact on Western education in the twentieth and even twenty-first century. No theory of learning or teaching today would seriously suggest that children are anything but active, capable of exploring their environment to develop cognitive structures though the processes of 'assimilation' and 'accommodation'. For Piaget (1964), learning happens through a process of 'disequilibrium'. Faced with novel knowledge that s/he cannot make sense of in terms of existing cognitive structures, there is a disjuncture or dissonance between assimilation (understanding the novel in terms of what is already known) and accommodation (a shift in knowledge due to the conflict that arises between the clash of what is unknown with what is known).[6] In the resulting cognitive dissonance, change and learning, becomes inevitable as the child seeks to overcome the discomfort of disequilibrium. The motor, if you like, for cognitive development then lies in disequilibrium and is located between the child and his/her transaction with a novel object. In the following quote, Piaget articulates how a child comes to know something:

> To know an object, to know an event, is not simply to look at it and make a mental copy or image of it. To know an object is to act on it. To know is to modify, to transform the object, and to understand the process of this transformation, and as a consequence to understand the way the object is constructed. An operation is thus the essence of knowledge; it is an interiorised action which modifies the object of knowledge.
>
> (1964, 176)

What is evident in this quote is that knowledge requires not only transformation of self but of the world's meaning too. It is here, in the notion of cognitive dissonance and transformation, that the work of Lev Vygotsky (1978) echoes Piaget's work.

Sociocultural (Cultural Historical) Theory: Consciousness in Society

As noted in Chapter 2, Vygotsky's (1978) theory is known in the West as sociocultural theory and in the East as cultural-historical theory. For clarity, in this book, I refer to his theoretical framework as cultural-historical theory. Although

Vygotsky (1978) died early and never met Piaget, he did read his early work. That Piaget recognized Vygotsky's work is also clear (Piaget, 1995). Many scholars suggest that the work of these two psychologists is incommensurable (see Shayer 2003 for an elegant argument to the contrary). While their positions are epistemologically distinct, there is, in fact, much that both theorists have in common and the ability to mobilize both, creates a more nuanced picture of development.

For Vygotsky (1978, 1986) higher cognitive functions are developed through social interaction; what is initially developed between people becomes internalized over development. Like Piaget, Vygotsky theorized that cognitive development required activity on the child's part. Unlike Piaget, however, his focus was on how mind is socially constructed through the mediation of a culturally more competent other. Conversely, for Piaget, social interaction is necessary, but not sufficient, for cognitive development and little of his theorizing focuses on the history or culture that the child brings to the classroom. Of course, this is not necessarily a drawback for his work; he was, after all, not concerned with cross-cultural comparisons in general, as his major interest was in studying universal characteristics of human learning, not context-specific differences.

However, in the South African context, where multi-cultural education is the norm, there is a need for a theory capable of accounting for the impact of culture on learning. In addition, unlike Vygotsky who viewed a teacher/more culturally competent other as necessary and sufficient for development, Piaget felt strongly that children were little scientists, capable of exploring the world and developing logico-mathematical thought along the way, without the explicit need of a more competent other to guide and co-construct meaning. What this has amounted to in schools is a focus on discovery-based learning, where children engage in research, often without the specific guidance of the teacher.

While I am not convinced[7] that Piaget intended his theory to be appropriated by teachers in this manner, this is indeed what has happened. As Karpov (2003) has indicated, discovery-based learning in the absence of structured instruction has the potential to cement students' misconceptions, rather than actually leading to the development of scientific concepts.[8] Gagne (1966) is even more critical of discovery-based learning suggesting that 'To expect a human being to engage in a trial and error procedure in discovering a concept appears to be a matter of asking him to behave like an ape' (143).[9] This is perhaps too harsh a critique when levelled at Piaget, who did recognize the importance of assistance in learning, but theorized that development was the basis for learning. From both theorists, however, we derive the notion of development as involving a clash, a conflict or contradiction that changes both the child and the object they are acting on. However, in the absence of a historical embedding of consciousness, Piaget cannot speak to teaching/learning in South African schools. In this context, where apartheid's effects continue to be felt at all levels of the education system, an understanding of the cultural deprivation emerging from years of oppression requires a theoretical grasp of the social, cultural and historical practices that people bring to bear on the tools they use (Feuerstein et al., 1981; Kozulin, 2001). Finally, while Piaget's theory provides an elegant description of 'internalisation', I would argue that its lack of an explicit[10] contextualist approach to knowledge development fails to adequately account for the acquisition of new knowledge without positing the pre-existence of complex structures. This difficulty is often referred to as the 'learning paradox' and is articulated in the following quote from Bereiter:

> What needs explaining from the standpoint of the learning paradox is not only how the child learns to test theories but also how the child acquires the theories to be tested. Statements to the effect that the child 'learns from experience' (…) dodge the issue and are often not very plausible. Out of the infinitude of correspondences that might be noticed between one event and another, how does it happen that children notice just those ones that make for simple theories about how the world works – and that, furthermore, different children, with a consistency far beyond chance, tend to notice the same correspondences?
>
> (Bereiter 1985: 204.)

For Bereiter (1985) this paradox lies in understanding how internalization takes place and for Cole (1996) this paradox is resolved by Vygotsky's general genetic law of human development, which indicates that mental structures begin as social relations between two people before being internalized by the child. That is, development begins as an inter-psychological relationship before becoming intra-psychological.

Essentially, the general genetic law indicates how to overcome the learning paradox by enabling us to conceptualize the prior existence of complex cognitive structures as existing in the child's culture, rather than in the individual child. That is, for Vygotsky the child never approaches the world as a 'clean slate'; rather, every experience the child has is mediated through culture. This model of learning implies a complex relationship between learning and development, with good learning happening only when learning leads to development. Acceptance of the Vygotskian viewpoint requires that we accept that there is a complex relationship between teaching and development, not implied by the other two models. Both the behaviourist and the Piagetian positions assume a view of teaching that is unproblematic and universal.

The third position, however, asserts a view of teaching that requires a degree of responsivity and guidance on the teacher's behalf. The behaviourist view leads us to envisage a child who is a passive recipient of knowledge. The second view provides a more active view of the student as developing along certain pre-established pathways. In the third view, we have a picture of a student whose cognitive development is socially constructed through the student's own active engagement with meanings in the world. The kind of curriculum that would be designed in this instance would be one that guided children's development of scientific concepts in a context where informed and supported acquisition and the transfer of control take precedence over transmission.

The difference between fundamental pedagogics and progressive pedagogics discussed in this chapter is graphically represented in Figure 4.1 below.

Figure 4.1 graphically depicts the move from fundamental pedagogics under apartheid to progressive pedagogics under a democratic government in South Africa. The move illustrated in Figure 4.1 towards a more inclusive, constructivist pedagogy underpins the current curriculum.

In a 2015 review of teaching and learning in South Africa, Hoadley outlines certain changes that have occurred in South African schools. This is re-iterated in part in her 2017 (Hoadley, 2017) book. Referencing the work of Taylor (2007, 2008), and Reeves and Muller (2005), she points out what is needed in schools in South Africa for students to acquire knowledge. Fairly tightly controlled pacing, that considers student progress, but is not determined by the slowest student, together with a focus on more reading and writing, more explicit and detailed feedback and greater content coverage are seen as necessary for learning gains. Hoadley's (2015) review is comprehensive and coherent, pointing to both gaps in primary school education as well as suggesting what kind of interventions are required to enhance learning gains. This kind of review of education in schools is important in determining what gaps exist in our knowledge base as well as indicating what types of interventions one may expect to benefit learning. What is missing in reviews and indeed meta-analyses of teaching/learning in South Africa is a detailed and nuanced understanding of cultural historical factors that are at play in any given classroom, making any general statements about what 'works best' or

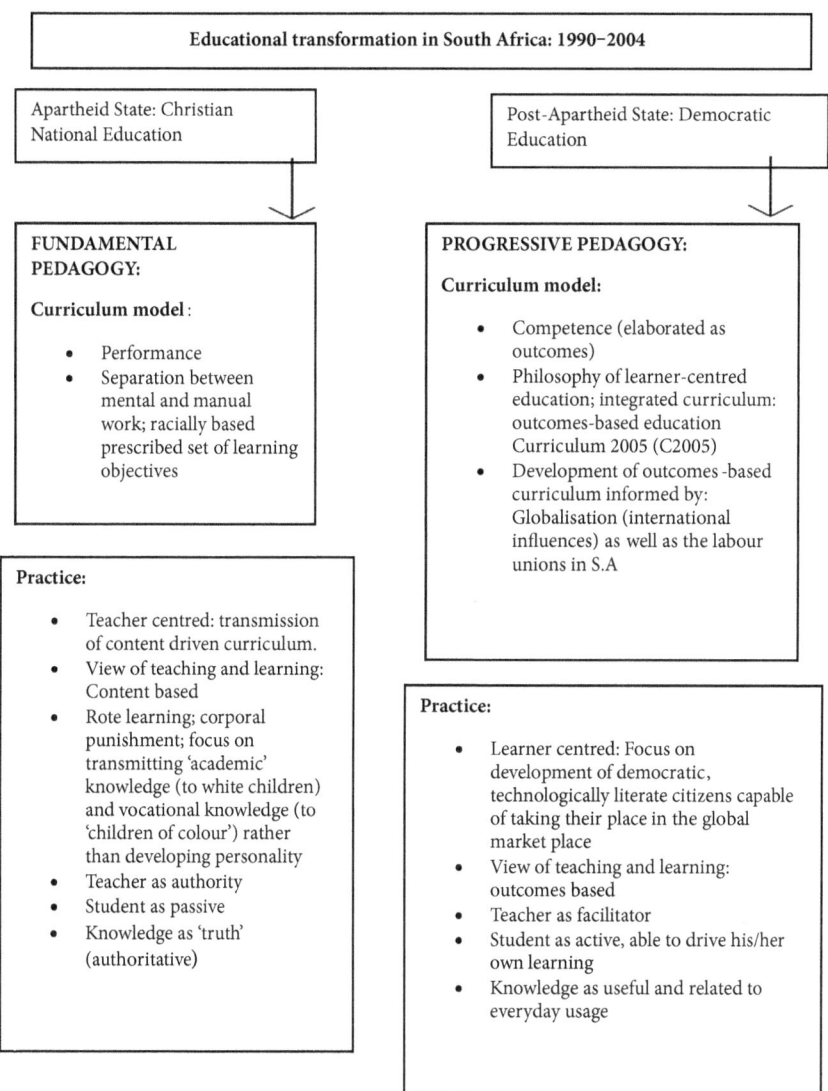

Figure 4.1 A change from fundamental to progressive pedagogy.

what needs to be improved problematic. What is needed is an understanding of how pedagogy has changed in classrooms over the twenty-seven years of democratic education. The answer to the question of pedagogical transition, as with all answers involving humans, is that it depends where you look. Below I present current empirical data from three classrooms, to highlight the contextual nature of pedagogy.

The More Things Change, the More They Stay the Same OR Has Pedagogy Really Changed from 1994 to 2021?

Extract 1: A Lesson about Fractions

This is the second teaching session the teacher has given on fractions to her grade 6 class, so they have been exposed to fractions before. The school is in a very disadvantaged rural area in the apple growing area outside of Cape Town and the building is made of mud bricks, insulated with straw. School fees are approximately USD 60 per annum. The teacher and students are all second language English speakers with Afrikaans as their first language. The language of instruction, however, is English. The teacher is a 52-year-old female with thirty-three years teaching experience. She has a diploma from a former teacher training college. The teacher, Mrs January, greets the class and settles them into their seats before beginning her lesson. She has written the fraction ½ on the blackboard. There is no technology in her classroom and her only teaching tools are the textbook and the blackboard and chalk. The children do not have textbooks of their own but share one textbook between two children, as they are waiting for more books to be delivered.

Extract 1: Mrs January and the Denominator

1. Mrs January: This is what we call a fraction. Now all of you … *Points at blackboard: ½ is written on the blackboard.*
2. Pupils: fraction
3. Mrs January: fraction
4. Pupils: fraction
5. Mrs January: fraction
6. Pupils: fraction
7. Mrs January: right, this is the top (*points at the numerator*). The top of the?
8. Pupils: fraction
9. Mrs January: right. Then if you go down you see this (*points at the denominator*) part, it is what we call what?
10. Pupils: we call it denominator.
11. Mrs January: denominator, denominator, denominator, denominator. Right.

The lesson continues with three more examples of fractions written on the board before children are required to do an activity where they create fractions from various pictures.

This lesson was recorded and transcribed in 2014, that is, after the move from transmission-based pedagogy to a focus on acquisition as highlighted by the curriculum statements. When asked about how children learn, Mrs January said the following: *'definitely active, they learn by doing. And that's the problem. They don't know their tables. Now, I say, every morning, say your tables. Stand up and say your tables'* (Interview Mrs January: 1 May). While indicating that she thinks children learn actively, which is in line with the policy documents suggesting children are active learners, it appears that what 'active' means for Mrs January doesn't equate with what the policy documents indicate. That is, for her, standing up and saying one's tables every morning is not seen as a rote endeavour, but rather as an activity. Let me be clear here; there is nothing inherently problematic with rote learning. However, the use of rote learning depends very much on what it is that you want a child to learn. Rote learning is extremely good at laying down memory tracts and cementing basic factual knowledge such as multiplication tables in mathematics or declensions in Latin. If, however, the desire is for children to acquire conceptual understanding, rote learning is not going to meet this objective. In the extract above, what we see is a performance of students learning the language of mathematics, rather than learning the concepts underpinning fractions. This is, perhaps, to be expected as these children are not operating in their first language and words like numerator and denominator are thus, quite foreign. As a mechanism for learning the name of parts of a fraction, rote learning, as illustrated in extract 1, may be useful. It is not, however, useful if one is expecting children to learn the concepts upon which fractions are based. Moreover, this kind of pedagogy is not different to what would have been observed under Bantu education during apartheid. In this instance, then, there is no difference in pedagogy post-1994 observed in this specific classroom.

Extract 2: And Another Lesson about Fractions

Our second extract is drawn from the class of Mr Botha. The school is a farm school, built of bricks and concrete and located in the wine farming district outside Cape Town. The area is peri-urban and relatively well built up with solid infrastructure. The children who attend this school speak Afrikaans as their first language and all students come from the neighbouring farms where their parents are farm workers. School fees are approximately GBP 200 per annum. The school has a computer lab, and the teacher has two computers in his classroom; one on his desk and one that students can use for google searches for projects.

Mr Botha is thirty-seven years old and has thirteen years of teaching experience. He has a matric[11] pass plus a four-year teacher training certification. He is very energetic and interested in his pupils. This is his second lesson on fractions, which, while they have been taught in lower grades, require a new introduction as the children are struggling with them. He has just finished explaining what a numerator and a denominator are; that is, what function they serve.

Extract 2: Mr Botha's Apples

1. Mr Botha: Question?
2. Wayne: explain the denominator again sir. (*puts up his hand*)
3. Mr Botha: Right, explain the denominator again.
4. Come let's go further. (*Gets an apple from a bag of apples he has brought to the lesson*)
5. Now, what is this? (*holds up an apple*)
6. Students: whole
7. Mr Botha: whole.
8. And I cut him exactly, exactly, in how many parts? (*begins to cut the apple in half*)
9. How many parts are there?
10. Students: two
11. Mr Botha: now, my denominator tells me how many parts I have divided my whole into (*holds up parts*)
12. In this case, it's two. (*holds up parts*)
13. So my denominator in this case will be?
14. Students: two
15. Mr Botha: two.

The teacher uses a discourse structure that is familiar in most schools and is characteristic of much of the teaching I have observed over twenty years in the field. This is the IRE structure, where the teacher poses closed, known answer questions to students, who respond with either a correct or incorrect answer (Cazden, 2001; Dillon, 1982; Littleton et al., 2005; Mehan, 1979; Sinclair & Coulthard, 1975). The IRE discourse pattern has been critiqued over the years because the acquisition of new knowledge requires more than asking simple, closed questions that do not open debate and places the teacher in the role of inquisitor who potentially hinders rich discussion in the classroom (Wood, 1992). Indeed, the work of Mercer and his colleagues at Spoken Language and New Technology project (SLANT)

(Hennessy et al., 2020; Howe et al., 2019) has shown how a rich, dialogical discourse in classrooms develops students reasoning capacity.

However, there are also those who argue, and I am amongst them, that the IRE structure is only problematic if the feedback or evaluation move is not elaborated by the teacher (Hardman, 2021; Song et al., 2019). When the follow up move is used to develop a shared understanding of the problem under discussion, the IRE sequence can be extremely useful for learning. This is especially so in context, such as the classroom in extract 2, where students are operating in a language that is not their own and who may not all share the understanding of fractions required by the teacher. The IRE structure does more than simply enquire about students' knowledge base and reinforce already learnt concepts; it provides space for a child to engage in the classroom discourse. Getting involved in classroom talk is difficult; it requires that you put your knowledge on display for your peers and the teacher. This is risky because you could be incorrect and lose face. Hence, giving students access to the classroom discourse through IRE is at least one mechanism for involving children in the classroom.

What is particularly interesting about extract 2, however, is not the IRE sequence; rather, it is the fact that the teacher alters the pacing and the sequencing of the lesson *in response* to a student question. Moreover, when Wayne asks a question, the teacher does more than simply repeat what he has said before, he makes use of concrete apples to illustrate the point he is discussing about fractions. That is, he provides a model of the concept under discussion. There is more student activity in this extract than in extract 1, but it would still be a stretch to say that this is representative of the kind of constructivist pedagogy outlined in this chapter, where the meaning of the concepts under discussion is co-constructed between teacher and taught through the linking of the abstraction with the everyday. This lesson was observed, videoed and transcribed in 2004, years after OBE had been rolled out in classrooms and yet the kind of pedagogy, we see in extract 2 is reminiscent of pedagogy one would see under apartheid. Again, although the curriculum and policy has shifted, as outlined in Chapter 1, pedagogy in these schools remains very much as it was under apartheid: a pedagogy that resonates more with a transmission than an acquisition model of teaching/learning. The schools in extracts 1 and 2 represent government schools that are funded by the government. While Mrs January's school is disadvantaged, Mr Botha's school caters to the aspirant. In the third and final extract explicating pedagogical change in South Africa post-apartheid, we locate ourselves in a very privileged, private school where school fees are around USD 7000 per annum.

Extract 3: Fractions – Change: It's All about the Context

Also known as independent schools, private schools are self-funded through trusts, religious organizations or for-profit companies. While not all private schools charge high fees, most do. The independence of these schools means that they are not obliged to follow the curriculum that the government stipulates. Generally, these schools are extremely well resourced, both materially and in terms of human resources. This specific school is in an affluent suburb of Cape Town. The classes are generally small and there is a wide selection of technology available to the teacher and students for teaching/learning purposes. Mrs Chambers, the teacher, is thirty years old with eight years teaching experience. She has an undergraduate degree, a postgraduate certificate in education and an Honours degree in education. All students have their own iPad. While some private schools do not require that children wear uniforms, this school is more traditional in its approach to dress, and children all wear school uniforms. There are seventeen children in Mrs Chambers' class. Today they are doing their third grade 6 lesson on fractions. The teacher introduces the lesson on equivalent fractions in the first 5 minutes of the lesson. She then sets them problems to solve using iPads. Students are put into groups of 3 or 4 and are allowed to occupy any space in the school that is not occupied, in order to make a short film where they solve the fraction problem given.

Extract 3: Fractions – How Cute!

1. Gail: So, plussing and Minusing fractions.
2. Eva: Addition and subtraction of fractions.
3. Gail: So first you've got to make sure the denominators the same.
4. Sara: Yes, so find the common multiple.
5. Eva: So, the first step you've got to do is the most common multiple.
6. And then you've got to add the tops.
7. It doesn't actually matter.
8. We don't have to do it; we've just got to show the steps.
9. Gail: Let's just do it.
10. So, the lowest common multiple between seven and three.
11. Eva: Seven, 14, 21.
12. And then we've got to times this by three, that by six and that by six.
13. Teacher: Girls, what topic is this?
14. Gail: Simplifying fractions.
15. Teacher: Simplifying fractions, great. Carry on.

16. Gail: Okay, so maybe I can do the second part of the step of simplifying.
17. Then I'll write the sum down and you can do the talk.
18. Zoe: Okay.
19. Gail: (Inaudible). And then one of us can write the sum up.
20. Let's ask.
21. Zoe: We're doing it on clips right? (Inaudible).
22. Eva: Today we'll be doing parts of a whole.
23. We'll be explaining how fractions make up a full whole.
24. Teacher: As I say, if you want to get a whiteboard, you can get a whiteboard from inside and write examples.
25. Or you can use the board inside the classroom. (Overtalking)
26. Eva: (Inaudible). I can't write neat.
27. Zoe: You can't insert a time-lapse in clips.
28. You can make it shorter, but you can't speed up how long it takes.
29. Eva: Okay, then you have to Zoe, you have to write (inaudible).
30. Shall we just write on the poster and then we'll just figure it out?
31. Zoe: There's only one way to start it.
32. I don't care how much you hate it.
33. There's only one way to stop it.
34. Gail: What are you going to do?
35. Zoe: We're making this movie.
36. Gail: No, we cannot put an image of a cat.
37. Come on.
38. Zoe: This is the best.
39. I'll show you.
40. If you don't like it, we don't have to have it.
41. Eva: Maybe you can just put a meme at the start.
42. Zoe: Look how cute that is.

In this extract, lines 2–6 illustrate how the children themselves are teaching, articulating the mathematical concepts and explicating them. Where Gail, in line 1, says they are 'plussing and minussing', she is corrected by Eva who gives her the correct mathematical terms for these operations, addition and subtraction. What is different from the other extracts in this section of the chapter is the fact that the teacher speaks very seldom and, when she does, it is not to explain but rather to query what the children are doing and re-iterate this [line 15]. We have a form of dialogue developing between Gail, Eva and Zoe as they attempt to develop a movie clip to illustrate the problem they are solving. The reason that talk in this lesson differs so much from extracts 1 and 2 is because these girls are sharing a cognitive tool, the iPad and must, therefore, work together to solve a problem. In terms of the understanding of constructivism developed in this chapter, we could say that this final extract is perhaps closest to a constructivist teaching/learning environment than the other two extracts. This, of course, is due to the differences in the contexts of these extracts. The different pedagogical praxes across different socio-economic contexts should alert us to the importance of context in research findings. There is no single solution to questions when studying pedagogy; the answers generated must always be qualified by the understanding that this answer holds for this time and in this context. It is for this reason that cultural historical theory provides such a fecund framework through which to study pedagogy in context.

Conclusion

This chapter outlined the shifts in pedagogical practices from the apartheid era to the present. Shifts in curricula, discussed in Chapter 3, must necessarily impact on pedagogy as pedagogy and curricula are intertwined. Hence, the move after democracy from fundamental pedagogy to a focus on more outcomes-based pedagogy, brought with it a focus on shifting teachers, from a predominantly transmission mode of pedagogy to an understanding of pedagogy in terms of acquisition. The extent to which pedagogy has changed in South Africa is a question we are not able to answer for the entire country. Culture, socio-economic background and context impact on how teaching happens in schools. The data presented in this chapter illustrate how different contexts, elicit different praxes. What we can conclude, however, is that is it possible to shift pedagogy and that if we understand learning in terms of acquisition instead of transmission, a move to more dialogical interaction between peers as well as teachers is necessary for cognition to develop.

Part Two

Cultural Historical Approaches to Pedagogy

5

School Science for Eight-year-olds: A Cultural Historical Analysis

South Africa continues to lag behind the rest of the world in benchmarking tests of mathematics and science (DBE, 2011d; Klinck, 2013; TIMSS, 2011). The changes in the curriculum discussed in Chapter 3 notwithstanding, South African children appear particularly bad at maths and science. The obvious question that comes to mind is why this should be so, given the huge investments both materially and in terms of human resources, the government has made in education. In fact, it isn't just in STEM subjects that South African children appear to fare poorly in South Africa. The Progress in International Reading Literacy Study indicated that 79 per cent of children in Grade 4 in South Africa could not read for meaning (Howie et al., 2017). This finding is particularly worrying as Grade 4 represents the developmental move from learning to read to reading to learn. If one is unable to understand what is read, learning is simply not possible. Given the interventions in schools aiming to better education, this is certainly a crisis for a developing country, where education is one of the few mechanisms for children to emerge from poverty.

While Chapters 1 to 4 dealt primarily with outlining theory foundational to this book, this chapter begins the section of the book that provides analysis of data using the theoretical concepts discussed earlier in the book. In this chapter and the next, I turn to Grade 2 science lessons to investigate two questions: Firstly, to what extent does the set textbook make scientific concepts available to students and secondly, what does actual pedagogy in a Grade 2 classroom look like when analysed using a Neo-Vygotskian conceptual framework?

From Theory to Analysis: Talk as Data

The foundation of Vygotskian thought is captured in his General Genetic Law which states that higher cognitive functions – thinking, reasoning and problem-solving – begin as real relations between people, *inter-psychologically*, before being internalized *intra-psychologically*. Dialogical interaction is thus posited as a crucial means of cognitive and pedagogical change. This idea, that communicative interchange can be said to provide a 'basis for thinking', is of clear importance for any communication strategy with a properly transformative agenda. The following quote from Halliday explicates the importance of language for learning:

> The distinctive characteristic of human learning is that it is a process of meaning-making – a semiotic process: and the prototypical form of human semiotics is language. Hence the ontogenesis of language is at the same time the ontogenesis of learning.
>
> (Halliday, 1993: 93)

What Halliday does not point to, but what Vygotsky elaborates on, are the cognitive effects of *semiotic mediation*. This chapter is not a language or linguistics chapter: I am an alien in those lands! My purpose here is to show how language, both verbal and written, has a cognitive impact on a child. Vital in this respect is Vygotsky's notion of *mediation*, namely, the utilization of cultural artefacts such as textbooks (tools, signs, symbolic and communicative activity) as a means of attaining higher mental functions. Not dissimilar to Geertz' notion of culture as 'a system of inherited conceptions expressed in symbolic forms by means of which men communicate, perpetuate, and develop their knowledge about and attitudes toward life' (1973; 89), Vygotsky's culturally more competent other is more embedded in the meaning of what they are teaching. A science teacher, for example, who is trained as a scientist and has a degree in teaching science is more culturally competent in her scientific knowledge than a child in Grade 2 who has yet to encounter the abstractions that underpin science.

In a bid to address the question of how knowledge develops within a Marxist psychology, Vygotsky (1978) articulated a developmental method capable of studying what cannot be seen – thinking for example – through identifying the 'germ cell' of development. While Marx analysed a 'cell' of capitalist society, Vygotsky considered the 'cell' of psychology as the interaction between the infant and the mother – the culturally more competent guide (Marx, 1857; Vygotsky, 1987). For Vygotsky *'the path from the object to child and from child to object passes through another person'* (1978; 30). In the development of higher cognitive functions, those uniquely human ways of thinking, we never approach the world as it is, but rather, our interaction with the world is *mediated* by someone else. Meaning is not something that resides in objects but rather is derived through interaction with others.

This leads to the pedagogical understanding of guided assistance within a space where this learning can fruitfully occur, the Zone of Proximal Development (ZPD) which is discussed in Chapter 2 of the current book in some depth. For the purposes of this chapter, the ZPD represents that social space where development occurs through social interaction between the novice and the more competent other through, predominantly, talk. Regarding the germ cell of schooling, Vygotsky's focus is on word meaning as the simplest instantiation of cognitive development; that is, word meaning captured in its simplest form, for the development of higher cognitive functions. While many theorists have subsequently pointed to the importance of action (Leontiev, 1978; Engestrom, 1999) as primary sources for this move in development, classrooms are essentially contexts in which language remains the primary tool for constructing meaning. For this reason, I focus on language, both spoken and written, as a source of data in this book. This is not to suggest that action and gestures are not developmental; certainly, they are. However, in this and the following chapter, language, both written and spoken, remain the primary tools mobilized in teaching and learning in the classes I discuss.

Sociocultural theorists such as Mercer (2010) have conducted several useful studies indicating how talk can be studied in classrooms using socio-cultural discourse analysis. A large body of research suggests that language in classrooms is developmentally crucial. However, as with all tools, it is not language itself that serves a developmental purpose, but rather *how* it is mobilized by teachers and students. It is useful to distinguish therefore, between the acquisition of content and the acquisition of forms of thought in a classroom: that is, what is taught and how it is taught in a manner that develops a child cognitively. The former relates quite narrowly to the actual content that students acquire in school, such as the notion of wild and domesticated animals, for example, which form the empirical context in the data reported later in this chapter. The latter, however, draws on Vygotsky's notion of higher cognitive functions as developing through the acquisition of scientific, abstract concepts. While content can be learnt quickly, forms of thought require mediation through the ZPD and are therefore, considered developmental. So, for example, a child could learn that a cow and a horse are mammals simply by being given a list of mammals to memorize. However, if the intention is to develop the child cognitively, that child must be able to accurately classify animals according to whether or not they are mammals. The ability to do this requires that the child has acquired the abstract understanding of the essential features of the concept, mammals. For Vygotsky, the *object* of mediated action in the ZPD is conceptual, not technical. The following quote highlights this:

> Instruction is only useful when it moves ahead of development. When it does, it impels or awakens a whole series of functions that are in a stage of maturation lying in the zone of proximal development. This is the major role of instruction in development. This is what distinguishes the instruction of the child from the training of animals. *This is also what distinguishes instruction of the child which is directed toward his full development from instruction in specialised, technical skills such as typing or riding a bicycle.* The formal aspect of each school subject is that in which the influence of instruction on development is realised. Instruction would be completely unnecessary if it merely utilized what had already matured in the developmental process, if it were not itself a source of development.
>
> (Vygotsky, 1987: 212)

For Vygotsky, the school[1] is that 'space' in which children learn to manipulate scientific concepts. It is in the school classroom that the child encounters abstract knowledge generally through the teacher and the prescribed textbooks. The importance, then, of accurate, detailed textbooks as mediating artefacts is clear. However, as Chaiklin (personal correspondence 08/06/2021) indicates, the content of science textbooks, for example, remains remarkably unchanged since at least the turn of the twentieth century. The quote from Mann (1917) below is illustrative of what he believes should be placed in a student physics textbook.

> If the teacher remembers that physics does not consist of a large number of detached fragments of facts and laws, and that elementary physics is not a totally different species from physics, but is the child who grows later into the man physics, he should be able to organise a course having unity, significance, simplicity, and real value in the lives of those who must enter the ranks of the world's workers.
>
> (Mann, 1917: 244–5)

What is interesting about this quote is Mann's insistence that science (physics) texts should not contain detached facts but that the knowledge presented should have 'real value in the lives of those who must enter the ranks of the world's workers'. It is in the notion of 'relevance' that the linking of the scientific to the everyday concept becomes essential in developing the child cognitively (Daniels, 2001; Karpov, 2003; Vygotsky, 1986). While everyday concepts arise through the child's interaction with the world, scientific concepts are taught. However, in the absence of the everyday, scientific concepts are meaningless and lack relevance in the child's everyday life.

> The development of the scientific [...] concept, a phenomenon that occurs as part of the educational process, constitutes a unique form of systematic co-operation between the teacher and the child. [...] In a problem involving scientific concepts, he must be able to do in collaboration with the teacher something that he has never done spontaneously [...] we know that the child can do more in collaboration than he can do independently.
>
> (Vygotsky, 1987: 168, 9, 216)

In the quotation, the development of understanding of a scientific concept arises in the relationship between the teacher and student in the ZPD *through communicative interaction*. Explicit guided instruction, then, is central to the development of scientific concepts. Acquisition of scientific concepts enables children to mediate problem solving and thinking. The abstract scientific concept 'descends to the phenomena that the concept represents' (Vygotsky, 1986: 130). That is, the abstract descends to the concrete by being used in local, everyday examples. It is in this sense then that the abstraction of the scientific concept can only make sense if it is displayed using procedural knowledge.

Vygotsky's differentiation between scientific and everyday concepts provides us with a mechanism for describing the object of school teaching: that is, scientific concepts. This understanding of scientific and everyday concepts enables us to view teaching in the ZPD as a double-move between the students' everyday concepts and their exposure to scientific concepts which facilitate an understanding of scientific concepts (or subject content concepts) as the object of schooling (Hedegaard, 1998). This double-move plays out as a finely tuned interaction between the teacher's model of subject-matter (scientific) concepts and the student's everyday concepts. By linking abstract knowledge to students' lived experience, students can own the concept in a meaningful way. Further, the 'radical-local' pedagogical model proposed by Chaiklin and Hedegaard (2013) indicates the complexity, yet achievability, of teaching in a manner that is truly transformative of both the child and the world. This is a profoundly different lens on pedagogy than the more traditional notion which views students as empty vessels waiting to be filled by the expert pedagogue.

In Chaiklin and Hedegaard's (2013) recontextualization of Vygotsky's central concepts, the expert pedagogue is essential to learning and this happens in a dialogical space where the active student participates in his/her developmental trajectory. The primary vehicle through which development happens in this pedagogical theory is language. This theory, however, leads to the potentially problematic issue of variation in semiotic mediation which leads to differential cognitive development (Hasan, 1992).

Variation in Semiotic Mediation and Its Cognitive Consequences

> the speech of those who surround the child predetermines the paths that the development of the child's generalisations will take.
>
> (Vygotsky, 1987: 143)

The quote above indicates clearly that the type of talk a child encounters determines the degree to which they will acquire scientific concepts. The importance of semiotic mediation in the development of higher cognitive functions leads us to ask about the cognitive outcomes of variation in semiotic mediation. What happens when children are not uniformly given access to the requisite semiotic mediation to help develop, for example, syllogistic reasoning or categorical thinking? In his famous studies in Uzbekistan, Luria (1976) found that:

> Categorical classification involves complex verbal and logical thinking that exploits language's capacity for formulating abstractions and generalizations for picking out attributes, and subsuming objects within a given category ... 'categorical' thinking is usually quite flexible ... The ability to move freely, to shift from one category to another, is one of the chief characteristics of 'abstract' thinking' or the 'categorical behaviour' essential to it.
>
> (Luria, 1976: 77)

Rather controversially at the time and since, Luria found that categorical, abstract ways of thinking were intricately linked with formal education, in particular, with schooling. Those participants in his study who had little or no access to formal schooling did not appear to think in the categorical ways outlined by Luria.

Much has been written about Luria's work and there is a pervasive ideological misunderstanding that people tend to place on his findings, suggesting that he made a distinction between literate thinkers and non-literate thinkers, thus privileging the thinking of literate over illiterate thinkers. This is a misreading of his work. He makes no claims of superiority of one mode of thought and in fact, refers to the performance rather than the competence of the subjects of his study. What his work suggests is that access to different semiotic mediation during development will lead you to perform tasks in very different ways. This does not mean that someone who has not attended school cannot think in abstract ways, rather it suggests that this competence needs to be developed. This becomes important in relation to pedagogical practices in South Africa, where the legacy of education under apartheid continues to permeate classrooms. The nature of talk in classrooms is therefore important in the child's development and needs to be considered when conducting research in different contexts. In the chapters that follow, talk becomes the unit of analysis and differences in teacher talk reflect difference in pedagogy and, consequently, potentially differential acquisition of scientific concepts. Classroom talk, of course, is not the only language that students are exposed to in the class.

Textbooks provide students with access, to greater or lesser degrees, to scientific concepts in a classroom. In what follows, I present a study in which I analysed the Grade 2 Department of Basic Education (DBE) textbook aimed at teaching science to school children. Science is not introduced as a discrete content subject in South African schools until Grade 4. Foundation phase children (Grades 1–3) are taught Life Skills, with a component of this focusing on science. Only one hour per week is given to teaching science in the topic of 'Beginning Knowledge'. Given that scientific – that is, abstract – concepts need to be taught, the question driving this study was:

> To what extent does the DBE textbook and CAPS policy document make scientific concepts available to students in Grade 2?

As discussed earlier in this chapter and in Chapter 2 of this book, scientific concepts are meaningless outside of a reference point: that is, unless linked to a child's everyday concepts, scientific concepts cannot be internalized meaningfully. Hence, a secondary question of this analysis relates to the extent that everyday concepts are mobilized in the textbook and how these are linked to the scientific concepts in a way that generates meaningful acquisition. The analysis reported here focuses on science texts for Grade 2 because science integrates literacy, numeracy and critical thinking skills. 'Science' in this sense refers to the subject and content of science as it is taught in schools, rather than referring more broadly to 'scientific' (or schooled) concepts.

My focus on the Foundation Phase of schooling is informed by the current understanding that young children can acquire abstract knowledge if this is mediated to them and the acquisition of schooled concepts potentially enhances cognitive development (Fleer, 2010; Harrison, 2011; Haynes & Murris, 2012). However, I am not suggesting that children at a Foundation Phase level are able to think in mature scientific concepts or manipulate formal operational thinking. The suggestion here is that children can learn a level of abstract knowledge, provided this is taught to them. Considerable research indicates that children can learn abstract concepts earlier than was initially thought in the twentieth century (Egan, 2002; Fleer, 2010, Ginsberg & Golbeck, 2004; Spelke 2013). Incidentally, these findings from neuroscience prove Vygotsky's (1986) early contention that learning precedes development, illustrating, as they do, that young children can be taught to think abstractly (to a degree) before they reach the stages that Piaget (1956) outlined. Moreover, learning scientific concepts provides an important foundation for the acquisition of abstract thought (Syla et al., 2004).

Beginning with Vygotsky's distinction between scientific and everyday concepts, this chapter draws further on Hedegaard's (1998) notion of scientific concepts as 'schooled' concepts while also drawing on Davydov's elaboration of scientific concepts as containing both 'procedural' and 'content' knowledge. As noted, when Vygotsky refers to scientific concepts, he is referring to fully formed concepts that generally only come fully into being in adolescence. However, research mentioned in this chapter indicates that young children can think abstractly and for this chapter, I use the term 'simple' scientific concept to describe what I am looking for in the data. This follows from my earlier work (Morris et al., 2016) that utilizes the notion of simple scientific concepts to distinguish this from a fully developed concept. For the purposes of this chapter, a simple scientific concept is outlined in table 5.1.

Table 5.1 Attributes of a simple scientific concept.

1. Has at least two essential characteristics
2. Employs scientific terms that represent specialised language. Although, in this chapter we are dealing with Grade 2 students who will not have the vocabulary of trained scientists, they are able to understand this specialized language when it is pitched at their level.
3. Simple scientific concepts are hierarchical and transferable across contexts.
4. Simple scientific concepts have two integral parts: content and procedural knowledge.

Table 5.1 illustrates the characteristics of simple scientific concepts that are analysed in the data that are reported in this chapter. Focusing on a grade 2 textbook and curriculum documents, I am looking for the extent to which simple scientific concepts are made visible and elaborated in the text. A secondary objective is to determine the extent to which everyday concepts are linked with the scientific concepts for the child to make sense of what is being taught. The analysis focuses on a specific science topic elaborated in the textbook. Very specifically, I focus on how the concepts of 'wild' and 'domesticated' animals are presented in this text and whether everyday concepts are linked to the scientific concepts.

Methodology

This chapter purposively samples the student Lifeskills workbook that is prescribed by the South African DBE for grades 2 and 3 as well as the CAPS policy document for Foundation Phase (DBE, 2011d). I focus on only one specific topic in this analysis because this is the topic that is taught by teachers in Chapter 6, which follows on from this chapter and gives context to the textbook analysis. These textbooks are given to teachers and students free of charge and one may therefore have some degree of confidence that each child has their own textbook.

Context

The student workbook that was analysed is written against a background of a South African curriculum that locates itself in a learner-centred pedagogy. That is, a pedagogy loosely based on constructivist principles, which understands that children are active cognizing agents who construct knowledge in collaboration with more knowledgeable others. As noted earlier in this book, the notion of 'constructivism' has become slippery, with authors such as von Glaserfeld indicating that constructivism must be 'radical' and that children construct their knowledge of the world in an individual, pragmatic way (1989). The problem with radical constructivism in my understanding of it is that it sees knowledge production as essentially idiosyncratic; for my own purposes, a concept can indeed be subjectively meaningful to a child, but this is a spontaneous concept. When one speaks of abstract concepts, these cannot have idiosyncratic meanings as their meaning is embedded in a history and culture of ideas. For our purposes in the current chapter, the DBE's understanding of constructivism does not go much beyond a focus on learner-centred pedagogy and an acknowledgement that learning is an active process.[2]

Analytical Framework

Drawing on the work of Morris, Hardman and Jacklin (2016) as well as the work on concepts outlined by Vygotsky (1986), the point of the analysis is to (1) ascertain the extent to which scientific concepts are made explicit to the students, (2) the extent to which everyday concepts are recruited in knowledge construction and (3) the linking between the scientific and the everyday. To achieve this, it is important to understand the 'big idea' or main understanding that lies behind why children in grade 2 learn about wild and domesticated/farm animals. Certainly, in a time of climate change, this knowledge is key for children to learn because ecosystems are impacted differentially, depending on whether an animal is wild or domesticated. The potential harm done to ecosystems through domestication of animals needs to be seen in relation to climate change as a real-world problem children are facing. When gaining knowledge about wild and domestic animals, then, children need to be asking questions such as: What is the impact of domestication on ecosystems? What impact does plant and animal domestication have on climate change? It is in this sense, of understanding the 'big idea' informing the content taught, that the everyday and scientific concepts need to be linked. The everyday concept gives relevance and places the abstract concept in a context that a child can make sense of the abstraction.

Analytical indicators were derived from the understanding of simple scientific concepts discussed above. These indicators are drawn from Morris et al. (2016) and are represented below.

Indicators

Indicator 1: To what extent do the selected texts make simple scientific concepts available regarding:

- Use of specialized language
- How the concepts relate to other concepts
- The concepts attributes
- How the concept is related to the wider context

Indicator 2: How do the texts describe the simple scientific concept in relation to content and procedural knowledge?

Indicator 3: How are the relationship between simplex and more complex scientific concepts represented in the texts?

These indicators must be present and must also be correctly defined in order to receive a score on the coding schedule represented in Table 5.2 below.

The six criteria above are drawn from the description of simple scientific concepts discussed in this chapter. A score of 12/12 indicates that that the criteria for the presence of a simple scientific concept have been met, are explicit, and complete. Scores between 5/12 and 11/12 indicate that not all criteria have been met, but sufficient criteria exist to suggest that a potential simple scientific concept is presented. A 'potential' scientific concept implicitly requires that the teacher develops this concept in more depth than is presented in the texts. This relates partially to Hedegaard's (1998) notion of an empirical concept that can potentially be developed into a simple scientific concept if the teacher has the content knowledge to do so. Note that the use of the word 'potential' here refers to pedagogy rather than development. Finally, a score of 4/12 and below indicates that the concept remains at the level of the everyday. While everyday concepts are necessary in classrooms, this is only so in relation to their linking to abstract concepts. A focus solely on everyday, spontaneous concepts is problematic because these concepts are empirical in nature and can lead to misunderstandings. Empirically, for example, fish and dolphins look like the same species because they have fins and live in water. However, these are completely different species, and a dolphin is more closely related to a cow than it is to a fish. Knowledge left at the level of the everyday does not develop the

Table 5.2 Rating scale for simple scientific concepts.

Rating Scale					
Criterion 1	**Criterion 2**	**Criterion 3**	**Criterion 4**	**Criterion 5**	**Criterion 6**
Contains two or more essential attributes that uniquely defines and differentiates the concept from all other concepts.	Employs two or more specialized terms.	Described in relation to other concepts on the scientific knowledge curriculum.	Transfers across contexts.	Structured as two integral parts i.e. content knowledge and procedural knowledge.	Underpins more complex scientific concepts.
/2	/2	/2	/2	/2	/2

(Morris, et al., 2016: 146)

child cognitively. Similarly, knowledge left at the level of the abstract, without reference to the everyday, serves no developmental purpose. The findings reported here then focus on simple scientific concepts, potential scientific concepts and everyday concepts.

Below, in Figure 5.1, I provide a hypothetical example of how one would begin to code a topic in a text in relation to the rating scale above.

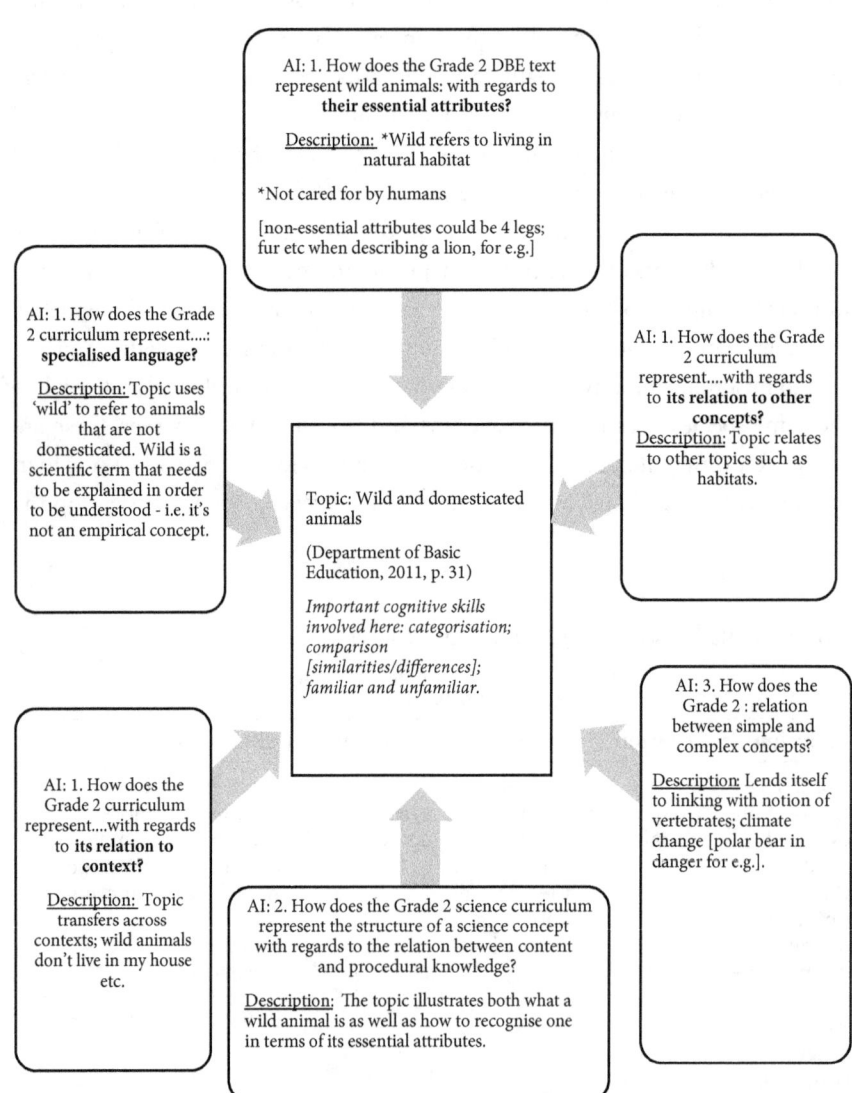

Figure 5.1 Analytic indicators: 'Wild animals'.

Findings and Discussion

In what follows I analyse the following topics: Wild and Farm/domesticated animals.

Table 5.3 illustrates findings in relation to how scientific concepts are presented to students in relation to farm animals in the student workbook for grade 2 Lifeskills. Drawing on the definition from Morris (1992), for our purposes a 'farm' animal is defined as:

1. Selectively bread by humans to meet their own needs
2. The domesticated animal lives in natural ecosystems that have been modified to ensure the continued existence and optimal breeding of the animals.
3. A domestic animal co-exists in a habitat with humans.
4. It relies on humans for its needs, such as a suitable habitat and food.

The word farm is defined as:

1. A place where buildings and land are used for agricultural purposes.
2. Animals on a farm are domesticated.
3. Farm animals are bred to meet human needs for milk, meat, eggs, etc.

Table 5.3 Farm animals: Old MacDonald and his domesticated animals.

Rating Scale					
Criterion 1	Criterion 2	Criterion 3	Criterion 4	Criterion 5	Criterion 6
Contains two or more essential attributes that uniquely defines and differentiates the concept from all other concepts.	Employs two or more specialized terms.	Described in relation to other concepts on the scientific knowledge curriculum.	Transfers across contexts.	Structured as two integral parts i.e. content knowledge and procedural knowledge.	Underpins more complex scientific concepts.
0/2	1/2	1/2	1/2	0/2	0/2
Total	3/12				

No definition of a 'farm' animal is provided for students. Of interest is the fact that farm animals are not defined as domesticated animals in this text, as the topic that follows on from farm animals is 'wild' animals and drawing the distinction between these types of animals is more easily effected if one can see that the central difference between them lies in their domestication. The topic begins with the book presenting a picture of animals that one could find on a farm and asking students to select the one that they like the most. The topic extends over three pages in the workbook and no definition is given either of a farm or a farm animal. The essential characteristics of farm animals, therefore, are absent from this text and this is scored in table criterion 1 as 0/2. On the second page of the topic, children are asked to fill in the correct answers on a table where the everyday name of say a male sheep, is given and they are required to write down that this is in fact called a ram. There is potential here to link the everyday concepts of gender to the scientific names given to genders of animals, but the teacher would have to do this as there is no explanation in the text to aid the students. Specialist terms, such as 'ram' and 'ewe', are used, but they are not defined in terms of their essences. The use of a specialized term to describe a male sheep means that criterion 2 is scored ½. Of some interest to this reader is the fact that students are asked to name the sounds that animals make, such as 'baa' for a lamb. This everyday knowledge is at a low level, as a three-year-old would be able to answer this.

The indication appears to be that in this learner workbook, at least, the understanding of children's cognitive capacity is quite limited and, indeed, limiting; this, in the face of evidence we have discussed earlier in the chapter indicating that children are able to think abstractly even in the Foundation Phase (Carey & Spelke,1996; Egan, 2002; Fleer, 2010; Ginsberg & Golbeck, 2004; Haynes & Murris, 2012; Morris et al., 2016; Winkler-Rhoades et al., 2013). On the final page of this topic students are given a written-out version of the nursery rhyme, 'Old MacDonald'. While this song may well be familiar to students, it doesn't provide evidence of what everyday concepts they may have about farm animals. It appears that the assumption may be that this nursery rhyme is familiar and, therefore, represents a form of everyday knowledge that students can use to understand the scientific notion of the 'farm'. A nursery rhyme, however, does not necessarily represent an everyday concept. Certainly, there are nursery rhymes that illustrate everyday concepts, such as 'Ring a Ring o'Rosies', which represents everyday concepts regarding the plague and its symptoms (that is, the red pustules that form on the skin). However, Old MacDonald's farm does not seem to relate to everyday concepts except in so far as the sound an animal makes when one listens to it. The ability of the concept of 'farm' to transfer across contexts then, is categorized as ½ because there is some sense in which knowing the sounds an animal makes contains a basis for understanding different kinds of animals. No procedural knowledge is given (for example, one could tell the children that we get wool from sheep) and this is then marked 0/2.

The final criterion for simple scientific concepts in relation to 'farm animals' relates to whether the concepts given in grade 2 are built on in Lifeskills in grade 3. In grade 3, no mention is made of farm animals, although two pages are dedicated to the life cycle of animals and one page to drawing one's pets. There is no observable link between the topic of 'farm animals' and any topics in grade 3, indicating a score of 0/2 for the simple scientific concepts underpinning more complex ones. In Table 1 the total score for the topic 'farm animals' is given as 3/12. A score below 4/12 indicates that the concept remains at the level of the everyday, indicating that in relation to the topic of farm animals, children in grade 2 are not being taught any abstraction and remain tied to context dependent concepts. I turn now to the topic of 'wild animals' as it is represented in the text. The notion of 'wild' is, like 'farm' an abstraction. Drawing again on Morris (1992) for our purposes we can define a wild animal as:

1. Untamed
2. Existing in its natural habitat
3. Does not rely on humans for its existence

Three pages of the text are devoted to teaching children about wild animals. No definition of what constitutes the essential characteristics of wild animals is given. Rather, children are given examples of five wild animals: a lion, an elephant, a buffalo, rhinoceros and leopard; that is, the African big five, a term originally coined by hunters in search of trophies but used today to highlight the need to protect these unique animals. As no definition is given of the term wild, criterion 1 receives a score of 0/2. In relation to describing the big five on pages 50 and 51 in the textbook, the picture shifts with specialized terms being used to describe some of the animals and their habitats. I have coded this 2/2 for criterion 2. Further, the descriptions of the animals link to other simple scientific concepts such as habitats as well as descriptions of the nature of the

Table 5.4 Wild animals.

		Rating Scale			
Criterion 1	Criterion 2	Criterion 3	Criterion 4	Criterion 5	Criterion 6
Contains two or more essential attributes that uniquely defines and differentiates the concept from all other concepts.	Employs two or more specialized terms.	Described in relation to other concepts on the scientific knowledge curriculum.	Transfers across contexts.	Structured as two integral parts i.e. content knowledge and procedural knowledge.	Underpins more complex scientific concepts.
0/2	2/2	2/2	2/2	1/2	1/2
Total	8/12				

groups/herds they live in. I have therefore scored criterion 3 as 2/2 because there is a sense in which the information about the wild animals is linked to other concepts such as habitat and camouflage.

Of particular interest is page 52 of the textbook that discusses how animals 'hide' themselves. When making use of the everyday term, 'hide' the text introduces the notion of camouflage, thereby linking the abstract notion to an everyday example. As the topic discusses camouflage in relation to hiding, it can be transferred across contexts where a child might understand camouflage in relation to soldiers in the army. For this reason, criterion 4 is marked 2/2. There is also some indication of how, for example, a zebra might camouflage itself, although this is not provided in much depth and how this might impact on the child's understanding of 'wild animals' is not developed. For this reason, criterion 5 is scored ½. Finally, criterion 6 is scored 1/2 as the grade 3 textbook builds on the knowledge of 'habitat' developed in this topic. With a total score of 8/12, what we have in relation to wild animals in this text is a potential simple scientific concept. As noted, 'potential' here refers to pedagogical potential. That is, depending on the teacher's input, a simple scientific concept may be developed. The challenge with potential simple scientific concepts, however, lies in the reliance on the teacher to develop this knowledge further. The assumption then is that the teacher has both the requisite content knowledge and the desire to assist learners to acquire this knowledge. Another assumption could be that the teacher has material resources available to her/him to draw on to bolster his/her knowledge. In a country like South Africa, however, with the highest Gini co-efficient in the world, it is problematic to make any assumptions about human and material resources. The difficulty of leaving concept development in the hands of teachers is discussed and illustrated in Chapter 6. For our purposes, I note that leaving the development of a concept in the hands of teachers is potentially very problematic. I turn now to the CAPS document that teachers rely on to inform their teaching to investigate the extent to which simple scientific concepts are made available in the text as well as to ascertain how these are linked to the everyday.

Analysis of the CAPS Document

The first thing to note is in relation to the amount of time given to Beginning Knowledge across grades 1–3. While English, for example, is allotted 8/7 hours per week in grades 1–3, beginning knowledge is given 2 hours per week. Further, as noted earlier, there is no specific subject called 'science'; rather, science is part of a body of knowledge called Lifeskills aimed at 'guiding and preparing learners for life and its possibilities, including equipping learners for meaningful and successful living in a rapidly changing and transforming society' (DBE, 2011: 8). Four hours in total is given to learning about farm and wild animals.

Table 5.5 Beginning knowledge in CAPS: Wild and Farm animals.

Grade 2: Beginning Knowledge	Simple scientific concept (adapted from Morris, 1992)
Wild animal	Untamed
• type	Existing in its natural habitat
• camouflage	Does not rely on humans for its existence
Farm Animal	Selectively bread by humans to meet their own needs
• types	
• uses (such as clothing and food).	The domesticated animal lives in natural ecosystems that have been modified to ensure the continued existence and optimal breeding of the animals.
	A domestic animal co-exists in a habitat with humans.
	It relies on humans for its needs, such as a suitable habitat and food.

There is a complete dearth of explanation in the CAPS policy document about what distinguishes a wild from a farm animal. In fact, nothing is mentioned to assist the teacher other than that there are different types of animals (everyday concept) and that they can camouflage themselves (a specialized term that, however, does not relate solely to wild animals as farm animals can achieve this). A rating of 1/12 is given to this topic, and it remains entirely at the level of the everyday. There is nothing in the policy documents for grade 3 that builds on this knowledge. The picture is similar in relation to farm animals as is illustrated in Table 5.6 below.

In relation to farm animals, there is some transference across contexts implied in the notion of the uses that farm animals have. This could also relate to procedural knowledge, in that knowing what use an animal has can help one to understand the concept of 'farm' animal. However, with a score of 3/12, again we are left at the level of the everyday and reliant on the teacher's own content knowledge to develop this topic further. However, as noted earlier, the assumption that teachers have content knowledge in science that goes beyond what is in the textbook or in the policy documents is problematic (Spaull, 2013).

Earlier in this chapter, I quoted Mann's (1917) suggestion that science textbooks should not contain decontextualized facts outside of the relevance they hold for the child's lived experience. Unfortunately, what the analysis presented above shows is that facts are presented in ways that do not link to the everyday

Table 5.6 Wild animals in the CAPS documents.

Rating Scale					
Criterion 1	Criterion 2	Criterion 3	Criterion 4	Criterion 5	Criterion 6
Contains two or more essential attributes that uniquely defines and differentiates the concept from all other concepts.	Employs two or more specialized terms.	Described in relation to other concepts on the scientific knowledge curriculum.	Transfers across contexts.	Structured as two integral parts i.e. content knowledge and procedural knowledge.	Underpins more complex scientific concepts.
0/2	1/2	0/2	0/2	0/2	0/2
Total	1/12				

and therefore, lack meaning and relevance for the child engaging with them. There is no sense in the data analysed that the 'big idea' or core issue behind learning about wild and domesticated animals comes through in the textbook. The notion that an ecosystem is impacted differentially depending on whether an animal is wild or domesticated is not found in the textbook. One mention is made of habitats, but this is not even taken up further in the grade 3 text to enable children to understand the impact of domestication on an ecosystem, or indeed, climate change. Presenting facts about what makes an animal wild or domesticated is insufficient for the child to get a bigger picture of why this is useful knowledge to have in their real-life situation.

Conclusion

This chapter examines how simple scientific concepts are made available to students in the Grade 2 Lifeskills workbook provided for South African children by the DBE. In particular, the chapter focuses on the topics of wild and farm animals. Findings indicate that in relation to farm animals, only everyday concepts are made available to students in this textbook, that is, there is no evidence of simple scientific concepts in relation to the notion of farm animals. In relation to the notion of 'wild' animals, potential simple scientific concepts are presented in the book. The challenge with potential simple scientific concepts, however, is that the onus on developing these concepts lies with the teacher. As discussed in this chapter, research indicates that teachers in South Africa struggle with their content knowledge in science and mathematics. Their ability, therefore, to develop concepts for students that they may not be confident with, can lead to serious misunderstandings. The analysis of the two topics further highlighted the low level at which science content knowledge is made available to Foundation Phase students. This is perhaps the most worrying thing about this analysis; the dearth of abstract concepts being taught. Research in the twenty-first century indicates quite clearly that even young children can grasp abstraction if they are taught in a way that they can make sense of the abstract concepts. Children in grade 2 are eight and nine years old and are not only able to think in logical ways but are able to manipulate objects to understand them. While Piaget (1976) indicates that children in what he calls the 'concrete operational stage' cannot think in abstraction, the evidence that this is possible in relation to specific types of pedagogy, suggests that the lack of abstraction in the topics analysed in this chapter is problematic in terms of cognitive development. Vygotsky himself indicates that: ... *as long as the curriculum supplies the necessary material, the development of scientific concepts runs ahead of the development of spontaneous concepts.* (Vygotsky, 2002: 190). Without the necessary material, which is evident from this chapter, we cannot expect to be developing children cognitively in our schools. If we are not providing students with access to knowledge that challenges what they currently know, creating dissonance and thereby leading the student to seek a solution, we are not developing students cognitively. What we appear to be doing at least in relation to the topics studied here is reinforcing children's everyday understandings of the world, without challenging them to develop. Schooling, then, becomes about reinforcing a cannon of knowledge, rather than developing critical thinkers capable of novel thought. This is perhaps an explanation for why we continue to see the IRE structure dominating classrooms; if school is about reinforcing knowledge, then teaching/learning becomes a question, response and feedback loop, often in a fairly rote way. In Chapter 6 we investigate pedagogy based on the two topics analysed here to see to what extent a teacher can develop potential simple scientific concepts.

6

Hedegaard's 'Double-Move' in Teaching in Grade 2

Chapter 5 presented an analysis of a Grade 2 textbook from the Department of Basic Education in South Africa. Findings from this chapter indicate that the prescribed text contains little to no actual scientific concepts and does not link the abstraction of institutional knowledge with the empirically derived, everyday concepts that children bring to the classroom. These findings are problematic because they assume that a teacher has access to material beyond what is provided by the government and that the teacher uses this to inform his/her teaching of abstract concepts. Secondly, the failure to link abstract concepts with everyday, spontaneous concepts will lead to what Vygotsky called mere 'verbalism'. That is, the child knows the word and perhaps even the definition of the concept but does not understand it in a way that can transform him/her cognitively or be used to transform the situation that s/he lives in.

In this chapter, I present an argument for the use of Hedegaard (1998) and Chaiklin and Hedegaard's (2013) 'radical-local' pedagogy as a recontextualization of Vygotsky's key understanding that concept development requires that everyday and scientific concepts are linked in developing the child cognitively. I do this by providing an empirical example of Hedegaard's (1998) 'double-move' in pedagogy in a science lesson with Grade 2 students who are learning about wild and farm/domesticated animals.[1] I begin with examining the current status of knowledge acquisition in schools in South Africa (and indeed, it seems to me, around the world).

The Status Quo

Currently, children are educated in school to obtain employment when they are adults. That is, schooling is predicated on a capitalist ideal; the production of a workforce (Brown et al., 2003). For over a century, the body of knowledge taught in schools has not changed extensively. For Michael Young (2013), children learn 'powerful knowledge' in schools. The notion of powerful knowledge has certain resonances with Vygotsky's notion of scientific concepts, in that this kind of knowledge enables us to approach the world with different 'heads' capable of abstraction outside of an empirical instance of what we are working with. Young notwithstanding, I am not convinced however, that this *is* what we teach in schools. Do we teach children in such a manner that we equip them with the cognitive functions to act creatively and critically on new knowledge? Certainly, if one looks at what is taught in a traditional classroom, the answer to this question is not obvious. Rather, traditionally, schools have aimed to provide students with a body of knowledge that they can reproduce on a test, which requires at best, the use of memory and at worst, simply the ability to regurgitate what was taught in the classroom.

As seen in Chapter 5, the knowledge we present to children in schools, at least in the context analysed, is itself not problem-free, as the abstract concepts presented to children cannot be acquired in the absence of them being linked to the child's everyday concepts. This is something that is not visible in my analysis of the selected text used in the schools where I carried out most of my research. It is quite useless to present children with abstract concepts without giving them a mechanism with which to own and understand the meaning of these concepts. 'Powerful knowledge' then, in the absence of everyday concepts, remains outside the reach of many school children. Conversely, a reliance on the everyday at the expense of scientific/schooled concepts (as shown in Chapter 5) will lead to empirical knowledge laden with misunderstandings. Relying on the everyday cannot lead to cognitive development.

The next question to address is the content of the knowledge we want children to acquire. There is a difference, I argue, between the form of thought we want children to acquire (higher cognitive functions, or what we would call executive functions today) and the content that is carried in the concepts acquired. Now in the twenty-first century, it is time for us to challenge what is taught in schools. Children need more than content knowledge to develop the cognitive skills required for this unique century. Furthermore, the type of content they need to learn surely differs from what has been taught for over a century? Unlike the twentieth century, our world does not require workers to facilitate the growth of capital. We have computers doing the jobs, such as factory work or car manufacturing, done by humans in the twentieth century. Today careers such as robotics or stem cell research are opening new fields of work. We live in the Anthropocene and face challenges to the very existence of humanity if we are unable to produce adults who can practically deal with climate change, desalinate water, overcome poverty and many other crises of our current age. It is time, I would argue, for us to challenge the established canon in schools and to begin teaching children in such a way that they develop the cognitive functions required to navigate life as an adult.

The challenge of fully changing educational content, curricula and pedagogy may seem insurmountable. However, in this chapter I illustrate how the pedagogical model developed in this book provides both a structure for effective pedagogy and points to the nature of content that should be learnt in school; that is, a model of pedagogy that can transform current traditional pedagogy. I illustrate the impact of the double-move as a pedagogical mechanism for developing concepts, by comparing the pedagogy of a traditional classroom where a teacher has had no training in this novel pedagogical model, with a classroom where a teacher has been trained to use this type of pedagogy. The chapter begins though, by unpacking the notion of how scientific and everyday concepts are linked throughout development.

Vygotsky's Notion of Concepts; Scientific and Spontaneous Concepts

As seen in Chapters 2 and 5, Vygotsky (1986) distinguishes between spontaneous, everyday concepts and scientific, abstract concepts. For the purposes of this chapter, scientific concepts refer to school concepts (Hedegaard, 1998) that, once acquired, develop a child's ability to think theoretically. Everyday concepts, on the other hand, are learnt through spontaneous interaction with the world and create richly meaningful, empirical knowledge for the developing child. While the meaning of abstract concepts is culturally embedded, and, importantly, shared amongst people, everyday concepts are more idiosyncratic and related to the child's lived experience. An example illustrates this. If I were to ask you to think of a flower, you would probably be able to picture something with petals, a stem, stamen and leaves. You may even go further in your thinking and recognize that this 'flower' can only grow if it has sunlight, soil and water, so that photosynthesis can occur. Now, you can picture the abstraction of what a 'flower' is, but each of us may have in mind a different flower. For me, when asked to picture a flower, the first image I have is of daisies. Daisies are meaningful to my lived experience because my grandmother's house was surrounded by daisies and, as a child, I thoroughly enjoyed visiting my grandmother. My everyday concept of a flower is very specifically linked to my lived experiences as a child. However, as an adult, I understand the abstraction 'flower'. It is in this way that the abstraction of scientific concepts is intricately interwoven with the lived experience produced by the everyday concept that idiosyncratically makes sense to me. For an abstract, scientific concept to make sense to a child then, it must link with the everyday concepts that the child already possesses. The mechanism for this linking is elegantly elaborated in Marianne Hedegaard's 'double-move' in pedagogy, outlined in Chapter 2.

Science for Eight-year-olds: The Context of the Study

Science is not an official subject in South Africa until grade 4 so the lesson presented in this paper is taking place under the topic of 'Lifeskills'. Within this broad topic, children in grades 1–3 are given access to science concepts in a one hour a week lesson which falls under the Life Skills curriculum called 'Beginning Knowledge'. As noted earlier in this paper, students in the Foundation Phase (grades 1–3) can acquire abstract concepts, and the need to do so at younger ages impacts on their successful interaction with science knowledge later in their schooling (Morris et al., 2016). The school in this research is in an affluent area of Cape Town and charges school fees of around USD 3000 per annum. This is, therefore, a relatively high socio-economic demographic as the average cost of school fees in South Africa is around USD 900 per annum, for schools that charge fees.[2]

The school uses the Department of Basic Education's texts for both teachers and students and follows the Curriculum and Assessment Policy Statement (CAPS) curriculum. However, as this is an affluent school, teachers often bring their own teaching material to classes and are encouraged to do so to supplement curriculum content coverage. The school is co-educational and runs from grades 1–7. Students wear a prescribed uniform and sign a code of conduct that places moral interaction and kindness as core principles.

Two teachers and fifty students participated in this study. Although there are fifty-three students across the two classrooms, three students did not return the consent form for the study and were, therefore excluded from participation. Ethics clearance was obtained through the university's ethics committee and both teachers gave informed consent to be part of the study. One of the teachers, Mrs Jenkins, has been trained to use the pedagogical model outlined in Chapter 2 (the programme for this training is available in Appendix B). She is a thirty-two-year-old teacher who has taught for ten years and has therefore, a solid base of experience. For four weeks, Mrs Jenkins attended a course for 2.5 hours per week in which she was introduced to various concepts that have been discussed in this book, such as mediation, scientific and everyday concepts, the germ cell, and the double-move. I am the primary lecturer on this course and therefore, in terms of ethical considerations, the data collected and discussed in this chapter were analysed both by myself and by a colleague. Inter-rate reliability on the coding was 84 per cent, which is satisfactory. The second teacher, Ms Naidoo is twenty-eight years old and has been teaching for six years. She too has a firm foundation of experience in teaching grade 2. Ms Naidoo did not complete the course that Mrs Jenkins did.

Mrs Jenkins teaches grade 2J and has twenty-seven children in her class: fourteen girls and thirteen boys. Ms Naidoo teaches grade 2N and has twenty-six students in her class: twelve girls and fourteen boys. One hour a week is devoted to the teaching of science content and concepts under the Lifeskills curriculum. These teachers were observed over the course of a topic (two and a half weeks) in which they taught about wild and farm/domesticated animals.

Analysis

The analysis involved coding teacher talk as this is viewed as a primary mediating tool in classrooms (Hennessy et al., 2016; Mercer & Littleton, 2007). The focus of the comparative analysis was on how teachers taught and specifically, whether they linked scientific and everyday concepts. In Table 6.1 below, one can see the codes and examples of how talk was coded.

The 'Big Idea'

The content of the observed lessons was domesticated/farm animals and wild animals. The 'big idea', the relevance behind learning this, lies in the impact that domestication can have on ecosystems. Because this case study plays out in the Western Cape which is water scarce it is relevant, therefore, for Western Cape pupils to know about the impact that say, domesticated plants can have on an ecosystem. When the British colonized this tip of Africa, they planted pine trees all along Table Mountain. Pine trees are alien to the Western Cape and sap the water table. The plantations are slowly being eradicated because there is simply

Table 6.1 Coding framework.

Code	Definition	Examples	Teachers
ECE	Everyday Concepts Elaborated	'The men {lions}, the boys, yes they have manes'	Mrs Jenkins
ECNE	Everyday Concept Not-elaborated	'… or we call it the wild where they are free'	Ms Naidoo
SCE	Elaborated Scientific Concepts	'So they are predators, they are hunters'	Mrs Jenkins
ST	Scientific Terms	'I'm a predator'	Mrs Jenkins
FE	Elaborated feedback	'Ok, so lions are large animals. They are big and house cats are smaller'	Mrs Jenkins
NEF	Non elaborated feedback	'Mr Lion is the King of the Jungle and he is the strongest animal'	Ms Naidoo
CQ	Closed question	'So this can be food, but food for what?'	Mrs Jenkins
OQ	Open Question	'Why do you say that?'	Mrs Jenkins

not enough water to sustain these aliens. Harnessing this everyday example in a lesson, therefore, would help a child to understand why it's important to learn about the differences between wild and domesticated plants and animals. Cognitively, children will have to apply the notion of comparison to understand the differences and similarities between wild and domestic animals. The ability to compare, that is, requires that one can differentiate along certain dimensions.

For the purposes of this chapter, a 'wild' animal is defined as: (1) In its natural state, untamed, animals *ferae naturae* (Harper-Collins, 2009: 2370). (2) growing and living without human aid or intervention and (3) related to or resembling corresponding domestic animals. A 'domesticated/farm' animal is (1) any animal that has been domesticated by humans to breed and live outside of a wild habitat. (2) generally requiring human intervention to survive in the habitat that the human selects for it (Morris, 1992). In Table 6.2 below, a summary of the differences in talk between both teachers is given to orient the discussion that follows.

What we can see in Table 6.2 is that both teachers do elaborate everyday concepts, with 17 per cent of Mrs Jenkins's talk focused on this and 6 per cent of Ms Naidoo's talk. In Table 6.2 we can see that Ms Naidoo makes very little reference either to scientific terms (ST – 1 per cent), or scientific concepts (SCE 2 per cent). This picture shifts in relation to Mrs Jenkins who elaborated scientific concepts in 16 per cent of her talk. Ms Naidoo's talk is dominated by

Table 6.2 Comparison between two teachers' talk when teaching science in grade 2.

Code	Mrs Jenkins % of teacher talk	Ms Naidoo % of teacher talk
Everyday Concept Elaborated	17	6
Everyday Concept Not Elaborated	0.4	22
Scientific Concept Elaborated	16	2
Scientific Term	8	1
Feedback Elaborated	22	-
Non-Elaborated Feedback	17	33
Closed Q	18	36
Open Q	2	-
Total	100%	

closed questions (CQ – 36 per cent) followed closely, as one would expect in an IRE sequence, by feedback (33 per cent). Note, however, that this feedback is not elaborated and generally takes the form of 'That's right' or 'Yes'. While Ms Naidoo makes use of everyday concepts, these are predominantly not elaborated on (ECNE – 22 per cent).

In contrast, we see that Mrs Jenkins not only uses more scientific terms (ST – 8 per cent) than Ms Naidoo, but importantly, she elaborates scientific concepts (SCE – 16 per cent) relatively often. The extent to which she links the scientific and everyday concepts is investigated later in this chapter in relation to the qualitative data. Note also that although 18 per cent of Mrs Jenkins's talk is taken up with closed questions (CQ), 22 per cent of her talk is aimed at elaborating on feedback she received from the class. The use of closed questions in an Initiate Respond Evaluate sequence (IRE) is well established in research as a didactic technique (Sinclair & Coulthard, 1975). While there is serious criticism levered against an IRE sequence in developing students' understanding of concepts, the use of the IRE sequence can only be adjudicated in relation to the evaluation move the teacher makes. Where evaluation is elaborated, the IRE sequence is more useful for learning than when it is not elaborated. Where feedback is not elaborated on, the sequence becomes merely an exchange of questions with known, closed responses. In Extract 6.1 below, we can see how Mrs Jenkins uses feedback to elaborate on what the children are learning – the difference between wild and domesticated animals. Mrs Jenkins is teaching them this topic by developing their thinking in relation to similarities and differences between the different types of animals. That is, as we shall see, she is not only intent on teaching content in the lesson, but also on teaching the form of thought that allows for comparisons between members of different classes.

Extract 6.1: Mrs Jenkins and IRE

Line	Talk	Analysis Code
1.	**Teacher**: I want you to tell me what you think the connection is? You're going to laugh at me. What is the connection between his stuff here (*points to cat food tin in her hand*) and that Jane? (*There is a picture of a zebra on the board. The teacher is pointing to the zebra and holding a tin of cat food. What she is looking for, which she will explain throughout the lesson, is similarities and differences between wild and domestic animals*).	CQ
2.	**Jane**: There's stripes on the cat	NFE
3.	Okay, that's a brilliant one, stripes.	FE
4.	So they have stripes in common, they share stripes.	CQ
5.	But that's not quite what I am looking for, Stan? *Stan has his hand up.*	
6.	**Stan**: Food.	
7.	**Teacher**: Ha, food. FE	FE
8.	Stan, explain it? CQ	CQ
9.	You're right, but explain what you mean.	FE

While a traditional IRE sequence can be quite restrictive in terms of developing concepts, this depends very much on the evaluation, or feedback move that the teacher makes during the sequence. In Extract 6.1 we can see how Mrs Jenkins uses closed questions to open a discussion through elaborating her feedback. This indicates that what she is looking for goes beyond what the children are offering as responses. In line 4, note how she uses the abstract notion of 'common' and immediately defines this word with a word children will understand: 'share'. While a relatively large amount (16 per cent) of Mrs Jenkins's talk elaborates scientific concepts and everyday concepts (17 per cent), in her lesson she goes beyond merely elaborating the content of the concepts, by discussing how one can think in relation to these concepts. I have distinguished between the content and form of thinking, by indicating that the contents of thought are 'subject content' facts, whereas the forms of thinking are 'cognitive functions'. In the extract below, this is illustrated when Mrs Jenkins begins to discuss the task that the children are required to work on in the lesson. In this instance, the task requires that children draw a mind map ('bubble map') *comparing* wild and domestic animals. This is a high-level task requiring that children can distinguish similarities and differences between the animals.

Extract 6.2: Make way for the queen

Dialogue

1. **Students:** Make way for the queen.
2. Make way for the queen. *The teacher (referred to as 'the queen' by her students) has stood up from her desk and walked towards the blackboard.*
3. **Mrs Jenkins:** So, we're going to do a bubble map. *Draws two intersecting circles on the board. Labels the one circle 'wild' animals and the other circle 'domestic' animals.*
4. Well, I haven't done a very good bubble around each one. *Laughs.*
5. On this side is the things that are only belonging to the lions, and this side only the cat, and the middle, the two joining, things that they can both do.
6. Right, Sadie? *Sadie has her hand up.*
7. It's something in the middle.
8. **Sadie:** They have very sharp claws.
9. **Mrs. Jenkins:** They've got sharp claws.
10. That's perfect, Sadie, you're working on the right idea here.
11. Sharp claws.
12. Love it.
13. Okay, they both have those. Pam?
14. **Pam:** Well, when we were talking about the mane, it's also so that they can stay, so that their mane looks like the dead grass colour so that they can hide.
15. **Students:** And they (over talking).
16. **Mrs Jenkins:** They're both?
17. **Students:** Predators.
18. **Mrs Jenkins:** Yes, they are predators.
19. Can you explain what the word predator means?
20. **Kyle**: It means they both hunt.
21. **Mrs. Jenkins**: So they are predators, they are hunters.

22. Let's put predators in here. Pre ... *Writes in the centre, shared space of the bubble map.*
23. **Nkosi**: De ...
24. **Mrs Jenkins**: Detor, pre ...
25. **Nkosi**: Predators.
26. **Mrs Jenkins**: Preda, thank you.
27. Okay, predators.
28. If I'm a predator, I'm hunting you.

In Extract 6.2 above, the teacher is beginning to illustrate how children can compare wild and domesticated animals by focusing on what they have in common and what differentiates them. She does this by means of a bubble map where two bubbles intersect each other with a space in the centre where similarities are recorded. What is interesting about this extract is how the teacher links the abstraction of comparisons, to a concrete, everyday bubble map that children can empirically interact with. What we have here is what Feuerstein would call the mediation of meaning; the recruitment of students' everyday knowledge to make sense of the abstraction being taught. Note too how she links the everyday concepts of 'hunting' with the abstract notion of 'predation', thereby giving the word 'predator' a meaning that students can share with her.

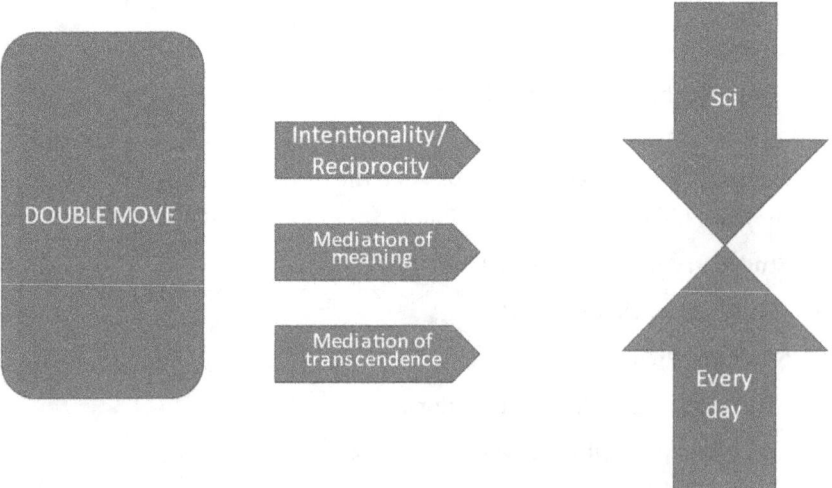

Figure 6.1 Pedagogy in practice.

What we have in Extract 6.2, then, is the teacher providing a what Gallimore and Tharp (1990) call cognitive structuring to enable children to compare animals. A cognitive structure is a structure for thinking that enables the children to adjudicate where certain content belongs. In this instance, in relation to a bubble map. The pedagogy enacted here is graphically illustrated in Figure 6.1 below.

What we see in Figure 6.1 is how the double move is animated by the mediated learning experiences in linking the abstract and the everyday. In Extract 6.3 below, we can see how Mrs Jenkins uses intentionality and reciprocity as mediating learning experiences to 'hook' children's attention and focus them on the task at hand.

Extract 6.3. Roaring into the Lesson

1. **Mrs Jenkins**: Rooooaaar (*children are all sitting at their desks, finishing a mathematics task. The teacher climbs onto her desk on all fours and begins to roar*).
2. **Students**: *laughter; Sidney roars back.*
3. **Mrs Jenkins**: I bet you want to know why I am roaring?
4. **Chloe**: You're a lion (*inaudible*)
5. **Mrs Jenkins:** I am a wild lion.
6. I am wild!
7. Put away your maths books and come to the mat everyone.
8. today we are going to learn about wild animals. *Mrs Jenkins moves to the front of the mat and begins to stick up pictures of wild and domesticated animals. The pictures are not placed in categories at the moment. Later in the lesson she will begin to do this when she does the mind map with the children.*

In Extract 6.3 in line 1, Mrs Jenkins grabs the students' attention by roaring; note how she goes on, in lines 5–8 to outline the intention of the lesson. Chloe's response in line 4 indicates a reciprocal interaction is opened between teacher and taught. It is through intentionality and reciprocity that the teacher begins to mediate the concepts to be learnt in the lesson.

When the Textbook Is the Only Resource

In Chapter 5 we saw a dearth of elaborated scientific concepts in the textbook that is used in this lesson by both teachers. While Mrs Jenkins has brought additional resources to her classroom, such as pictures and a mind map, Ms Naidoo relies entirely on the textbook for teaching. What follows is the beginning of the lesson on wild and domesticated animals.

Extract 6.4: Ms Naidoo – Old Macdonald and His Farm

1. **Teacher:** Huh-uh, huh-uh, huh-uh I'm gonna point it out. I, we'll sing it together. Ok. Face the front. Don't look at the camera. Don't look at the camera. One, two …
2. (Students sing along with Teacher)
3. Old MacDonald had a farm,
      E-I-E-I-O.
4. And on the farm he had a dog
      E-I-E-I-O.
5. And a woof, woof here,
      … *sings the entire song going through: Birds, ducks, cats and sheep.*
6. **Teacher:** Ok. Did you enjoy that?
7. **Students:** Yes.
8. …
9. **Teacher:** Right sweetheart. Shhtt.
10. Can you tell me name me some animals that's where you get in our homes.
11. An animal that you get in the home. Ollie?
12. **Students:** A dog.
13. **Teacher:** A dog. …
14. **Students:** A meerkat.
15. **Teacher:** A meerkat.
16. Will you get a meerkat in your home?
17. **Students:** No.
18. **Teacher:** Will you get him in the home?
19. **Students:** No.
20. **Teacher:** Where will we find a meerkat?
21. In the …
22. **Students:** Wild.
23. **Teacher:** In the wild yes, in the bush.
24. And where do you get a pig?
25. **Students**: In the farm.
26. **Teacher:** Yes, he is certainly on the farm.
27. But the farm, you see why do we get it on the farm in because a farm has space.

28. A farm is a little house, then they have big land hey where the animals can go on.
29. But we also call it domestic animals.
30. We also call it a home animal. Ok. Right.

The lesson begins with the teacher and students singing the nursery rhyme, Old MacDonald. This is the 'hook' the teacher uses to get the students to engage in what she will be teaching: the farm. For Feuerstein, this is the moment when the teacher makes known her intentions and looks for reciprocity from the students, but intentionality, the reason for singing this song, is absent. The children sing along, indicating some sort of engagement, although this couldn't be seen as reciprocity because they have not been given any reason about why the song is important. For example, they could have been told that today's lesson will be about animals, such as farm animals, that have been domesticated specifically to live on a farm.

As a scaffolding 'hook' to recruit students' attention, the singing of this song lets the children know that they will be learning about the farm. However, it does not make clear what the teacher's intention behind the song is, nor does it necessarily capture students' attention because as grade 2 students, they may not be that interested in singing a nursery rhyme that they know very well. As noted in Chapter 5, the textbook Ms Naidoo is using begins this section with Old MacDonald's farm and the teacher sticks strictly to this in her lesson. In Chapter 5, findings indicated that there were some potential simple scientific concepts in the DBE textbook on Beginning Knowledge, in relation to the teaching of the concept of 'wild'. The challenge with potential simple scientific concepts, however, lies in the fact that they rely on the teacher to elaborate them in more depth, ultimately developing simple scientific concepts. In Extract 6.4, we see that sticking very closely to the textbook does not aid Ms Naidoo in developing the scientific notion of what a farm animal is. In fact, she is trying to get students to understand the notion of farm animals as domesticated, which is a key distinction between wild and farm animals. Yet nowhere in the extract, or in the lesson, does she elaborate or define what a farm is or what a domesticated animal is. This echoes what is in the textbook she is using.

No definition of the essential attributes of domesticated animals is provided and it becomes clear in line 14 that at least one student is not clear about the differences between wild and domestic animals as he indicates that one would find a meerkat on a farm. As the lesson progresses, the only feature of a farm that the teacher mentions is space. However, this is not what distinguishes a farm from the wild, as space is available in the wild too. However, in lines 29 and 30 the teacher begins to attempt to define farm animals in terms of their domestication. While she does not explicitly define domestication, she likens it to a 'home' animal, presumably a pet. The children in this school are relatively affluent and many have pets, so their everyday concept of a pet is a useful concept to harness to define domestication. The scientific concept of 'domestication' is linked here to the child's everyday understanding of his or her own pet. Unfortunately, there is a missed opportunity to make this high-level concept more meaningful in relation to what kind of animals live on farms. While one may indeed have pets on a farm, it is unlikely that a cow, for example, is seen as a pet in the same way that a dog might be. Moreover, the opportunity of making the term 'domestication' useful and meaningful in a child's lived experience is not fully developed as domestication is linked in this extract only to pets, rather than more broadly. In Extract 6.5 below, we see how Mrs Jenkins achieves this transcendent leap from the classroom to the wider world that children live in.

The Double-move as Geared towards Authentic, Lived Experience

As noted in Chapter 2, the double-move requires a linking between the scientific and everyday concept in such a way that the concept acquired can be used beyond the confines of the classroom. In Extract 6.5, Mrs Jenkins attempts to make the work the children are learning relevant to their everyday lives.

Extract 6.5 'Cow Farts' and Global Warming

1. **Mrs Jenkins:** So, uh, so Shane, why do you think it's important to learn about wild and domesticated animals?
2. **Shane:** Lions can kill you and eat you!
3. **Mrs Jenkins:** yes, yes they can.
4. But I'm thinking of something else.
5. Who's heard of global warming?
6. Hands up, no shouting. *8 hands go up*
7. Felix?
8. **Felix:** It is um, it gets very hot and there's fires like the fires on the mountain.
9. **Mrs Jenkins:** It gets hot.
10. Yes, it gets hot.
11. Well, I read this story in the newspaper about how cows gas makes it get really hot. *children laugh at the word 'gas'.*

12. Hey ok, it's very funny.
13. Yes Iris?
14. **Iris:** Farts *laughing. children start laughing loudly*
15. **Mrs Jenkins**: Yes, farts. And that fart has something in it it's called methane gas.
16. This gas makes the climate hotter.
17. **Shane:** From farts?
18. **Mrs Jenkins**: Yes Shane, I know it's funny but it's also very serious.
19. It makes the planet hotter and that's not good for us to live in, is it?

Extract 6.5 above is of interest because we can see Mrs Jenkins making a link between the heat of summer and global warming. This she relates to cows and their 'gas'. While she doesn't go further to illustrate how domesticating animals can have severe climatic effects, she has opened the relevance of why children should be learning about wild and domesticated animals. Quite simply, this topic is of interest to their lives in a very real way. In this move, she is providing a bridge between the classroom and the outside world, what Feuerstein would call the mediation of transcendence.

In both Table 6.2 and the four extracts in this chapter, one gets a sense of two teachers who teach quite differently. As noted earlier, Mrs Jenkins has been trained to teach using the double-move and has learnt Vygotsky's pedagogical principles, while Ms. Naidoo has not. A cursory glance at the empirical data suggests that these teachers do indeed teach quite differently. In education, it is impossible to isolate a single variable when discussing the cause of teaching/learning because classrooms are populated with a variety of different 'heads', each with his/her own history, culture, and social embeddedness. However, we can tentatively suggest that given that the study was carried out in one school, in one grade and that the teachers had access to similar students and classroom context, the differences between the pedagogical praxes may speak to the differences in the teachers' training in regard to this pedagogical model.

One cannot generalize this finding to other classes because, as I have noted, schools and classrooms in South Africa are incredibly different, with children drawn from many different cultural groups. All that we can say in relation to this study is that for Mrs Jenkins and Ms Naidoo, there is a difference between how they use talk in their grade 2 classrooms. We know that Mrs Jenkins has been trained to use the double-move and has a firm grounding in Vygotskian principles so we can say that there is a possibility that the training she has received has influenced her pedagogical practice. More research, with a larger sample, is required to make any further statements about the impact of the double move in pedagogy.

Conclusion

This chapter set out to illustrate how someone who is trained in Vygotskian pedagogical principles and in using the double-move to teach teaches in a grade 2 science lesson. Effective pedagogy, for Vygotsky, is that pedagogy that moves beyond what a child can do on their own. It is a form of praxis that aims at developing the developmental 'buds' in the child. Two teachers in a single school formed the subjects of this study with the aims being to investigate whether teacher talk would differ between a teacher trained in the double move versus a teacher not trained in this. Findings indicate that Mrs Jenkins trained in the double-move and Vygotskian pedagogical principles elaborated more scientific and everyday concepts than Ms Naidoo who did not have this training. Further, while much of Ms Naidoo's talk featured closed questions and unelaborated feedback, Mrs Jenkins's use of closed questions is generally followed by elaborated feedback, aimed at developing the child's idea of the topic under discussion. A brief caveat is in order, however. This study took place in a relatively affluent school with well trained teachers and a relatively affluent student body. The findings here cannot be generalized outside of these two classrooms. What we can conclude though is that this case study provides tantalizing evidence of the possibilities of the double-move in pedagogy as capable of developing scientific concepts in the ZPD.

Part Three

Towards a Pedagogy of Inclusion

New Technology, New Pedagogy? Investigating Shifts in Pedagogy in Disadvantaged Grade 6 Mathematics Classrooms

Pedagogical Transitions with Computer Technology: New Tool, New Pedagogy?

What happens when you introduce computers into disadvantaged schools in peri-urban and rural areas? This is the question that led me to investigate the impact that computer software and hardware could have on pedagogy, at the turn of the twenty-first century. The context for this technological intervention was the Western Cape Province of South Africa and the rationale behind this was that teachers in disadvantaged schools lacked content knowledge, specifically in mathematics, and the computer software, in the form of CAMI[1] math's could benefit children's acquisition of mathematical concepts (Spaull, 2014). The need to focus on mathematics in this context was highlighted by the fact that South Africa performed (and indeed, continues to perform) extremely badly in mathematics benchmarking tests such as the Trend in International Mathematics and Science Study (TIMSS) tests (Gufstafssen, 2019; Howie & Plomp, 2006). National achievement scores have been way below the TIMSS centre point of 500 since 1995, and South Africa continues to perform at the lower end of the rank order table of participating countries.[2] The introduction of computer-based lessons in mathematics appeared to provide an answer for the poor results South African children achieved in mathematics and, consequently, under the Khanya initiative, computers were rolled out into previously disadvantaged schools in the Western Cape Province of South Africa. In this chapter, I take a historical look back to that intervention before looking forward, in Chapter 8, to what potential, if any, technology has to impact both on pedagogy and, subsequently, on cognitive development.

The introduction of computer software to improve mathematical performance is informed by a well-established relationship between learning outcomes and learning resources (Schollar, 2001). The theoretical foundation of this book, in fact, posits that tools can impact on cognitive development through their use (Cole, 1996; Hardman, 2016; Saljo, 1999). A computer is a very specific type of tool; it contains not only hardware, but software that is designed by a human, with the intention, in the case study discussed in this chapter, to improve children's mathematical outcomes. One could reasonably argue that certain computer software can mediate children's access to mathematical concepts if it is designed in a manner that provides structured, guided assistance in the child's Zone of Proximal Development (ZPD). As discussed in Chapter 2, the kind of software capable of achieving this is founded in what many call 'constructivism', referred to in Chapter 2 as being founded in the work of Vygotsky and Piaget. The foundation of this theory lies in its acceptance of active cognizing agents, co-constructing meaning through interacting/transacting with the world.

Initiated by the Western Cape Government, the Khanya project was rolled out in 2001. This was a province-wide initiative involving several primary and secondary schools that aimed to 'promote learning and maximise educator capacity by integrating the use of appropriate, available and affordable technology into the curriculum process' (Khanya, 2001: 1). All project schools received a computer laboratory equipped with sufficient computers so that no more than two children worked at a computer at any one time. A computer was allotted to the teacher and was networked to the other computers in the classroom. While connectivity was ensured, the school had to pay their own internet ill, constraining internet usage. This chapter reports on four schools located in previously disadvantaged areas of the Western Cape, South Africa. While most research that investigates computers in schools concerns itself primarily with the impact the computer software has on *learning* rather than focusing on teaching (Cox & Abbott, 2004), this chapter focuses very specifically on teaching to address the question of how, across what dimensions, pedagogy potentially transforms with the introduction of computer software into grade 6 mathematics classrooms.

Cultural Historical Activity Theory: A Chat about CHAT

While there is little argument in psychological and educational settings about the primacy of teachers in developing students' knowledge, surprisingly few Information and Communication Technologies (ICTs) studies focus exclusively on pedagogy with computers and even fewer studies of this nature come from developing contexts (exceptions to this are Spencer-Smith & Hardman, 2014; Hardman 2008; Hardman 2005; Chandra & Paktar, 2007). The focus of this chapter, therefore, is on understanding pedagogical transitions with the use of computer hardware and software in disadvantaged schools in a developing country. The aim is to try to understand whether teachers in this context interact with this technology as a tool for learning and what impact this has on their pedagogical praxes. Studying teaching/learning in a classroom is extremely difficult as there are several complexities one needs to account for, such as for example, social background, cultural and historical influences on the child and the teacher and a number of extraneous variables that influence what happens in an actual classroom. To make sense of pedagogical change with computers, I use Engeström's (1987) Cultural Historical Activity Theory[3] (CHAT, sometimes referred to as third generation activity theory). The strength of this development of Vygotsky's project lies in Engeström's understanding of human activity as a multifaceted activity system.

The Foundation

Referred to by some as Third Generation Activity Theory, Engeström's initial articulation of an activity system as a site of research is captured in Figure 7.1 below.

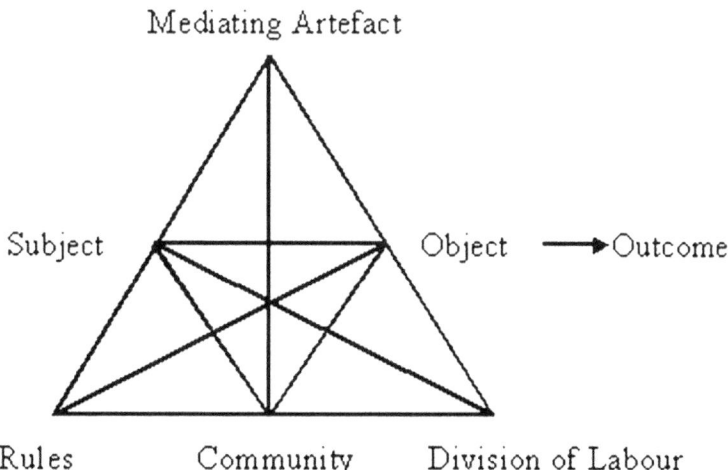

Figure 7.1 An activity system. (Source: Engeström, 1987: 75).

In Figure 7.1, the subject (the teacher, in this study) uses mediating artefacts to act on the object of the activity to reach a desired outcome. The subject's actions play out in a system that is rule governed and forms part of a community, who each have certain roles (division of labour) that they enact in the activity. An example animates this figure: in this chapter the teacher (subject) uses the computer, language and the blackboard (mediating artefacts) to act on the object (students' acquisition of maths concepts) in order to produce mathematically literate students (outcome). The teacher's actions are mediated by the rules of both the classroom and rules prescribed by the curriculum, for example in relation to pacing and sequencing of content. The teacher occupies the role of expert while the student occupies the role of novice (division of labour). The community refers to those people who share a common object, in this instance, the teacher, the software designers and the students. Parents may form part of the community, but this would need to be proven through parental involvement in the activity of teaching mathematics. Of course, it is disingenuous to suggest that teachers and students necessarily share the same object, and this is one of the strengths of CHAT in that it recognizes that people can hold conflicting motives yet be acting in the activity system. A brief caveat in relation to understanding the notion of object in CHAT is useful before progressing to the study.

Some confusion has arisen in writing regarding the notion of the object as for Engeström (1987) the object is the problem space that is worked and transformed during an activity, while for Leontiev (1981) the object is very specifically the motive driving the activity (Hardman, 2007). While these two approaches may appear at face value to differ, one can appreciate their complementarity if you consider that the object of activity for Leontiev is very specifically an individual psychological motive (Kaptelinin, 2005) which Engeström develops into a collective, shared object in his articulation of CHAT. Whereas for Leontiev the object of activity is related to motive, the object of activity, for Engeström is related to production (Kaptelenin, 2005). Moreover, pointing to a contextual elaboration that is analytically absent from Leontiev's work, there is a need to focus on object construction in the context of an activity. It is only possible to distinguish between the object of an activity and material artefacts in the 'constellation of the activity' (Engeström & Escalante, 1996: 362).

Learning as Expanding

Arising from Engeström's doctoral work (1999) CHAT is premised on the notion of learning as 'expansive'. The bi-directional arrows in Figure 7.1 indicate the dynamic nature of the nodes of the triangle. The individual action represented at the pinnacle of the triangle is situated within a context in which power relations and rules influence the subject's actions (Wells, 1999). According to Engeström, there are *three* mediating relationships within this triangular representation (see Figure 7.1). M*ediating artefacts* (tools and signs) mediate between the subject and the object; *rules* mediate between the subject and the community; and *division of labour* mediates between the community and the object. These mediating relationships need to be seen in terms of the larger triangle (or context). For Engeström (1987/1999) an activity unfolds over time and is not generally equated with something as brief as a lesson that unfolds in a school (Roth & Lee, 2007).

The strength of Engeström's (1999) work for this book lies in its elaboration of a social background for actions. However, I note here that Engeström is mainly concerned with studying expansive learning, that is learning that ultimately changes the activity system, leading to the development of a new form of praxis within a new activity system. Expansive learning can be likened to Bateson's (1972) notion of evolutionary learning, where the learning is so profound, that the activity is entirely changed. The premise of this book is that such learning *can* take place in schools, but that currently, this is not what we see in most classrooms that adopt a form of pedagogy that tends to reinforce the knowledge required from the curriculum at the expense of developing truly critical thinkers who can change the world as they change themselves. In the absence of a re-structuring of teaching/learning, as argued for in this book, Engeström's work is constrained to being used in this chapter as an analytical framework, rather than as a transformative theory, which is precisely what it needs to be. This is not an issue for Engeström, who does not use CHAT as a static framework to study praxis. Indeed, Engeström's work is articulated best in his Change Laboratory methodology that intervenes in static activity systems to transform them. This being said, his work has been used by numerous authors as an analytical framework for studying teaching/learning in classrooms and as we shall see in the findings presented below, the framework is useful for situating psychological processes in the social world (Anthony, 2011; Hardman, 2008; Hardman, 2019; Kain & Wardle, 2014; Nussbaumer, 2012).

The Study

Four schools and four teachers participated in this study. Two teachers were female and two were male. Mrs De Wet teaches at Newtown primary which is a peri-urban school situated in a low socio-economic area. Mr. Botha teaches at Merryvale, a rural school situated in the apple growing district of Cape Town. Ms Todd teaches at Siyazama primary, located in a peri-urban, low socio-economic area. Finally, Mr Abel teaches in a large rural school. All teachers spoke Afrikaans as their home language although all teachers except Mrs De Wet taught in English. Mrs De Wet taught in both English and Afrikaans; that is, she had an English mathematics class and an Afrikaans mathematics class. It is worth noting that at the time of this study, only one teacher, Mr Botha, had a personal computer at home. The three other teachers, Mrs De Wet, Ms Todd and Mr Abel did not own personal computers. The grade 6 classes studied ranged in size from a minimum of thirty students at Merryvale primary where Mr Botha taught to a maximum of forty students at Newtown where Mrs De Wet taught. Given that these schools were the beneficiaries of the Khanya computer initiative in the Western Cape, each school had sufficient computers for each child to use the computer on his/her own.

To understand the multiple cases and uncover patterns of similarity and difference between them, the sample was drawn to ensure both balance and variety (Denzin & Lincoln, 2011; Stake, 2013). While a comparison requires common features, ensuring variety requires that these features differ along a least one criterion. To ensure comparable data, demographic variables such as language of instruction, home language and socio-economic status were comparable across the study. To ensure variety, the sample includes two schools from urban and two schools from farming areas. That is, the cases selected differ in terms of their urban or rural setting. Cases were selected based on the following criteria:

- Students access the computers for at least one hour per week and no more than two children share a computer during the mathematics lesson.
- The learner profile is one of disadvantaged, Afrikaans-speaking predominantly 'coloured'[4] children (where 'disadvantage' refers to low socio-economic status as determined by the proxy variable of school fees).

- The school functions well, where 'functioning' refers to:
  - good management (there is a principal who is generally at the school during the school day; there is a school governing body that meets at least once a term; staff meetings take place once a week);
  - structured timetables (school begins and ends at a determined time; lessons run for a fixed period of time).
  - material resources (there is electricity; classrooms have sufficient space for each student to have a desk and a chair; there is at least one computer for two children; children have access to paper and pencils/pens);
  - human resources (teachers have at least a diploma from teachers' training college; teachers have access to in-service education and training programmes (INSET); there is at least one administrative staff member; there is at least one cleaner).
  - schools that are designated as functional by the provincial education department

A Mechanism for Sampling Data

Twenty-six hours of video data were gathered, transcribed and where necessary, translated into English. This generated a large body of data that required the ability to sample sections of the data to do justice to a thorough analysis of the lessons. To this end, I developed a sampling mechanism that I call evaluative episodes that enabled me to select specific, representative portions of data to analyse. Evaluative episodes[5] were used to (1) select episodes from classroom interactions to analyse in more depth; (2) elicit the object of the episode in the absence of direct intervention; and (3) provide an analytical space to investigate tools, rules, division of labour, object and outcome. An evaluative episode is a space in the lesson where the teacher stops what she is doing and returns to explain what it is that the children should be working on. In this sense, then, an evaluative episode illustrates what the teacher's object is in a specific lesson. An evaluative episode is a coherent classroom activity in which the teacher elaborates the evaluative criteria required to produce a legitimate pedagogical script. This refers to the production of work that is recognized, in the local classroom context, as correct by the teacher. These episodes are marked out because they represent disruptions in the intended pedagogical script. That is, they indicate a break in the flow of the pedagogic plan where the teacher is called on to restate and make explicit the requisite evaluative criteria in response to student productions (Hardman, 2005a, 2005b, 2007a, 2007b). The reference to disruptions and restatement of content draws on the body of knowledge that has developed out of Flanagan's (1954: 33) definition of a critical incident as 'a classroom episode or event which causes a teacher to stop short and think' as well as Wragg's (2001: 11) description of a critical incident as an event that appears to 'help or impede children's understanding', and Goodwin's (2001: 11) understanding of these events as turning points in the lesson 'where the teacher's utterances influence the shape and tone of the subsequent interaction'. Evaluative episodes in this data were generally opened by a teacher's question or, more rarely, by a student's question. Twenty-eight evaluative episodes across the four schools were identified. Following the identification of evaluative episodes, teacher and student talk was coded using a schedule developed by drawing on the work of Mercer (2005) and Wells (1999). Finally, a coding schedule drawing on the CHAT nodes of an activity system (viz. object, subject, rules, tools, community and division of labour) was used in the form of a Likert-type scale to analyse pedagogical practices along a continuum. This is not an actual Likert scale because respondents are not asked to select a response to a given statement. Rather, the researcher observes pedagogical practices and assigns a value to these practices. Once talk had been coded and counted, percentages of talk were generated so that a picture of talk in the classroom could be generated on the Likert scale developed from the CHAT schedule. The full schedule is in Appendix A but for ease of reference an example is provided below:

In Table 7.1 you can see how percentages of talk were placed into a Likert-type scale to generate a picture of what is happening in the classrooms. For

Table 7.1 Linguistic tools: Mathematical questions.

Indicator	Mathematical content questions		
1 Most Restricted Principles and procedures implicit	**2 Moderately restricted**	**3 Moderately elaborated**	**4 Most elaborated** Principles and procedures explicit
0–24 per cent of questions teach (i.e. mostly testing questions that close interaction and don't facilitate explication)	25–49 per cent of questions teach explicating the mathematical content	50–75 per cent of questions teach explicating the mathematical content	76–100 per cent of questions teach: explicating the mathematical content. Questions used mainly to teach.

example, if 25–49 per cent of mathematical content questions were recorded in the lesson, this would be marked on the CHAT schedule as [2]. All nodes of the activity system (namely rules, tools, division of labour, object, community and outcome) were analysed in relation to the schedule for which Table 7.1 serves as an exemplar. What follows is a discussion of the types of pedagogy emerging in the face-to-face and computer-based lessons. As we shall see, pedagogy does shift in the computer-based lessons, but whether this shift leads to progress or whether it regresses the lesson, needs to be interrogated in relation to the data.

Findings and Discussion

Four ideal pedagogical types were identified in the data. These types are 'ideal' in the sense that they do not inhere in one single teacher and any single teacher may move between one 'type' and another depending on the motive of the lesson.

Reinforcement Pedagogy

The first pedagogical type identified in the data I have called 'Reinforcement Pedagogy' (RP), because the object of these episodes is to develop and reinforce students' content knowledge using direct teaching methods. This type of episode is characterized by an Initiate, Respond and Evaluate (IRE) discursive structure that is used to teach, rather than to exclusively test students, and has a didactic form that promotes a relatively high percentage of student verbal interaction. In an RP episode, direct teaching is aimed at the *elaboration* of mathematical content rather than the development of novel mathematical (scientific) concepts and teachers adopt a predominantly didactic model of teaching, which is informed in places by a cognitive constructivist epistemology that views knowledge as actively constructed by the student when he/she is developmentally ready to do so. This epistemic stance towards knowledge is suggestive of a particular type of tool use, as can be seen below. The belief that children learn through practice, repetition and activity leads teachers to seek to actively recruit students' attention, using mediating artefacts as tools to generate active participation in the lesson and reinforce students' knowledge. In Extract 7.1 Mr Botha is engaged in teaching students about fractions. This is a grade 6 class who have learnt about fractions for the past three years. The knowledge being covered, then, is not novel.

Extract 7.1 Explain again: Reinforcement pedagogy

1. **Mr Botha:** Right, explain the denominator again.
2. Come let's go further. *Teacher walks over to the bag of apples he has and selects an apple to cut.*
3. Now, what is this? *Holds up apple. Reference to the everyday- students' understanding of parts of a whole.*
4. **Students:** Whole
5. **Mr Botha:** Whole.
6. And I cut him exactly, exactly, in how many parts? *Teacher cuts apple using the knife.*
7. How many parts are there?
8. **Students:** Two
9. **Mr Botha:** Now, my denominator tells me how many parts I have divided my whole into *holds up parts*
10. In this case, it's two. *holds up parts*
11. So my denominator in this case will be?
12. **Students:** Two
13. **Mr Botha:** Two

As the episode progresses, the teacher moves from using the concrete object (the apple) to representing the parts of the whole on the blackboard. His primary material tools in this episode, then, are the apple which he produces in line 2 and which he subsequently goes on to cut and the blackboard, which he uses to visually represent the abstraction he has been discussing. By cutting the apple in two and going on to represent this visually on the board as ½, the teacher uses these tools to illustrate properties of fractions with the purpose of reinforcing students' content knowledge about fractions. By manipulating these tools to uncover the properties of the denominator the teacher is concerned here with developing students' content knowledge, specifically their understanding of the function of the denominator. The use of material tools then enables the teacher to present the concept he is transmitting in more than one way, in this instance, visually on the board and concretely by cutting the apple. While relying on material tools to accomplish his object, the most prevalent tool used in these types of episodes is the teacher's language. In Extract 7.1 the teacher uses mathematical utterances to elaborate content knowledge such as in line 9 when he defines the denominator's function. Of interest in these episodes is *how* these mathematical utterances function. Line 9 (Extract 7.1) represents the culmination of an explanatory episode in which the teacher cuts an apple to illustrate parts of a whole in his bid to explicate the denominator's function (the object of this particular episode). Throughout the episode the teacher links abstract knowledge (such as fractions) to students' everyday understandings of parts and wholes to develop students' understanding of fractions.

A further, central feature of linguistic tool use in these episodes is the high levels of questioning in which the teacher cues students' engagement to facilitate their successful engagement with the task. In Extract 7.1 there is a standard IRE sequence (lines 3–13) where the teacher poses a question, students respond and the teacher evaluates the response. Note how the teacher uses these types of questions as tools to teach students the content. The questions posed grab students' attention, focus their attention on the unfolding problem and enable them to have at least some access to the unfolding discourse, although it is recognized that this engagement is limited to responses. In Extract 7.1 one can see how the teacher uses questions as cues to elicit the answer he wants from the students, moving them towards an understanding of how parts make up a whole. It is interesting to note how this particular use of IRE structure serves a teaching, rather than a testing function. The teacher uses questions in lines 6, 7 and 11 to cue students' correct responses. This IRE sequence is used to clarify concepts and prevent breakdowns in the flow of the lesson and is an effective method for leading students through a discussion when they do not possess the requisite skills to engage without assistance.

Thirteen episodes from the twenty-eight were coded as RP episodes (ten face-to-face and three computer-based lessons). In these episodes teachers use linguistic tools to elaborate mathematical content knowledge. The episodes are characterized by the representational use of tools to elaborate subject content knowledge and a lack of generative use of tools to elaborate mathematics. The evaluative criteria are elaborated; that is, what counts as a 'correct' answer is made clear and explicit to students. Another feature of instruction in these types of episodes is the relatively low levels of control exercised by the teacher over pacing and social order rules. Direct teaching has, unfortunately, become associated with the simple transmission as opposed to meaningful acquisition of knowledge. However, didactic approaches do not necessarily imply a dull transmission of facts but, at their best, these approaches involve children in actively learning concepts (Siraj-Blatchford, 1999) as can be seen in Extract 7.1 above.

We turn now to a second type of pedagogy identified in the data, Collaborative Pedagogy.

Collaborative Pedagogy: The Beginnings of Co-construction of Meaning

In these episodes evaluative criteria are elaborated and the teacher exercises weak control over pace and social order rules. These types of episodes demand that students adopt a critical, reflective role in relation to the pedagogic text and even, in one instance, an active enquiring role. The teachers' role in these episodes is one of mediator. This role is characterized by the explicit elaboration of evaluative criteria, the use of mathematical explanations (that is, the elaboration of scientific concepts), probing questions and material artefacts as generative tools and the weakening of teacher control over rules of the social order and pacing. Students have a level of control over communication relations. Space in these episodes is not as rigidly demarcated as in the RP episodes and there is some fluidity between learning and teaching spaces. The object of these episodes is the development of specialist knowledge.

These episodes are labelled 'Collaborative Pedagogy' episodes (CP) because the teacher and students work together to construct a deeper understanding of the pedagogic text. Students in these episodes are encouraged to develop novel ways of solving problems, provided they can give reasons for how they arrive at their methods.

The collaborative pedagogy episodes come closest, in this study, to the kind of pedagogical practice outlined in this book; that is, a decolonial inclusive pedagogy. That is, even in the absence of formal training in the novel pedagogical model proposed in this book, we see that there are signs in some classrooms, at least, of teachers and students collaborating in meaning making. We see a level of collaboration, some dialogue, the inclusion of the child's voice and a weakening of the teacher's control over pacing. However, in relation to evaluative criteria, the teacher is very clearly in possession of the types of knowledge that count as valid in this instance. Five of the episodes indicated the pattern identified as collaborative episodes. No computer-based episodes fitted this pattern. Extract 7.2 below, which is drawn from Newtown Primary, illustrates how the teacher uses probing questions to promote reflection as well as to illustrate how students provide elaborated reasons for how they arrived at their answers. Cliff has been called on to present his group's answer to the class. One student, Ishmael, has discovered a pattern while folding the card and the teacher calls on him to share this with his classmates.

Extract 7.2 Collaborative pedagogy

1. **Mrs De Wet**: Now I want another group to tell me what they did in their group, folding. *(hands go up from 3 groups)*
2. Ok, Cliff come. *Cliff goes to the blackboard and begins to fold his piece of card.*
3. **Cliff**: Miss we took our rectangle miss
4. and we fold it in half miss
5. and we fold it 8 times down miss
6. **Mrs De Wet**: Why did you do that Cliff?
7. **Cliff**: Because the principle is you have to times it by 2 miss
8. So we folded it 8 times down miss, miss miss,
9. and we folded it miss
10. and we had to times it by 2 miss
11. and we open it
12. and we got 16, miss.
13. **Mrs De Wet**: So 1/8 of ½ is 1/16?
14. Ok.
15. **Ishmael**: Miss, (unclear) *puts hand up*
16. **Mrs De Wet**: Hmm?
17. **Ishmael**: There's a pattern miss.
18. You don't have to fold it
19. **Mrs De Wet**: Ishmael says, Ishmael says he did not have to fold it,
20. He saw a pattern there,
21. He did not have to fold it.
22. Ok, Ishmael, tell us.
23. **Ishmael**: A ½ of ½ miss is equal to ¼ miss and then I said ¼ of ½ is 1/8
24. So whenever you give your answer you times it by two like four times two and equal and just times the denominator miss

In this extract the teacher uses a probing question in line 6 to encourage Cliff to provide a reason for why his group solved the problem in the ways they did. In line 7 Cliff refers to a mathematical pattern underlying his solution of the problem, namely that one must 'times by two'. This principle, however, is too closely tied to Cliff's actual empirical problem to serve as a general principle for solving multiplication of fraction problems. In line 15 Ishmael bids for talk time to indicate that he has seen the pattern emerging in the solution of the even-numbered denominators they have been solving. The ability to bid for and receive talk time is indicative of a level of power sharing between teacher and students, that is, more symmetrical power relations. Ishmael has used a piece of cardboard as a tool to *generate* a rule for solving these kinds of questions. In lines 23–6, Ishmael elaborates how one might solve for ½ x ½ by multiplying the denominator by two. Ishmael's answer echoes Cliff's and yet, his identification in line 26 of the importance of the denominator lifts his explanation out of the realm of the current empirical problem and provides a general principle for solving these types of problems: one must 'times the *denominators*'. There are three points to be drawn from this extract: first, the teacher uses probing questions to encourage students to reflect on their answers, second, in the elaboration of content, tools are used to generate thinking and third, students can elaborate the evaluative criteria for the production of a mathematical text as Cliff does in lines 3–12 and Ishmael does in lines 23–6. This kind of engagement from students, coupled with the teacher's use of probing questions and material artefacts to develop students' reflective engagement with mathematics, is one of the key features that distinguishes this type of episode from a Reinforcement Pedagogy episode.

The third pedagogical type identified in the data I have called Directive Pedagogy (DIR), because the teacher maintains strict control over the environment, directing students' actions. For this pedagogical type, very little talk is used to elaborate mathematics as most teacher language is used to elaborate task skills. For example, in Extract 7.3 below, we see the teacher directing students in relation to work on the computer.

Extract 7.3 Directive pedagogy

1. **Mr Botha:** Ok, it seems some of you are lost.
2. Let me show you again *He sits down at a computer and 7 students stand behind him as he illustrates how to do the task. This is the third time he's discussing the task- this is the first time he's using the computer*
3. Listen to me, this group here
4. Listen to me quickly
5. Click outside the block *Looks up from the computer and looks at the group of students*
6. And the block disappears *Illustrates this on the computer- moves the mouse- he repeats the action three times so that students can see what he is doing.*

These types of episodes are characterized by strong teacher control over pace and social order rules, and low levels of elaboration of evaluative criteria. Spatial boundaries are relatively porous, with the teacher moving around the teaching area checking students work. The teacher's role is 'director', characterized by the fact that teacher talk functions as a tool to facilitate students' access to technology through developing their technical task skills. The kind of knowledge being imparted takes the form of technical skills that are localized and situated. That is, these skills appear to be tied to specific task situations and are geared to producing technically proficient students.

Four computer episodes, one computer episode in Merryvale, one in Newtown and one in Thandokhulu and one face-to-face episode in Merryvale fit this pattern. The final ideal type identified in the data is Defensive pedagogy and refers to a mode of pedagogy where the teacher is entirely in control and asymmetrical power dominates the classroom. The term 'defensive pedagogy' is drawn from the work of Garrison and Bromley (2004) who characterize this kind of pedagogy as defending against student control in a classroom.

Defensive Pedagogy: Power and Control

Defensive pedagogy (DP) is characterized by a pattern of practice in which the teacher, acting in his/her role of manager, uses language to regulate students' actions in a context in which evaluative rules are not elaborated and where the teacher exercises a high degree of control over rules of pacing and social order rules. Students are verbally passive in these types of episodes and do not occupy much of the talk time (less than 10 per cent of the overall discourse comprises student utterances). Their roles tend to be as performers. The teacher's role is predominantly to manage students' behaviour.

Five of the recorded twenty-eight episodes were categorized as DP episodes and all were computer-based episodes. Three of the four schools taking part in the study had episodes that fall into this category. DP episodes are characterized by high incidences of behavioural prescriptions and low incidences of mathematical explanations. Teachers dominate talk time and there are few if any mathematical utterances in these types of episodes and the object of the episodes is a regulative, rather than an instructional one. Results are summarized in the Table 7.2 below.

The findings presented in this table indicate very clearly that pedagogical transitions can be expected with the introduction of novel technology, in this

Table 7.2 Comparison of types of episodes across the schools: Face-to-face and computer lessons.

Type of episode	Schools								Total
	Merryvale		Thandokhulu		Siyazama		Newtown		
	Comp	F2f	Comp	F2f	Comp	F2f	Comp	F2f	
Reinforcement pedagogy		4	4			1	3	1	13
Collaborative pedagogy				2				3	5
Defensive pedagogy	2		2		1				5
Directive pedagogy	2	1	1				1		5

instance, the use of a computer. The data indicate that no collaborative pedagogy appears in the computer-based lesson, and, in fact, pedagogy in these contexts becomes directive and, in some cases, even defensive, with children given no chance to explore or co-construct meaning in the lesson. Collaborative pedagogy, where students and teachers engage in the co-construction of meaning through dialogical interaction is, in my understanding, close to the kind of pedagogy that Vygotsky had in mind when he outlined his General Genetic law. Indeed, the kind of pedagogy outlined in this book, an inclusive, decolonial pedagogy has collaboration as its foundation. Yet we see no collaborative pedagogy in the computer-based lessons. Perhaps most problematic is the occurrence of DP in the computer-based lessons that effectively shuts down any student's engagement in meaning construction. What we can see in this table is that the object of the lesson changes in the computer-based lesson from being the reinforcement of mathematical concepts, or in the collaborative episodes, the development of understanding of the mathematical concepts, to being the technology itself. Rather than expanding students' acquisition of mathematical concepts, then, in this multiple case study it appears as if technology has narrowed students' capacity to acquire these concepts. The question now becomes, what can we make of these findings? Are computers potentially damaging to the acquisition of mathematical concepts in this context?

The obvious answer, from these findings, is that the computer software in this study changed pedagogical practices, which impacted on the teaching/learning of mathematics, in regressive rather than progressive ways. In fact, in the computer laboratory, the object of mathematics becomes the computer technology, rather than a deeper understanding of mathematical concepts. However, the reasons for this are multifaceted. The teachers used software that was either drill and practice (CAMI maths) or very basic software that enabled children to make shapes, and, in one case at least, the use of a word document to draw shapes and colour them in. That is, the software utilized in these schools did not allow for the co-construction of knowledge in any way. In fact, something like CAMI maths is a drill and practice piece of software that is extremely useful for reinforcing knowledge that has already been taught but cannot teach novel content in the absence of the teacher. This is because this software is based in a Behaviourist theory of learning that sees learning as progressing through intermittent reinforcers and being located solely at the level of observable behaviour, that is, performance on the software tasks. Findings from a large body of research indicate that attainment in mathematics increases with ICTs when a constructivist pedagogy underpins the software used (Fisher et al., 2013; Hardman, 2019; Hardman 2021; Hardman & Ntlhoi, 2021; Rosen & Salomon 2007; Tamim et al. 2011; Tay, 2016). Further, it is worth noting that teachers in this study had very little training in how to use computers and only one teacher, Mr Botha, owned his own computer at home. What we have then is a situation in which we expect teachers to be defensive around a novel technology that they have not been trained to adequately use, either as a cognitive tool or indeed simply as an administrative tool. As we shall see in Chapter 8, this picture shifts significantly when the teacher is familiar with the technology and allows students to interact with it to co-construct knowledge.

Conclusion

This chapter investigated the extent to which pedagogy altered with new technology (computers in this instance) in specific disadvantaged schools in South Africa. Findings indicate that pedagogy does indeed shift when novel tools, such as computer technology, are introduced into the classroom, However, the way pedagogy shifts depend on what kind of software is used and what kind of learning theory underpins this software. Drawing on Engeström's Activity Theory, this chapter illustrates how one can study pedagogy as an activity system, accounting for change in terms of dynamic contradictions that emerge within and between the various nodes of the activity system. Four ideal pedagogical types emerged from the data. Reinforcement pedagogy is the kind of pedagogy that we see most often in traditional schooling. It is characterized by an IRE sequence, where students and teacher stand in very distinct roles when producing an outcome of the activity. There is nothing inherently wrong with this type of pedagogy, just as there is nothing wrong with say, rote learning, if the teacher is aware of what this kind of pedagogy achieves. RP cannot lead to conceptual understanding; it is rather about the reinforcement of knowledge that has already been acquired. Collaborative pedagogy, in contrast, is more open and teacher and students come close to co-constructing knowledge through engaging in dialogue in a context where the rules of the activity are not very firmly controlled by the teacher, enabling children to work at their own pace to a certain degree. This kind of pedagogy is, in many ways, a constructivist pedagogy, in that it recognizes the child as an active cognizing agent who co-constructs meaning with the teacher. Finally, we have directive and DP, which both predominated in the computer-based lessons. Directive pedagogy is concerned more with directing students' behaviour then with developing students cognitively while DP stands out because of the rigid division of labour and asymmetrical power relations that predominate. The outcome of the study reported here highlights the importance of what pedagogical theory animates a classroom. Where teachers rely on a Behaviourist approach to learning, then their teaching will not go beyond what they observe in the child's performance. Conversely, where a teacher believes that children co-construct meaning with him/herself, the focus becomes more on the child's competence than merely on their performance. What this chapter illustrates is that there is a change in pedagogy when a novel tool, in this instance, a computer, is used. None of the teachers in this study had been trained in the use of the pedagogical model described in this book. In Chapter 8 we investigate how pedagogy shifts when teachers have been trained in this pedagogical model and they use technology as a tool to teach.

8

The Transition from Face-to-face to Computer-based Pedagogy

Throughout this book, we have discussed the importance of pedagogy that is actively able to link the child's everyday and scientific concepts within the ZPD, through the process of mediation. In the twenty-first century, use of Information Communication Technology (ICT) as teaching tools has become ubiquitous. A large body of literature has investigated ICTs' ability to develop children cognitively, with a research focus being on a movement in assessment scores pre and post technology use (Dalby & Swan, 2019; Papadakis, et al., 2016; Goos, 2020; Tay, 2016; Yeow & Henderson, 2012). Indeed, the findings in the literature, especially in relation to mathematics learning, indicate that ICTs can lead to better student attainment (Haßler et al., 2015; Kirkpatrick et al., 2018). Research has also shown that at primary school level, ICTs (especially mobile ones such as iPads) increase students' motivation to learn (Ibrahim et al., 2019; Manuguerra & Petocz, 2011; McFeetors & Palfy, 2018). As motivation is key to learning, the mobile devices' capacity to raise levels of motivation is worth noting in relation to teaching/learning in schools. Adding to this positive picture of ICTs as tools for teaching/learning especially in primary school, is Hilton's (2018) finding that the use of ICTs improves students' attitudes towards mathematics. As mathematics has a long history of provoking anxiety in children, which inhibits learning, this finding speaks to the possible benefits of ICTs in mathematics classrooms (Harari et al., 2013; Namkung et al., 2019).

Given the cultural-historical foundation of the current book, the question emerging in relation to ICTs in this chapter is the extent to which they can serve as mediating tools, capable of developing children cognitively. To answer this question, the current chapter provides empirical evidence of ICT use in two distinct contexts: a school where computers are used in a laboratory setting and two schools that use iPads in a classroom setting. All three teachers involved in this research have been trained in the pedagogical model outlined in this book. The purpose of this chapter, then, is to ascertain how two different types of technology are used in two different contexts, with a view to understanding the technologies' capacity to mediate higher cognitive functions.

We begin this investigation with a look at what research says about how technology must be used to lead to attainment in schools. Interestingly, the research is quite clear in this area: it is not technology itself that leads to learning gains, but, rather, how technology is used pedagogically that accounts for student attainment (Hardman, 2019, 2021; Webb & Cox, 2002). The literature is clear that 'constructivist' pedagogy is the most effective pedagogy for using technology to ensure student engagement and attainment (Hardman, 2019). The unstable meanings attributed to constructivism have been discussed in Chapter 2; here I note that the use of constructivism in this context relates to an understanding of children as active cognizing agents who learn through mediated engagement with a more competent other; in this instance, the teacher with the use of mediating tools.

For Vygotsky (1986) and many Neo-Vygotskians, language is the primary mediating tool through which cognitive development happens (Mercer, 2005, 2012). In fact, for Mercer (2005), explanatory talk that can develop in problem solving situations develops students' reasoning. This is discussed later in the chapter. For now, though, I focus on how language used in and with ICTs can give us an idea of what kind of cognitive processes are being developed through interaction with ICTs. The focus on language as a unit of analysis forms the basis for the investigation in this chapter. To adjudicate the impact of ICTs as potential mediating tools, we need to investigate how they are currently used in context. The following empirical questions are addressed in relation to the data presented:

1. What kind of talk do we observe in an ICT lesson during problem solving? Is there any evidence of exploratory talk that leads to reasoning?
2. To what extent are scientific and everyday concepts visible and made explicit in the lesson?

The theoretical foundation of this chapter lies in the work of Vygotsky (1978) and Mercer's explication of exploratory talk as evidencing reasoning.

Pedagogy with ICTs

Pedagogy, as discussed throughout the book, is premised on a relationship between teacher and student in which one leads the other from a place of not knowing something to a place of new, co-constructed knowledge. This process of mediation, or guidance by a culturally more competent other, occurs in the Zone of Proximal Development (ZPD), that unique social space that opens in dialogue between teacher and taught or expert and novice. This space draws on what the child can do without support and offers support to enable the child to go beyond what they are currently capable of doing on their own, in much the same way that a bud must be tended before it becomes a flower and then fruit. While gestures, tone of voice and material tools are all useful in developing a child cognitively within the ZPD, language, for Vygotsky (1986) and many Neo-Vygotskians, is the most significant mediating tool. This is especially so in a classroom where teaching/learning happens predominantly through language. The type of language that moves development is quite specific though: it requires that a dialogue is opened between teacher and taught where the meaning of the abstract concepts being studied is co-constructed. As noted earlier in the book, however, this does not lead to a relativist notion that abstract knowledge differs from place to place. The co-construction of meaning that happens in the ZPD in dialogue lies in the student relating and linking their everyday, spontaneous concepts to the abstraction being taught in such a manner that the abstract makes sense to them. Abstract concepts without everyday concepts are hollow and meaningless, changing neither the child nor the world.

Studying Talk in Classrooms: From Traditional Pedagogy to Dialogic Pedagogy

If we can change the quality of classroom talk, we can change the quality of education.

– Mercer (2012: 23)

Real concepts are impossible without words and thinking in concepts does not exist beyond verbal thinking.

– Vygotsky (2002: 107)

Language in traditional classrooms is characterized by an IRE (Initiate-Respond-Evaluate) discourse, where the teacher asks predominantly closed questions (or known answers) to which the students provide single, correct answers (Cazden, 2001; Dillon, 1982; Mehan, 1979; Nystrand et al, 1997; Wells, 1993). While this type of classroom talk has been heavily criticized for not taking the child's knowledge into account and for basically teaching static, rote recall-type knowledge, I am cautious to suggest that the IRE structure is necessarily problematic for teaching/learning. This is especially so in disadvantaged contexts or in specific cultural contexts where children are afraid to ask questions themselves. It takes courage to ask a question in a classroom because doing so reveals what you do not know, thereby putting your knowledge (and you) in question. Hence, I would argue that when studying the IRE structure, we must do so in the context in which it unfolds, rather than by judging it automatically as problematic (Applebee et al., 2003; Burbules, 1993; Dillon, 1982; Mehan, 1979; Mohr & Mohr, 2007; Nystrand, 2006; Nystrand et al., 2003; Wells, 1993). A closed question, for example, can lead to an opening of a discussion, depending on the feedback given by the teacher (Hardman, 2001). It is the teacher's response that provides students with feedback that can either open or close a dialogue. However, many classrooms still tend towards using the IRE framework that does not promote dialogue (Chick, 1996; Fleisch, 2008; McKinney et al, 2015; Msimanga & Lelliott, 2012; O-saki & Agu, 2002; Verspoor, 2006; Wedin, 2010). In this chapter, the focus is on the extent to which ICTs can develop students' ability to reason using 'exploratory talk'.

The notion of exploratory talk with ICTs as capable of developing a child's reasoning capacity comes from the work of Mercer and his colleagues in the Spoken Language and New Technology project (SLANT) (Hennessy et al., 2020; Howe et al., 2019). They have spent nearly two decades researching student talk in relation to ICTs, seeking to understand in particular, 'exploratory talk', which Mercer (2012) argues is indicative of reasoning (Hennessy et al., 2020; Howe et al., 2019).

They identify three types of peer talk in a computer-based environment: 'disputational talk', 'cumulative talk' and 'exploratory talk'. Technologically based lessons are likely to exhibit all types of talk in single lessons. Disputational talk is very individualistic and involves disagreement and ultimately, the need for the individual to 'win' or be correct. There is no collaboration here. This type of talk is characterized by challenges and short exchanges. Conversely cumulative talk is very collaborative however, it lacks critical engagement from team members who may agree to an answer even though they do not think the answer is correct. This is characterized by elaborations, repetitions and confirmations. Finally, exploratory talk involves peers critically engaging with each other's ideas. There is a level of co-construction of meaning here where meanings are negotiated and agreed upon. Where there are disagreements, a different hypothesis is given and justified. According to Mercer and his colleagues, exploratory talk is characterized by joint problem solving, reflection and constructive criticism in which students are encouraged to challenge their peers constructively through offering alternative hypotheses. It is this that develops students' reasoning skills (Mercer, 2000a; Mercer, 2000b; Mercer & Fisher, 1997a, 1997b; Mercer et al., 1999; Mercer & Wegerif, 1998; Wegerif, 1997a; Wegerif, 1997b; Wegerif & Mercer, 1997c; Wegerif and Dawes, 1997; Wegerif & Mercer, 2000; Wegerif & Scrimshaw, 1997c). Exploratory talk then, is truly dialogical in nature as meanings are co-constructed and justified with evidence and, moreover, dialogical enquiry has been shown to positively impact on student outcomes (Hennessy et al, 2020; Howe et al, 2019).

Mercer's (2005) interest in how talk facilitates the joint construction of knowledge is outlined in his project linking the presence of exploratory talk to improved educational outcomes. To this end, he developed Socio Cultural Discourse Analysis which differs from a purely linguistic analysis as it focuses on the *function* that language serves in a context such as a classroom. It does, however, share some features with a purely linguistic analysis in that it focuses on lexical content and the cohesive structure of language, as these characteristics of talk point to how knowledge is co-constructed. Mercer (2005) uses software such as *Wordsmith* or *Monoconc* to analyse large bodies of data quantitatively, within a qualitative paradigm. In this research we use NVIVO to generate a picture of how terms are used and what terms are used most frequently. Mercer (2005) points to the interesting kind of work that can be done using quantitative measures, especially when addressing the extent to which new terms are taken up in the context of the school. The current chapter draws on this methodologically.

Methodology

Research Design and Methodology

Cultural-historical theory's understanding of meaning as mediated lends itself to a qualitative research approach, where ontologically, multiple realities are accepted (Twining et al., 2017). Epistemologically, a qualitative paradigm following from the dialectical logic of cultural-historical theory recognizes that meaning is culturally determined and subject to change. There is not one, single objective meaning available outside of the participants interpretation of it. The design I adopt in this study, therefore, is a case study design, enabling the development of a thick description of peer talk in a computer-based lesson and two iPad lessons across three schools (Yin, 1981). Although firmly based in a qualitative paradigm, I use both numerical (quantitative) and non-numerical data to understand talk in a classroom. That is, I use quantitative and qualitative *methods* to understand the data, recognizing that although the methods differ, they are both located firmly within a qualitative paradigm underpinned by cultural-historical theory. It is this theory, then that underpins our research design.

Triangulation and Researcher Reflexivity

I would argue that all research, even that located in a positivist, quantitative methodology, is informed by the values, assumptions and biases of the researcher. This is particularly so in qualitative research where interpretations are constructed from the data by the researcher. One way to address this is to openly situate yourself in the research and outline your assumptions from the beginning; what Elliott et al (1999, 221) call 'owning one's perspective'. While this research was undertaken by me, the analysis was carried out by myself and a fellow researcher; and both of us locate ourselves epistemologically in a cultural-historical framework. We understand that meaning is constructed in cultural context and is often open to negotiation. While we believe theoretically that schooling should be about cognitive development, we have seen very little evidence of this in much of our research. We were therefore, not anticipating finding evidence to answer our questions. However, in a bid to be open and ensure our data spoke to participants' own ideas about what they were doing in the classroom, we shared our data with both students and teachers reported in this chapter. Getting participants to check our interpretations of the data is a form of triangulation that helps to ensure accuracy of interpretations. Further triangulation was obtained through collecting various types of data ranging from interviews, student questionnaires, and teacher questionnaires and observations, although this chapter deals only with video data. Finally, we used investigator triangulation to ensure that both researchers arrived at the same interpretations of the data.

Procedure

I videotaped three classes of approximately 60 minutes each and the videos were then professionally transcribed. I checked the transcription against the video and analysed the data both quantitatively using NVIVO and qualitatively. The research focus was to study communication between peers, hence we used NVIVO to track specific terms that we felt opened discussion. These were:

1. **Why** questions. This kind of question requires an explanation and is therefore open, potentially leading to communicative interaction.
2. **What else** statements and questions. When someone asks 'what else' they are also opening a potential discussion rather than closing discussion.
3. **How** questions also potentially open communication by calling on the speaker to explain the processes used in problem solving.
4. **Explain** statements lent themselves to opening communication by requiring the speaker to explain their thinking.
5. **Give a reason** statement. These statements, like explain statements, require that the speaker externalize their thinking processes in problem solving.
6. **Because, if, I think, would and could:** These terms we draw directly from the work of Mercer (2004) which he uses to assess primary students' reasoning. (Hennessey et al., 2020)

Inter-researcher reliability was established through both my colleague and I coding the data with 87 per cent agreement. Once we submitted the transcripts to the quantitative NVIVO analysis, we then investigated the data qualitatively to determine what kind of talk was generated in the iPad and the computer-based lesson. We reasoned that the categories submitted for quantitative analysis point very much towards exploratory talk. Quantitatively, we were interested to see what terms came up most frequently in the lesson and whether these were related to mathematical concepts or to something else. However, this needed to be confirmed through qualitative analysis. We take the utterance, rather than the speech turn as our unit of analysis where we define the utterance as a part of speech that makes sense on its own and can be understood logically out of context. For example, 'A rectangle has four sides'. That is, our analysis focuses on the micro-level of classroom talk before moving to the meso-level of classroom talk to qualitatively investigate the nature of the dialogue found (that is, explanatory or disputational, etc.).

Given that mediation is about the acquisition of scientific concepts in the ZPD, we also qualitatively and quantitatively analysed the data for incidences of scientific and everyday concepts. We applied the following categorical framework to analyse the data for these concepts:

Table 8.1 Categorical framework for conceptual acquisition.

Code	Definition	Example
Mathematical term – MT	The use of a maths term.	T: 'Improper fractions'
Mathematical concept – MC (Scientific concept)	The explication of the mathematical concept in relation to its essential attributes.	T: 'You need to change the whole number to a fraction. So what am I doing if I change that whole number to a fraction?'
Everyday concept – EC	The use of an everyday example to make the abstract concept more meaningful to students.	S: 'But it's like *sharing*, fractions, like sharing. They must be equal.'

Sample, Participants and Context

Purposive sampling was used to select three schools for this study. The criteria underlying the selection of schools were as follows: Firstly, one school should utilize only computers while the other two should use iPads, and secondly, schools should function well where 'good' functioning refers to there being a management structure in the school, timetables were followed, teachers were present in the classrooms and ensured use of technology, all schools should be sufficiently affluent that iPads and computer laboratories are available for use and, finally, all teachers in the sample should have completed the Honours course run by myself outlining how to teach using Vygotskian principles and the double-move (see Appendix B for the structure of this course). Furthermore, the schools had to be willing to let us video tape their teachers and students. This also required obtaining ethical clearance from our university together with informed consent from the three teachers in the study and the parents of the children in the study. Consent to be studied was obtained from students. The fact that we wanted to study both a classroom using computers only as well as a classroom using iPads only, limited our sample to schools with this technology. Three teachers and seventy-one students took part in the study. All teachers attended an Honours course I run over a four-week period which introduces them to Vygotskian concepts and outlines the pedagogical model elaborated in this book. The research focused on a grade 6 mathematics lesson for two reasons: Firstly, research indicates that ICTs have most impact in mathematics lessons and secondly, grade 6 is an interesting developmental period for children on the cusp of what Piaget (1976) calls formal operational thought, that enables abstract reasoning.

We received consent forms from both teachers and sixty-six parents for their children to be audio recorded, provided confidentiality was assured. It took two weeks for parents to return the consent forms and three reminders were sent out for them to do so. The five students whose parents did not return the consent forms were not part of the study.

School A

School A is a private school located in an upper middle-class area of Cape Town. Also known as independent schools, private schools are self-funded through trusts, religious organizations or for-profit companies. While not all private schools charge high fees, most do. The independence of these schools means that they are not obliged to follow the curriculum that the government stipulates. Generally, these schools are extremely well resourced, both materially and in terms of human resources. As such, we note that these schools are not representative of schooling in South Africa in general. The purpose of this chapter is therefore, not to generalize but merely to investigate the extent to which talk differs with the use of a computer versus the use of a mobile device, in this case, iPads. School fees at this school are high in relation to average school fees in South Africa (USD 6 070.40 where the average for a good government school is between USD 800 and USD 3000). The school is in a large old house, renovated to accommodate classrooms. There are approximately 310 students at this co-educational school from grades 1 to 7. Children do not wear uniforms and call their teachers by their first names. While asymmetrical power exists in all spaces where someone has more knowledge than the person they are teaching, there was very little overt asymmetrical power observed between teacher and students in this school. The teacher is a young man of twenty-seven, Mr Jules, who has been teaching for five years. He has an undergraduate degree, and a postgraduate teaching certificate and is currently studying for his Honours degree in education. There are twenty-three students in his class of whom ten are boys and thirteen are girls. Children are noisy in the class, although they all appear to be on task. Mr Jules permits children to talk and engage with each other. When he addresses the class, students become quieter but do not entirely stop talking. He has a very good rapport with the children.

School B

School B is located in an affluent suburb of Cape Town. The school has 472 students and charges USD 4155 per annum. It is a private school, one of the oldest schools in Cape Town. The grade 6 teacher, Mrs Smit, is a mathematics specialist teacher and teaches only mathematics at the school. She has been teaching for thirty-two years and has an undergraduate degree as well as well as a higher certificate in teaching and an Honours in education. The school is very traditional in its ethos and children wear a full uniform, including a blazer to school. There are twenty-five students in Mrs Smit's classroom, fifteen girls and ten boys. Mrs Smit gets on very well with the students who clearly have a lot of respect for her and remain quiet throughout the lesson unless called on to speak. The school has a computer laboratory where children each have access to their own computer.

School C

Situated in a leafy Cape Town suburb, school C is a relatively small private school. Like schools A and B, as a private school C follows its own curriculum, while still covering the core issues dealt with in the CAPS curriculum. There are approximately 450 students in this school from grade R to 7. The students wear school uniforms, and the school is co-educational. School fees are USD 2045 per year. There are twenty children in the grade 6 classroom, eleven boys and nine girls. The teacher, Ms Jones has been teaching for seven years. She has an undergraduate degree, a postgraduate teaching certificate and an Honours degree in education. While the students wear school uniforms, the school is rather informal and the power dynamics between teacher and taught are quite fluid, with children easily accessing talk time in lessons.

Findings and Discussion

Table 8.2, below, illustrates the analysis results from NVIVO across the three lessons observed and recorded.

We began this research to answer the following questions about iPad and computer use:

1. What kind of talk do we observe in an ICT lesson during problem solving? Is there any exploratory talk evident?
2. To what extent are scientific and everyday concepts visible and made explicit in the lesson?

Table 8.2 NVIVO and coding Analysis – Talk time and concepts overall.

Code	School A iPad		School B Computer lab		School C- iPad	
Length of lesson	59 mins, 03 seconds		1hr 3 minutes. 40 seconds		59 mins 06 seconds.	
Turns of talk	635		401		550	
Teacher talk	307	48%	348	87%	272	49%
Student Talk	328	52%	53	13%	278	51%
MT- Teacher	215	70%	306	88%	210	76%
MC-Teacher	85	28%	40	11.4%	50	18%
EC-Teacher	7	2.%	2	0.6%	12	4%
NVIVO word frequencies of % of STUDENT talk						
Why?	14	5%	3	0.9%	18	6%
What else?	64	24%	0	-	56	20%
Explain?	1	0.4%	0	-	15	5%
How?	43	16%	5	1.4%	30	11%
Give a reason	5	2%	0	-	5	2%
If	19	7.%	0	-	22	8%
Because	19	7%	0	-	7	3%
I think	1	0.4%	0	-	8	3%
Would	6	2%	0	-	20	7%
Could	20	7%	0	-	3	1%
TOTAL		71%		2.3%		67%

In the following analysis and discussion, I address these questions.

In Table 8.2 we see that in school A more than half of the talk in the class is student talk (52 per cent) and 28 per cent of talk is geared towards the explication of mathematical (scientific) concepts while only 2 per cent of talk is related to the students' everyday experience. The picture is similar in school C where 51 per cent of talk time is occupied by students. This is because, as we shall see in the qualitative data, the students are engaged in problem-solving together using iPads. This picture shifts when looking at student talk in school B's computer laboratory. Only 13 per cent of talk in the classroom is student talk and 87 per cent of talk is generated by the teacher. All three teachers utilize mathematical terms more often than they elaborate mathematical concepts.

In school A, 70 per cent of teacher talk is about mathematical terms, in school B, 88 per cent of teacher talk uses mathematical terms and in school C, 76 per cent of teacher talk is mathematical terms. Mathematical concepts, that is, explication of abstract concepts in the teachers' talk takes up 28 per cent of teacher talk in school A, 11.4 per cent in school B and 18 per cent of teacher talk in school C. The fact that less teacher talk is geared towards explicating mathematical concepts in these contexts is not necessarily problematic, as all lessons were revision lessons that did not require the introduction and explication of novel concepts.

If we look at the terms, we input into NVIVO to determine frequency of terms used, we can see that in School A 58 per cent of talk is taken up with terms that we have argued point to the development of true dialogue in exploratory talk. This drops in School B where 2.3 per cent of teacher talk is characterized by terms that we have argued lead to dialogue. However, this picture presents overall teacher and student talk. If we focus only on student talk, as in Table 8.3 below, we generate a picture of student engagement with these terms.

We can see in Table 8.3 students in school A make scientific concepts explicit, indicating that our third posed question, 'To what extent are scientific and everyday concepts visible and made explicit in the lesson?' can be answered in the affirmative in relation to iPad usage in this classroom. Moreover, the nature of the talk (question 1: 'What kind of talk do we observe in an ICT lesson during problem solving?') appears to point towards the development of dialogue, at least in School A. We have argued that the terms selected for analysis via NVIVO point to where potential dialogue happens. In Table 8.3, we can see that 58 per cent of the terms utilized in school A are dialogical pointers. This pattern is similar in school C where they also use iPads. In fact, 67 per cent of student talk in this lesson utilizes the terms identified as pointing to dialogical interaction and, indeed, exploratory talk. There are no dialogical pointers in school B. This should not lead one to think that students in school B do not engage in dialogue. What we have here is a situation, in school B, where children are sitting behind a computer. Each child has their own computer and there is, therefore, no need to work together to solve a problem. The students are using CAMI maths software, which poses drill and practice type questions that have right or wrong answers and there is no need to negotiate or dialogue to solve these problems. What is of interest though in school B is how much of student talk is using mathematical terms (91 per cent) and mathematical concepts (7.5 per cent). The reliance

Table 8.3 Student talk.

Code	School A		School B		School C	
Length of lesson	59 mins, 03 seconds		1hr 3 minutes. 40 seconds		59 mins 06 seconds	
Student Talk	328	55%	53	14%	278	51%
MT	223	68%	48	91%	180	63%
MC	82	25%	4	7.5%	74	27%
EC	23	7%	1	2.5%%	24	9%
NVIVO Student talk- Indicators of exploratory talk						
Why?	12	3.7%	-	-	18	7%
What else?	64	20%	-	-	56	20%
Explain?	1	0.3%	-	-	15	5%
How?	40	12.2%	-	-	30	11%
Give a reason	5	1.5%	-	-	5	2%
If	19	5.8%	-	-	22	8%
Because	19	5.8%	-	-	7	3%
I think	1	0.3%	-	-	8	3%
Would	6	1.8%	-	-	20	7%
Could	20	6.1%	-	-	3	1%
TOTAL		58%		0		67%

on mathematical terms, which are just facts, is slightly problematic as was discussed in Chapters 2 and 6. A fact, devoid of the relevance it has to the child's life, is essentially not developmental. Schools A and C, however, do have some very definite pointers towards dialogue with iPad use. This finding is of interest to us for two reasons: Firstly, teachers traditionally favour an IRE sequence when teaching which gives very little talk time to students and secondly, student talk utilizes terms suggestive of dialogue and, in fact, reasoning. Of course, terms out of their context can tell us little other than the frequency of their use. We turn now to a qualitative analysis to investigate how and indeed, if, these terms suggestive of dialogue do indeed open a dialogue between peers. Specifically, we are interested in instances of exploratory talk opened, we argue, by the terms listed above. Below we answer our second question: 'Is there evidence of exploratory talk that leads to reasoning?' in these two schools.

Qualitative Analysis of Types of Talk

The Lesson Context: School A

School A is engaged in learning about geometry. What we notice from Table 8.1 is that a large amount of talk time is taken up by the students (55 per cent). This is because students are solving problems together in small groups using the iPad while the teacher moves around the classroom helping them. In our own research, we have never encountered such a high percentage of student talk in any lesson over eighteen years of researching in schools. More interesting for us, however, is the amount of talk that uses the terms we argue point to exploratory talk. Fifty-two per cent of all students talk in this lesson was coded as having the terms that signal potential dialogue. In the following extract, students have been set a task to revise different types of fractions and make videos of their problem-solving actions on the iPad. Each group of three students has one iPad between them. The teacher gives them the topic (such as addition of fractions), but they are required to come up with their own example. What follows is the interaction between three boys working on defining and explaining equivalent fractions. They have a small handheld white board that they write on and then they move to record their answers on the iPad.

Extract 8.1: 'Genius takes time'

1. **Greg:** So, equivalent fractions.
2. So, we should times the denominators?
3. I've got it.
4. So how many times do you times by two to get to 100?
5. And then that will equal the numerator.
6. You times four by 25.
7. **Brad:** So, what would you write it as?
8. **Greg:** I have no idea.
9. **Brad:** You can't times the denominators because four over eight …
10. **James:** Maybe 100 divided by two, 50 divided by one.
11. **Greg:** We know how to work it out, but how do we explain this?
12. **Brad:** Okay, so two times 50 is equal to 100.
13. Just times the denominator.
14. **James:** Maybe we should get another example, like how do we get four eighths?

15. Because that's easier.
16. **Greg:** Yes, eight sixteenths or something like that.
17. **James:** No, but this is an easy example.
18. Much easier.
19. **Brad:** So are we doing this or not doing this?
20. **Greg:** Because this is easier
21. **James:** So, we are doing this? (Inaudible).
22. We know how to do it, we just don't know how to explain it. *As they are problem solving they are writing on a white board. James is holding the iPad.*
23. It's times'ing, so it's easier.
24. How many times can two go into 100?
25. How many times can one go into 50?
26. **Greg:** Or maybe divide the numerators?
27. **James:** I think it's how many times.
28. Because two can go into 100 50 times.
29. One can go into 50 …
30. **Greg:** I think it's if you divide both the denominators, on the fraction with the higher denominator, if you divide the two and it equals the same as the top numerator, it should be equal.
31. **Brad:** How would we write it then?
32. **Greg:** I think we just record our steps, instead of just writing them down.
33. **Brad:** Step one.
34. I'll just write step one. Now, let's (unclear).
35. So, who's explaining this?
36. **Greg:** Do you want to?
37. **James:** But I'm videoing.
38. Ja. I'm very good at videoing
39. **Greg:** So just divide the two denominators.
40. **Brad:** I'm so confused.
41. **Greg:** Because two divided by four, 100.
42. Two divided by 100 is 50.
43. **James:** One divided by 50 is …
44. **Greg:** Okay, James will explain it all.
45. We're like glass.
46. We're starting to crack, but we're actually not cracking at all.
47. **Brad:** I've got it!

48. So, if you divide four by 100, you get 25 and then you times that by that three to get 25.
49. And if that works ...
50. **Greg:** No, do this.
51. Do this one.
52. **Brad:** So you divide two by 100, you get 50.
53. Times that by 1, still 50. Same here.
54. Divide (overtalking).
55. **TE:** Okay, two minutes and then back in the class.
56. **James** Two minutes.
57. Okay, Greg.
58. **Greg:** Genius takes time (overtalking).
59. **TE:** Genius takes time, yes.
60. **James:** So, one half is equal to 50 over 100.
61. If you divide 100 by 50, it becomes (inaudible).
62. If you divide the two denominators, you should get this one.
63. Then you times 50 by one.
64. And if that equation works (inaudible).
65. So equivalent fractions is a ... fraction that is equal to another fraction.

One of the key characteristics of exploratory talk lies in the externalization of reasoning. One of the ways to see this in data is through the externalization of negotiation, where parties, in dialogue, come to an agreement about the meaning of a problem. In Extract 8.1, we can see several markers for reasoning such as 'if' and 'because'. The students first negotiate what problem they will solve (14–21) until they agree on a set problem. In lines 21–7 James and Greg discuss whether to divide or multiply to solve the problem. While Greg thinks division is appropriate, James outlines why multiplication is more effective to solve the fraction. In lines 37–43 Greg and James agree on using division to solve the equivalent fraction before the three boys discuss how they will practically use the iPad to show their calculation. In line 40, Brad indicates he is 'confused' which prompts Greg and James to externalize their thinking to assist him until in lines 47–9 Brad indicates he has now 'got it'. Working together and externalizing their problem-solving actions, the three boys completed the task together. Mr Jules has been trained in the pedagogical model outlined in this book and has elected to allow students to control talk time more than he does. As a pedagogical strategy, this appears to have enabled students to problem solve in a collaborative manner. This picture is very different in the computer-based mathematics lesson described below.

Extract 8.2: The Computer Laboratory

Students in school B are working with fractions. They are all sitting at individual computers in a dedicated computer laboratory. The teacher sits at her own computer at the front of the classroom. The teacher can track individual student's work through her own computer. When students have a question or a problem, she generally sits at her computer and engages with them on the screen, rather than getting up and walking to their computers. There is little talk in the classroom but when there is talk it tends to be what we see in Extract 8.2 below; that is, talk generated and guided by the teacher rather than the student. Students have been asking questions about how to solve the problems on the computer and Mrs Smit stops the class and asks them to follow her on their computers. She sits at her computer and solves a problem for them. What follows below is her solution of this problem.

Students are working CAMI maths on their computer. The teacher stops to explain something to them.

1. **Mrs Smit:** Watch on your monitors.
2. You multiply your numerators.
3. One times one gives me one,
4. your denominators, 3x2 gives me 6
5. and that's my answer
6. and then, when you get your final answer, it must be simplified.
7. Space bar
8. and then we go to the next one.
9. I'll do one more.
10. Numerators, 2x1 gives me 2
11. 3 x 4 gives me 12.
12. OK?
13. Now they they indicating I have to simplify.
14. So how'm I going to simplify?
15. Brenda can you help me?
16. **Brenda**: divide by two
17. **Mrs Smit**: divide by two. The numerator and the denominator.
18. OK I'm going to divide by two.
19. Two,
20. OK, watch on your screen,
21. two divide by two gives me 1
22. 12 divide by 2 gives me?

23. **Students:** 6
24. **Mrs Smit:** 6. OK.
25. I want you to do a few of those.

In Extract 8.2 above, we can see that the teacher acts in quite a traditional manner in the computer-based lesson, in that she stops the children to explain to them how to solve particular problems on the computer monitor. There is little chance for children to engage in discussion with each other because they each have their own computer and they are busy doing a drill and practice exercise on the computer. The fixed computer, then, points to a potential hindrance to the development of dialogue and exploratory talk. The picture with the iPad lessons across schools A and C, however, indicates that iPads can potentially open discussion and exploratory talk. In Extract 8.3 below, we see children engaged in problem solving using the iPad in school C.

Extract 8.3

Students are revising geometry. The teacher asks them to get into groups of three. Each group has an iPad and is allotted a geometrical problem to solve. They are required to video their solution. This group is outside on the lawn trying to solve the problem set about angles around a point.

Extract 8.3: 'I forgot how to math'

1. **Jane:** Oh, yes.
2. Angles around a point.
3. **Rob:** I thought it was angles on a straight line.
4. **Jane:** No, he's going to do angles around a point. (Overtalking).
5. **Stan:** Get the pen.
6. Where's the pen?
7. **Jane:** Angles around a point.
8. **Rob:** Are you going to say the things?
9. **Jane:** Okay, I'll tell you when to go.
10. **Rob:** If we get it wrong, we can do a new one.
11. **Stan:** We can just do the same one.
12. **Jane:** Is it the same one?
13. A plus B plus C will equal …
14. **Rob**: 45 and something. *Other two look at him and shake their heads.*
15. I forgot how to math (*laughs*)

16. **Stan**: A plus B plus C.
17. Angles around a point.
18. Can't be 45.
19. **Rob:** But I think it's 45 plus something.
20. **Stan**: Look, it's A plus B plus C
21. **Rob**: Ja, but.
22. **Stan:** because you have to add them all.
23. OK?
24. **Rob:** oh, OK. Oh angles around a point.
25. **Jane:** Tell me when to go.
26. **Rob:** Three, two, one.
27. Go.
28. **Jane:** So, there'll be A here and so since it's vertically opposite, there'll be A and then around there, it will have to be equal to 360.

In line 14 Rob offers an answer which neither Jane nor Stan agrees with. As the discussion continues, Rob maintains that his answer is correct. This shifts in lines 20–4 where Stan illustrates with a pen on paper how you must add all angles together and gives the reason for this. Rob then agrees and the group begin to video their answer. Although this is a very short exchange, it illustrates students (Stan) externalizing their reasoning and persuading their peers to agree with them by giving reasons for the answer. This is indicative of exploratory talk.

This chapter set out to investigate what kind of talk characterizes iPad and computer-based mathematics lessons in grade 6, investigating whether scientific concepts are elaborated on and whether exploratory talk is visible in this context. The quantitative analysis indicates that phrases and words that point to exploratory talk are present in the data in relation to iPad use but not in relation to the use of the computer. What appears relatively absent in the data across all contexts, however, is the lack of linking between everyday and scientific concepts. I have argued throughout the book that abstraction makes no sense in the absence of the everyday. However, a possible reason for the lack of everyday concepts in the data set lies in the fact that all lessons were revision lessons. We might assume, therefore that the students already had a sense of what the mathematics meant and did not have to link it to their everyday concepts. In relation to the type of talk found in the lessons, we found instances both quantitatively and qualitatively of the development of exploratory talk in the iPad lessons but none in the computer-based lessons. For Mercer (2005) this type of talk is directly related to reasoning and dialogical interaction; hence, it leads to learning.

Findings in this chapter indicate that using an iPad in a small group can promote a kind of dialogue, which has characteristics of what Mercer (2005) has termed exploratory talk; that is, talk that leads to reasoning. This picture shifts when the research gaze focuses on students working with drill and practice software at individual computers. This shift is expected, however, as the conditions for dialogue do not exist if children are sitting at individual computers working through mathematics sums. The portability of iPads, coupled with problems which require that shared solutions are negotiated, appears to offer the potential for exploratory talk and, consequently, reasoning. Although located in only three schools, these findings suggest that the iPad provides more chance for interaction than a fixed computer. A caveat is in order, however; the software used in many South African schools, such as *CAMI maths*, *Mathletics* and *MasterMaths* is premised on a behaviourist notion of learning, where children are presented with a stimulus (question) to which they provide a response (answer). Given different types of software, it is entirely possible that a computer, fixed in a laboratory, could lead to dialogical interaction. This requires future investigation.

Conclusion

The focus of this chapter was an investigation of the extent to which ICTs could be used as mediating tools for development. In this instance, three grade 6 mathematics lessons in three separate schools were studied. In schools A and C, the teacher utilizes iPads as teaching/learning tools and in school B, the teacher uses a computer with drill and practice type software. There is a body of literature that suggests that iPads can be used to facilitate exploratory talk in a classroom, and the findings from school A and C are supportive of this research. School B uses fixed computers and drill and practice software in their mathematics lessons. This kind of software is prohibitive of dialogical interaction because it is premised on a behaviourist notion of stimulus-response. What we have found in this analysis is what research over a twenty-year period has already elaborated: ICTs themselves cannot impact on learning, rather, it is how they are used pedagogically, that impacts on learning (Hardman, 2019; Webb & Cox, 2004). The question driving this chapter was the extent to which ICTs could mediate the development of higher cognitive functioning, operationalized as exploratory talk that leads to reasoning. The findings are that, yes, it is possible that ICTs (in this instance iPads) have the potential to develop students cognitively, but this is dependent on how they are used as pedagogical tools. A further point is worth making. All schools in this study are privileged private schools. Children who attend these school are generally well off and results regarding iPad or computer usage in these school cannot be generalized.

Conclusion: The Case for Hedegaard's Radical Local Model of Pedagogy

Introduction

In the twenty-first century humanity is faced with the greatest challenges of any century. Climate change literally threatens our species with extinction, ongoing war, poverty, homelessness, a serious pandemic and a rise in racist ideology are some of the burning issues of our time. While people like Pinker (2019) may believe we are entering a new Enlightenment, with a promise of progress and prosperity, for some of us at least, there is a feeling that the world is on the brink of serious change. But this is not necessarily a bad thing; change, although difficult, ushers in new possibilities, as has the twenty-first century. The advent of the new century brought with it calls for developing new competencies in children in schools. Authors argue that the core competencies of creativity, communication, collaboration, computational thinking and critical thinking must be taught in schools and some call for the development of a novel pedagogy to achieve this (Shahroom & Hussin, 2018). The argument and empirical data presented in this book have been aimed at addressing what kind of pedagogy is useful for the twenty-first century, by tracing pedagogical transitions in South Africa from 1994 to 2019. In this, the final chapter of the book, I discuss some of the central theoretical principles outlined in the book before returning to the data presented in this book that illustrates how the proposed pedagogical model can lead to cognitive development that can meet the unique challenges, we face in the world today.

The context for this book is the South African education system, which, because of apartheid, continues to be extremely unequal. The focus on South Africa is informed by the enormous educational changes that have happened over the past twenty-seven years in this country. It is in times of change that the mechanisms forcing change become visible and can be studied. While the focus on only one country may seem narrow, it is the underlying conflicts and contradictions that arise in times of change that have informed the pedagogical and curricula work that has emerged in South Africa, but which speaks to any developing country and, indeed, any developed country. Moreover, the decolonial movement that gained such traction in South Africa in 2015 has been echoed all over the world, making the development of a decolonial pedagogy of use for a wider audience. This book outlines a pedagogical model that aims to meet the needs of school aged children in the twenty-first century. To present this model, it is necessary to trace the history of curriculum and consequent pedagogical change across time in South Africa, to understand what pedagogy currently looks like and whether the model proposed in this book could be developmentally useful.

Under apartheid, South African education was rigidly controlled by the state, with a differential curriculum being taught to white and Black children. In Chapter 2, we discussed the transition from a traditional curriculum that viewed children as passive recipients of knowledge, to an Outcomes Based Education (OBE) curriculum that saw children as active cognizing agents involved in constructing knowledge as they transact with the world. C2005 (curriculum 2005) was rolled out in 1997 as a progressive response to the systematic exclusion of Black children from good education under the apartheid regime. OBE, however, failed to achieve the results that were anticipated due in large part to the fact that human and material resources simply were not available for teachers and students in most schools, due to the legacy of Bantu education. Considering the failure of C2005, the Revised New Curriculum Statement proposed a more structured curriculum, with more teacher control and in 2012 the Curriculum and Policy Statement (CAPS) was launched in schools. The pedagogical praxis underpinning CAPS is still focused on the learner as an active participant in constructing knowledge but is more defined than C2005. The curricula transitions discussed in Chapter 2 provide the context for discussing pedagogical transitions that emerged with the introduction of new curricula.

In Chapter 4 the pedagogical shifts consequent on the curricula shifts in South Africa illustrated a move from fundamental pedagogics to progressive pedagogics. Based on a behaviourist notion of children as passive recipients of knowledge, fundamental pedagogics gave way to progressive pedagogics, that viewed children as active cognizing agents, capable of co-constructing meaning with a teacher. The argument was developed, there, that the theoretical foundation best suited to explain learning as a developmental exercise lies in the work of Vygotsky (1978, 1986) and the Neo-Vygotskians. While recontextualized in schools as 'constructivism', Chapter 4 indicated the power that this theoretical foundation provides for developing children cognitively in a multicultural society such as South Africa. Rather than being underpinned by a behaviourist notion of a child as a blank slate, constructivism views children as active acquirers of knowledge through mediation. However, as with many theories that are recontextualized at the level of the classroom, constructivism has been used in South African schools as a basis for discovery-based learning, which views the child as constructing knowledge and problem solving without the need of a teacher. As discussed in Chapter 4, discovery-based learning is highly problematic as it relies on a child's empirical interaction with the world and, at best, can lead to the acquisition of everyday concepts and at worst, can reinforce misunderstandings. Everyday knowledge, in the absence of abstraction, has little use outside of the specific context in which it is acquired. The foundations of constructivism lie in the work of Vygotsky and reclaiming the meaning of his work provides the basis for the pedagogical model outlined in this book.

New Pedagogy? Vygotsky, Chaiklin and Hedegaard

The notion of pedagogy adopted in this book understands that learning precedes development and that a child can accomplish more with assistance than they can on their own. This is articulated as mediation, or structured guidance by a culturally more competent other, in the Zone of Proximal Development (ZPD) (Vygotsky, 1978). This zone is a uniquely social space that opens between teacher and taught in a classroom scenario. Through dialogue, the teacher and taught co-construct meaning through the linking of everyday and scientific concepts. While scientific concepts are abstract, systematic and generalizable, everyday concepts are spontaneously developed through the child's empirical interaction with the world. In the classroom setting, the scientific concept is only meaningfully acquired by the child if it is linked to the child's everyday concepts. It is important to note that a focus solely on everyday concepts in a class will not lead to cognitive development; rather, for the child to develop these, everyday concepts need to be linked to the abstraction that is taught in the classroom. For some authors (see, for example, Wink & Putney, 2002) mediation is seen as task specific guidance, not unlike Wood et al's (1976) notion of scaffolding. However, mediation is not scaffolding; it is developmental and is geared towards the child's acquisition of higher cognitive functions, such

158   *A Cultural-Historical Approach towards Pedagogical Transitions*

as language and number concept for example. What is mediated, then, is not skills for solving a task at a specific time, but concepts that alter the way the child ultimately thinks

To mediate, a teacher must be able to externalize, generally verbally for the child, the concepts that s/he is teaching. Figure 9.1 below is an example of a task I do with my Honours students to get them to think through what concepts they use to solve complex problems. This task forms part of the training in the pedagogical model outlined in this book and elaborated in Appendix B. This figure aims to get students to reflect on what steps they take, practically, to solve a complex problem.

Students in my postgraduate teaching class are given 90 seconds to look at this figure. They are then required to reproduce it from memory on a piece of paper in 90 seconds. Once they have drawn their rendition of the figure, we compare what they have drawn with the actual figure in a bid to ascertain

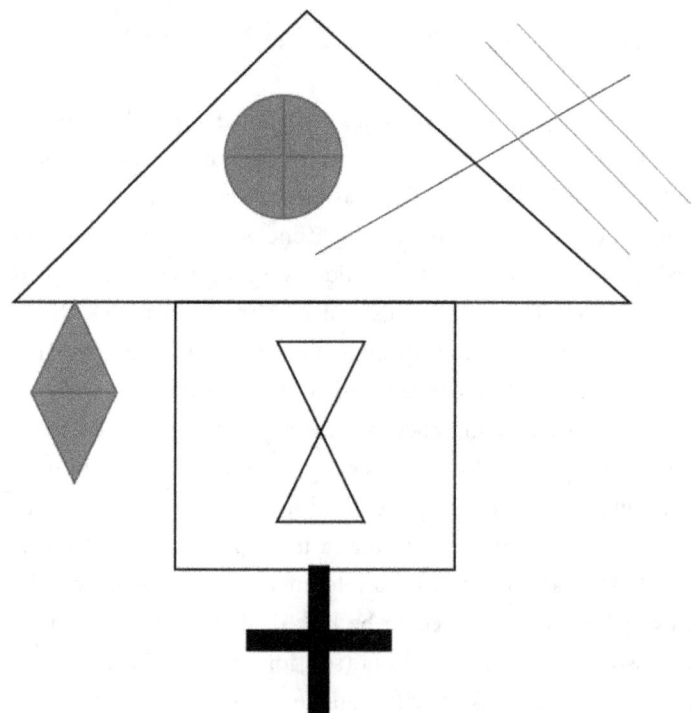

Figure 9.1 Hardman's conceptual figure.

what concepts they utilize to solve this memory task. A normal human brain can hold around seven items in short-term memory at one time, making it impossible to remember every feature of this diagram merely using memory (Van den Berg et al., 2012). What is needed is cognitive tools to assist you to solve this task effectively and efficiently. My students are required to tell me what cognitive tools they use to solve this task. The most obvious tool used is shapes. Clearly this diagram consists of various shapes and to reproduce this diagram, you need to know, conceptually, what a shape is. But there is more that is needed to remember this accurately; one needs number concept. How many shapes are there? How many lines? Mathematical concepts like 'parallel lines' are also useful when reproducing this figure. However, one doesn't simply use abstract concepts as tools to remember this figure, one also uses everyday concepts. For example, the picture looks like a house. The diamond hanging off the triangle looks like an outside light one might have on a house. Remembering the cross requires that one draws on cultural knowledge, as this symbol is extremely well known not just to Christians but to a much wider audience. The meaning of this cross, however, for the person doing the remembering will depend on their cultural context. Finally, one needs to have the concept of 'colour' to reproduce the blue triangle and blue circle. Figure 9.1, then, illustrates how one mobilizes concepts, acquired throughout development through the process of mediation, as tools to aid in memorizing a diagram. Mediation, then, is not the scaffolding of skills but rather the acquisition of concepts. How this happens pedagogically is outlined by Chaiklin and Hedegaard (2005) who propose a radical local pedagogical model that is capable of operationalizing Vygotsky's work in classrooms, using the double-move in pedagogy.

The double-move requires that the teacher link the scientific/schooled concept with the everyday concepts the child brings to class. It does this to achieve cognitive development while also equipping students with the cognitive structures to alter their lived experiences. This 'move' then can be seen as double in two ways: first, there is the movement between the linking of the scientific and the everyday and then there is the movement from the child's 'head' to the engagement with the environment in ways that equip the child to transform their lived experiences. Pedagogically, the double-move enables the teacher to develop the child in the context of the classroom, while paying attention to dealing with authentic problems that the child faces in their everyday situation. In the current book, the double-move operationalizes Vygotsky's (1986) notion

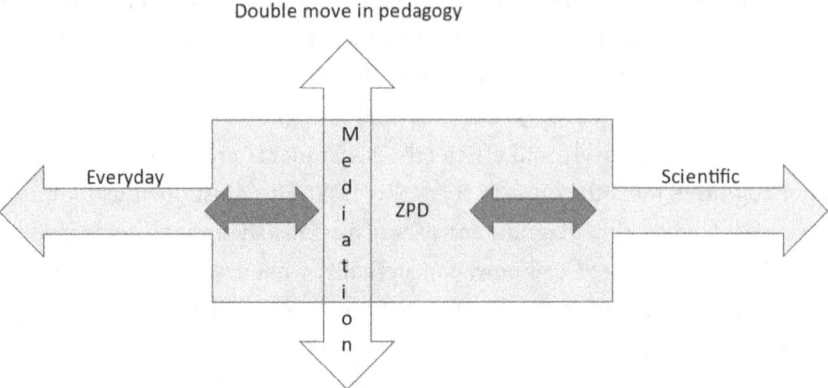

Figure 9.2 The double-move in pedagogy.

of the necessity of linking spontaneous and scientific concepts. This pedagogical approach is particularly interesting in relation to teaching/learning in the developing world context, where children face various challenges in their lived experiences. Mediation in the ZPD is illustrated in Figure 9.2 below.

Figure 9.2 graphically illustrates how mediation operates in the ZPD through the double-move, linking the child's everyday concepts to scientific concepts being taught in the classroom, using a radical-local model of pedagogy.

While the term 'radical' in Chaiklin and Hedegaard's (2005) pedagogical model refers to 'root' rather than the use of 'radical' to signal a departure from a traditional to a different pedagogy, there is a sense in which this work is radical in both senses: radical as it traces the root of concepts as well as implying a radical turn from traditional ways of teaching. It is in the latter sense of radical that I turn now to how this model can speak to the South African multicultural context.

Neo-Vygotskian Work and the Decolonial Turn or Back to the Future

What can African philosophy or psychology tell us about pedagogy in the wider world? Indeed, why is it useful to look at teaching/learning in South Africa if we are talking about a general pedagogical theory? These are both useful questions. For centuries, Africa and South Africa have accepted the psychology, sociology, science and pedagogy of the West. Few complaints were raised about the colonial epistemic project because it was accepted that the West surely knew what was best. If this book has illustrated anything about pedagogy in classrooms, it is that no two classrooms or teachers are the same. Different contexts require different approaches to teaching. I would even go further and suggest that no single curriculum can be a 'one-size fits all' curriculum. While postcolonial theory did indeed challenge the monolithic knowledge of colonialism in the twentieth century, this critique was less powerful than the decolonial movement's twenty-first-century attack on colonial education. This was particularly clear in South Africa where the #FEESMUSTFALL movement closed the country's universities and demanded free and decolonial education (Fataar, 2018; Francis & Hardman, 2018; Long 2018). Exactly what 'decolonial education' means is fairly opaque and indeed, Long (2018; 20) has referred to it as an 'empty signifier'. Of course, the problem with empty signifiers is that everyone seeks to populate them with their own interpretation of what the term means. This leads, at best, to epistemic vagueness and at worst, to a relativist notion that all knowledge is equal, regardless of where it originates. Chapters 1 and 2 in this book articulated my understanding of decolonial pedagogy, to which I briefly return here.

Decolonial Education and Decolonial Pedagogy

For Mignolo (2021), the decolonial knowledge project is aimed at the 'enunciation and expression of non-Western cosmologies and for the expression of different cultural, political, and social memories' (2000: 183). Decolonial thinking challenges the Western canon by asking it to reveal what has been left out and calling on disciplinary knowledge to develop epistemological diversity. It also challenges modernity, the sister of colonialism, by surfacing contradictions in modernity's notion of 'progress' by asking 'whose progress'? And, at what costs? Decolonial thinking is not postmodernist, I would argue (in fact, how could it be with its focus on inclusion, community and an ethics of care?). Rather, it critiques modernism, surfacing contradictions in this system. In education, for Zavala (2016), decolonial education in particular focuses on 'place-based pedagogies in grass roots and educational sites' (1). For Long (2018), decolonizing education is an ideological venture that has yet to provide a coherent theoretical or knowledge base. While definitions of decolonial education differ, one central theme appears to be the reclaiming of indigenous knowledge. However, as Muller (2009) has pointed out, not all knowledge has the same epistemic weight. Nor, indeed, should it. Therefore, when we seek to define decolonial education and to animate decolonial pedagogy as praxis, we need to do so with an understanding of what counts as knowledge; that is, what knowledge has the 'epistemic weight' to be considered general, abstract, and shared by a disciplinary 'home'. It is in the sense of recruiting community knowledge (what I refer to as everyday concepts following from Vygotsky's work) that the indigenous becomes part of abstract, scientific knowledge (Zippin, 2017). An example animates this: For centuries the San[1] have used the hoodia[2] plant to treat eye infections, stomach aches and other ailments. Scientists became interested in the Hoodia plant because it has another characteristic that is of use for a wider population: it curbs one's appetite. Of course, the San know this and have used the herb to help fight hunger in lean times. In 2003, a landmark agreement was signed between the San and researchers at the Council for Scientific and Industrial Research (CSIR) that recognized the San's intellectual property rights in relation to Hoodia, so that they could benefit from the drugs being developed to curb obesity in the West. This is an example of how indigenous knowledge can be linked with science to promote health among the world's population.

Another central issue for decolonial education's critique of the Western cannon lies in the silencing of indigenous populations' contribution to this cannon. It is in the sense of re-populating this established knowledge with the voices of those who initially devised certain knowledge that has become colonized that decolonial education needs to be seen as additive, rather than subtractive. To sum up decolonial education as utilized in this book: it is education that draws on communal fonts of knowledge; it challenges and critiques modernity's claims of progress and calls for epistemic diversity. In its focus on communal knowledge and on the collective rather than the individual, decolonialism resonates with the African notion of Ubuntu, which stresses that one is human only amongst others. This is not unlike Vygotsky's notion of cognitive development as happening in a social space, through mediation and echoes the Marxian notion of collective rather than individual development. In this book, Ubuntu underpins decolonial education and pedagogy by providing for an ethics of care. If this is what decolonial education is in this book, what does decolonial pedagogy look like?

It is in the actual practice of teaching/learning that children can develop cognitively, provided they are taught in specific ways. It is here, in praxis, that I draw on the work of Vygotsky (1986, 1978), Hedegaard (1998), Chaiklin and Hedegaard (2005), Freire (1970) and Feuerstein (1980) to elaborate the model of pedagogical practice argued for in this book. The central principles derived from Vygotsky's work are the notion of mediation and the distinction between everyday and scientific concepts. For Vygotsky, good learning, that is learning that leads to cognitive development, happens in the ZPD through the mediation, or structured guidance of a culturally more competent other. The ZPD represents a unique social space that opens between teacher and taught during mediation. This 'space' denotes a developmental space in which the 'buds' of developing knowledge are nurtured into the 'fruits' of conceptual understanding. It is here, in this space, that cognition develops when scientific concepts are linked with everyday concepts. Scientific concepts are abstract, systematic and general. They are necessarily taught and cannot be learnt through empirical engagement with the world. Everyday, or spontaneous concepts, conversely, are related to the child's everyday experience. These concepts assist the child in making sense of the abstraction they are taught in schools. It is in the sense that the abstraction can only be understood through practice that Freire's (1981) work echoes some of Vygotsky's ideas. The mechanism for linking the everyday and scientific is best operationalized, in my view, by Hedegaard's (1998) use of the double-move. She illustrates in this pedagogical mechanism, a way to link the abstraction of school concepts with the real-life lived experiences of the child. The intriguing thing about the double-move in relation to decolonial pedagogy lies in its focus on changing both the child (cognitively) and their environment. That is, the kind of knowledge that is taught in schools must be able to alter the child cognitively by equipping the child with conceptual tools to deal with real life problems they face. For example, if one is teaching the child the water-cycle, you must go further and illustrate how a child, living in a water insecure area (such as Cape Town where I live) can use the notion of precipitation and condensation to collect water when there is no rain. What concrete actions must the teacher enact to develop the child in the lesson? That is, how can we animate this notion of a double-move in an actual lesson? What actions must the teacher and taught take to establish the link between the everyday and the abstract? The pedagogical praxis is of huge importance here as we are dealing with real children, not with hypothetical data points whose development can be tracked objectively on summative, benchmarked tests. The understanding that pedagogy deals with real children requires a solid ethical foundation, that acknowledges that children have backgrounds that they bring to the classroom, that no two children are the same, and that children need to be treated with care and respect. This has implications for teaching. Here I turn to the work of Feuerstein and his notion of Mediated Learning Experiences (MLE).

MLE proposes a mechanism for mediating knowledge. In this respect, MLE is not unlike Vygotsky's notion of mediation in the ZPD. However, it is important to note that Feuerstein did not draw on Vygotsky's work and his understanding of cognition as modifiable through mediation arose from his own work in Israel. Twelve parameters are outlined for MLE, the first three of which are universal. In the current text, I draw only on these three universal parameters which are: mediation of intentionality and reciprocity; mediation of meaning and mediation of transcendence. These very concrete strategies can serve to scaffold a child's problem-solving activity. The word 'scaffold' is used here to denote the fact that these mechanisms of teaching/learning can be related to specific tasks and need not be related to cognitive development in the sense that mediation is in Vygotsky's work. Intentionality refers to the teacher's desire to teach and is intricately linked to reciprocity which refers to the students' desire to learn. Mediation of meaning requires that the teacher elicit students' understanding of the topic under discussion. That is, the teacher includes the students' voices and everyday[3] concepts in developing meaningful concepts in the classroom. The mediation of meaning also requires that the teacher can reflect on their own assumptions about what they are teaching. Finally, the mediation of transcendence requires that the child can bridge the ideas discussed in class to other contexts. This echoes the work of Chaiklin and Hedegaard (2005) in their radical local pedagogical model. For them, what is taught in class must be useful outside of the classroom too. So, schooling is not only about developing and changing the child's cognition but also equipping them with the tools to change their environments.

Empirical Evidence of the Model-in-praxis

While Chapter 2 makes an argument for the decolonial pedagogy outlined in this book, Chapters 6 to 8 illustrate the potential of this pedagogical model to develop children in a classroom. A central premise of this book is that schooling is about the acquisition of scientific (abstract) concepts. However, abstraction cannot be meaningfully attained without being linked to a child's everyday concepts, which help the child to make sense of abstraction. Teaching only scientific concepts leaves the child unable to understand and use concepts while focusing solely on the everyday leads to misunderstandings at traps the child in their immediate context. Pedagogy, therefore, requires that the teacher can elaborate scientific concepts and link them to everyday concepts. Chapter 5 in this book presents the analysis of a science topic for grade two students. This analysis focuses on the textbook children use as well as the curriculum document that teachers have access to, enabling them to elaborate the concepts being taught. Findings from this chapter indicate that neither the prescribed textbook, nor the curriculum documents provide access to scientific concepts. This is problematic given that schooling requires that children acquire concepts, not merely content knowledge that is not fully understood. The prescribed textbook analysed in Chapter 5 contains predominantly everyday concepts with very little mention of any abstraction. This leaves the need to elaborate the scientific concepts squarely on the shoulders of teachers, who are not necessarily able to do this due to a lack of content knowledge (Spaull, 2013). The danger of leaving textbooks at the level of the everyday concept is further illustrated in Chapter 6 in relation to two lessons taught by two separate teachers.

In Chapter 6, a comparison between a teacher who has been trained to use this novel pedagogy and one who has not been trained, illustrates that this model has the potential to open dialogue by linking the scientific and the everyday. Moreover, Mrs Jenkins, who was trained in this method, outlined the 'big' idea or central notion behind the lesson. The lesson was a science lesson on wild and domesticated animals. No reason for learning these two categories of living creatures is given in the textbook. A child might usefully ask why it is necessary to know the differences between wild and domesticated animals because there are few, if any, wild animals in the city and the child is not likely to encounter wild animals in their daily life. So, a child might reasonably question why they must learn this. What, indeed, is the relevance of knowing the difference between wild and domesticated animals? Well, domestication of plants and animals has greatly altered ecosystems, contributing towards global warming and climate change. Mrs Jenkins discusses this in her lesson by referring to the impact that methane from cows has on the environment. That is, she goes beyond the mere textbook and illustrates why this knowledge is useful to the children in their lived experience. Ms Naidoo, who is not trained in this pedagogical model sticks very strictly to the textbook and does not often elaborate scientific concepts or link them to the everyday. Ms Naidoo sticks so closely to the textbook that she adds no information in the lesson that is not derived from the textbook. This leaves the lesson at the level of everyday, empirical concepts. Findings from this chapter suggest that the pedagogical model outlined in this book can develop the teaching/learning scenario in ways that (1) incorporate children's voices, (2) develop children's understanding of scientific concepts by relating them to everyday concepts and (3) provide a linking of school knowledge to real-life situations.

Pedagogical practices are context dependent and in Chapter 7 the use of computers as pedagogical tools painted a picture of what pedagogical types emerge in the presence of static technology (as opposed to mobile technology). Located in disadvantaged schools, the research reported in Chapter 7 illustrates that the object of teaching narrows in the presence of computer-based teaching/learning. One interesting finding, however, was the discovery of a collaborative type of pedagogy that occurred in some face-to-face lessons observed in the project discussed. This pedagogical type formed the basis of my thinking around decolonial pedagogy as a mechanism for promoting dialogical interaction in classrooms using mediation. The fact that no computer-based lessons were classified as collaborative in this study should not be taken to assume that computer-based technology cannot facilitate collaboration through dialogue. The type of software used in the lessons observed was drill and practice software that lends itself to reinforcing knowledge rather than developing new knowledge. The findings that some face-to-face lessons provide the space for a model of pedagogy that is collaborative, inclusive and mediated, led me to compare the practice of teachers who were taught to use the decolonial model outlined in this book in the context of (1) the computer lesson and (2) a lesson using mobile technology.

Three private schools were the site of data collection in a grade 6 mathematics classrooms that focused in depth on how pedagogy shifts in the presence of novel technology, very specifically, in the use of iPads. Two schools use iPads as tools for teaching and the third uses computers in a computer laboratory. Children in the laboratory each have their own computer and do not generally talk to each other. Little overt pedagogy is visible in the three classrooms. However, the absence of the teacher's voice doesn't mean that there is no pedagogical model operating and indeed, allowing children to problem-solve within set parameters is a sound pedagogical strategy. There is evidence of high student engagement and dialogical interaction in both iPad lessons across two schools but very little evidence of student talk in the school where students use individual computers in the laboratory. There is little student talk and limited teacher talk in this scenario. This, however, is due not to the teaching, I would argue, but rather due to the selection of CAMI maths software which is a drill and practice type tool for reinforcing concepts that have already been learnt. As such, we anticipate no development of concepts in this lesson. What this research points to, however, is the potential an iPad has as a cognitive tool in a classroom. More research is required because this study took place in privileged private schools where children are relatively affluent and have material and human resources to assist them in schooling. Research with iPads in different contexts is needed to confirm this finding.

The Final Model

What we see in Figure 9.3 is a graphic representation of the pedagogical model described in this book. This is a graphic representation of a lesson from a grade 6 history class where the children are learning about hoodia, an indigenous plant that grows in Cape Town and has been shown to have appetite suppressant properties (this lesson is available in Appendix C).

On the right-hand side of the figure, in the square, under the heading 'lesson' you can see the object of the lesson – the development of children's cognitive ability to understand hoodia, an indigenous plant. On the far left of the figure is the theoretical foundation of the pedagogy used in this lesson: the work of Vygotsky, Hedegaard, Feuerstein and Freire. These theories, represented in this block, underpin the decolonial, inclusive pedagogy. The arrow from the theory to the lesson indicates the kind of praxis being used, that is, dialogical with a specific focus on the double-move being used to link everyday and scientific concepts. The actual outcomes from implementing the double-move are shown as broken arrows pointing at the development of executive functioning, reasoning, dialogical interaction and motivation. The practical mechanism through which linking between the scientific and everyday concepts happens lies in the MLE techniques of intentionality and reciprocity, mediation of meaning and finally, mediation of transcendence. The inclusion of the students' voices allows for a co-construction of meaning and brings new voices into the colonial

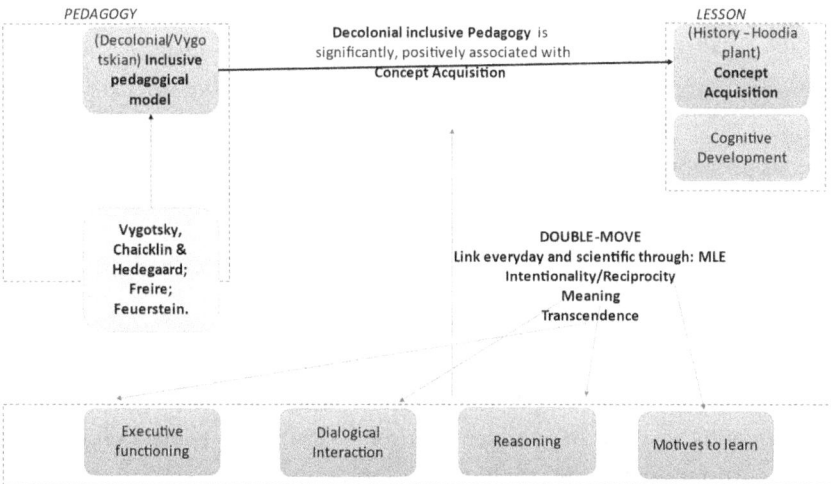

Figure 9.3 Decolonial inclusive pedagogical model.

cannon, decolonizing knowledge as it does so. What this pedagogy achieves is the development ultimately of executive functioning. Appendix C contains a practical example of a lesson plan, using this pedagogical model to enable the reader to visualize this model in practice.

Caveat Emptor

A final point needs to be made in relation to the use of cultural-historical theory as a basis for a pedagogical model in schools. One might reasonably ask why, given the evidence of success we have from Hedegaard (2020), and Chaiklin and Hedegaard (2005) (to name only two), this model has failed to gain traction in schools. Much like the kettle we buy at the shops, education is a product we purchase in good faith. Unlike a kettle though, education is not value free or a-political and the Latin phrase caveat emptor (literally: buyer beware) needs to be borne in mind when we purchase education. Pedagogy is political. There is perhaps, no clearer example of how political pedagogy is than the South African education system under apartheid (Kallaway, 2002). Vygotsky recognized this as illustrated in the following quote:

> *Pedagogics is never and was never politically indifferent, since, willingly or unwillingly, through its own work on the psyche, it has always adopted a particular social pattern, political line, in accordance with the dominant social class that has guided its interests.*
>
> (Vygotsky, 1997b: 348)

While there are no doubt many challenges to a cultural historical model of pedagogy, not the least being the level of training required of teachers, it is the political will to alter the traditional system that needs to change if we are to see serious pedagogical changes in our century.

Conclusion

The twenty-first century has brought with it many challenges that require the development of school leavers who are able to think critically and collaborate in attempting to solve the problems currently facing the planet. While some have called for a novel pedagogy to develop these skills in schools, this book outlines a decolonial, inclusive pedagogical model based not on new theory but on the work of twentieth-century scholars. What is new, however, is the call for decolonial education that allows for the voices of others to be heard in the construction of knowledge. This book has outlined a pedagogical model that aims to achieve just this. The decolonial turn taken here is not a subtractive one; rather the argument is made that decolonial pedagogy must include the knowledge and voices of marginalized groups in the co-construction of meaning and new knowledge. This does not require a rejection of Western knowledge, but an understanding of where local knowledge can grow and develop our current understanding of the world. Decoloniality calls on us to critique modernism by identifying contradictions in it so that we can move forward. Drawing on the work of Vygotsky, Chaiklin and Hedegaard, Freire and Feuerstein, I have outlined a pedagogy that includes students' voices in so far as their everyday concepts enable them to make sense of the abstractions taught in schools. Humanity stands on a precipice; we cannot live, think or learn the way we have in the past. We need to be able to address central issues that threaten our very survival as a species, not the least of which is climate change. To do this, to meet the challenges of the twenty-first century, we need to start with schooling, mobilizing a pedagogy that develops critical, creative, collaborative thinkers. This book has theoretically outlined what such a pedagogy can look like and has provided empirical evidence that is suggestive of its capacity to achieve this. What is needed now is the political will to change the traditional classroom to reflect the novelty of the twenty-first century.

Appendix A

AT Coding Schedule

TOOLS	Linguistic tools			
Indicator	Mathematical content statements			
1 Most Restricted Principles and procedures implicit	**2 Moderately restricted**	**3 Moderately elaborated**	**4 Most elaborated** Principles and procedures explicit	
0–24 per cent of teachers' discourse explicates/elaborates mathematical content.	25–49 per cent of teachers' discourse explicates/elaborates mathematical content.	50–75 per cent of teachers' discourse explicates/elaborates mathematical content.	76–100 per cent of teachers' discourse elaborates mathematical content.	
Indicator	Mathematical content questions			
1 Most Restricted Principles and procedures implicit	**2 Moderately restricted**	**3 Moderately elaborated**	**4 Most elaborated** Principles and procedures explicit	
0–24 per cent of questions teach (i.e. mostly testing questions that close interaction and don't facilitate explication)	25–49 per cent of questions teach explicating the mathematical content	50–75 per cent of questions teach explicating the mathematical content	76–100 per cent of questions teach: explicating the mathematical content. Questions used mainly to teach.	
TOOLS	Linguistic tools			
INDICATOR	Task skill talk: directive talk in relation to technical task			
1 Most Restricted	**2 Moderately restricted**	**1 Most Restricted**	**2 Moderately restricted**	
0–24 per cent of teachers' talk directs students' task engagement skills. Students work on their own and don't need a lot of teacher input in regards to going about completing tasks.	25–49 per cent of teachers' talk directs students' task engagement skills.	0–24 per cent of teachers' talk directs students' task engagement skills. Students work on their own and don't need a lot of teacher input in regards to going about completing tasks.	25–49 per cent of teachers' talk directs students' task engagement skills.	

Appendix A

TOOLS	Material tools			
Indicator	Function of tools: generative function			
1 Not elaborated Never/seldom	2 Sometimes	3 Mostly		**4 Elaborated** Always
The teacher never uses a material tool to generate novel thinking in relation to the problem.	At least once in the episode the teacher uses a material tool to generate novel thinking in relation to the problem.	The teacher often (more than three times) uses a material tool to generate novel thinking in relation to the problem.		Teacher consistently uses a material tool to generate novel thinking in relation to the problem
Indicator	Function of tools: representational function			
1 Most Restricted Never	**2 Moderately restricted** Sometimes	**3 Moderately elaborated** Mostly		**4 Most elaborated** Always
Tools are never used to represent verbal knowledge graphically/visually.	At least once in the episode the teacher uses a material tool to represent verbally encoded knowledge	The teacher often (more than three times) uses tools to represent verbally encoded knowledge.		Teacher consistently uses tools to represent verbally encoded knowledge.
RULES: evaluative rules				
Indicator	Teacher's evaluative talk			
1 Most Restricted Implicit	**2 Moderately restricted**	**3 Moderately elaborated**		**4 Most elaborated** Explicit
0–24 per cent of teachers' *evaluation of students work* explicates/elaborates why an answer is right/wrong. The teacher merely repeats the students' response, without illustrating why it is a good/bad answer or indicating what counts as a valid answer.	25–49 per cent of teachers' *evaluation of students work* explicates/elaborates why an answer is right/wrong The teacher merely repeats the students' response, without illustrating why it is a good/bad answer or indicating what counts as a valid answer.	50–75 per cent of teachers' *evaluation of students work* explicates/elaborates why an answer is right/wrong.		Over 76–100 per cent of teachers' *evaluation of students work* explicates/elaborates why an answer is right/wrong. The rules for what counts as a valid answer are explicit.

RULES: Pacing rules			
Indicator	Teacher talk controlling students' actions in time		
1 Very low teacher control	2 Low teacher control	3 High teacher control	4 Very high teacher control
0–24 per cent of teachers' utterances function to *hurry* students up or to direct their task oriented actions in time (keep the lesson flowing and avoid disruptions to the pace of the lesson). Students influence when to move onto the next exercise.	25–49 per cent of teachers' utterances are geared to directing students' actions in time.	50–75 per cent of teacher utterances are geared towards directing students' actions in time.	76–100 per cent of all teacher utterances are geared towards controlling students' actions in time. Students are always told how long they will be given to work on a task. Students can't disrupt the pace set by the teacher who frequently says things like 'Hurry up' or 'Time is short'. Where students do ask questions these are ignored or deferred.
RULES	Social order: Disciplinary norms		
Indicator	Teachers verbal use of disciplinary norms		
1 Very low teacher control Implicit	2 Low teacher control	3 High teacher control	4 Very high teacher control Explicit
0–24 per cent of teacher utterances contain overt behavioural rules. Students may have internalized certain routines and disciplinary norms; they are able to control their own behaviour without the teacher having to tell them what to do. The instructional context demands certain ways of acting.	25–49 per cent of teacher utterances contain overt behavioural rules. Students are generally able to control their own behaviour in the absence of instructions from the teacher.	50–75 per cent of teacher utterances contain overt behavioural prescriptions. Teacher often instructs children about how to behave. The teacher explicitly identifies unacceptable behaviour and states rules for appropriate behaviour.	76–100 per cent of teacher utterances contain overt behavioural prescriptions. The teacher frequently uses commands to discipline the students; identifying unacceptable behaviours.

Appendix A

RULES	Social order: Communication relations			
Indicator	Percentage of talk time			
1	2	3	4	
Teachers exercise low control			Teachers exercise high control	
76–100 per cent > of talk time is utilized by students. Lots of student verbal participation.	50–75 per cent of talk time is utilized by students. Quite a lot of participation. Students are quite active	Teacher mostly has control over who initiates and participates in communication as well as duration of interactions. 25–49 per cent of talk time is utilized by students. Some participation	Teacher always controls who talks and for how long they talk. Not much verbal interaction from students (0–24 per cent of talk time is student talk time).Not much participation. Students tend to be passive	

RULES	Social order: Communication relations			
Indicator	Levels of questioning			
1	2	3	4	
1 Very low teacher control	2 Low teacher control	3 High teacher control	4 Very high teacher control	
Teachers actively recruit student engagement by frequently asking questions (76–100 per cent of teacher utterances is questioning) prompting engagement.	50–75 per cent of teacher utterances are questioning prompting engagement.	25–49 per cent of teacher utterances comprises questioning prompting engagement.	0–24 per cent of teacher utterances comprises questioning prompting engagement.	
Teacher's questions elicit student interaction: 76–100 per cent of questions open interaction.	50–75 per cent of teacher questions open interaction.	25–49 per cent of questions open interaction.	Few questions asked; 0–24 per cent of questions open interaction	

DIVISION OF LABOUR	Boundaries between teaching/learning spaces			
Indicator	How much time teacher spends away from board.			
Weak boundary between teaching and learning space. Not clear where the teaching space ends and learning space begins. Fluidity between spaces.		Strong boundary between learning and teaching space. Definite space for teaching (front of the class near the board) and learning (seating area where children are positioned).		
1 symmetrical	2	3	4 asymmetrical	

| Teacher spends more than 76–100 per cent[1] of the episode away from the board. No clear boundary between teaching and learning space; teacher moves around in space. | 50–75 per cent of the episode the teacher spends away from the board; relatively fluid boundary between teaching and learning space; students can approach the board. | 25–49 per cent of episode is spent away from the board/teachers desk. Although it is clear that the board area is the teacher's space and the classroom desk area is the students' space, teacher and students frequently move between these spaces. | 0–24 per cent of episode teacher spends away from the board/desk. Clear demarcation between teaching and learning space. Teacher and students remain in their own spaces – teacher at blackboard and students in their desks. |

Division of labour: teacher and student roles

Power	Role	Tool use	Object	Rules
Symmetrical	1. Mediator	Over 10 per cent of questions promote reflection. More than 25 per cent of teacher's overall talk is teaching questions; More than 25 per cent of teacher talk elaborates math concepts. 0 per cent of teacher's talk is technical task skills Over 20 per cent of overall discourse is children engagement. Material tools serve predominantly generative function	Development of metacognitive skills	Elaborated evaluative rules; Low degree of teacher control over pacing and social order rules
	2. Instructor	0 per cent of questions promote reflection. More than 25 per cent of teacher's overall talk is teaching questions More than 25 per cent of teacher talk elaborates math concepts	Development and reinforcement of students' understanding of mathematical content knowledge.	Elaborated evaluative rules; Low degree of teacher

		0 per cent of teacher talk is technical task skills		
		10–20 per cent of overall discourse is children engagement		
		Material tools serve primarily representative function		
Asymmetrical	3. Director	0 per cent of questions promote reflection.	Development of students' technical task skills	Evaluative rules not elaborated; High degree of teacher control over pacing and social order rules
		0–10 per cent of teacher's overall talk is teaching questions		
		0–10 per cent of teacher talk elaborates math concepts		
		Over 25 per cent of talk is technical task skills		
		0–10 per cent of overall discourse is children engagement		
		Material tools serve primarily representative function		
	4. Manager	0 per cent of questions promote reflection.	Control of students' actions	Evaluative rules not elaborated; Very high degree of teacher control over pacing and social order rules
		0–10 per cent of teacher's overall talk is teaching questions		
		0–10 per cent of teacher talk elaborates math concepts		
		0 per cent of talk is technical task skills		
		0–10 per cent of overall discourse is children engagementNo use of material tools		

Division of labour: Teacher and student roles				
Power	Role	Tool use	Object	Rules
Symmetrical	1. Enquirer	25–50 per cent of student talk is answering questions Over 10 per cent of student talk is mathematical questions 0 per cent of talk is elaborating mathematical content. Students occupy over 10 per cent of discourse	Mathematical understanding	Low/very low teacher control over pacing and social order rules
	2. Reflector	25–50 per cent of student talk is answering questions 0 per cent of student talk is mathematical questions Over 10 per cent of student talk elaborates math content Students occupy over 10 per cent of discourse	Metacognitive skills	Low/very low teacher control over pacing and social order rules
Asymmetrical	3. Respondent	25–50 per cent of student talk is answering questions 0 per cent of student talk is mathematical questions 0 per cent of student talk elaborates math content Students occupy over 10 per cent of discourse	Math understanding	Low teacher control over pacing and social order rules

	4. Performer	0–10 per cent of student talk is answering questions 0 per cent of student talk is mathematical questions 0 per cent of student talk elaborates math content Students occupy 0–10 per cent of discourse	Technical skills and conduct	High/ very high teacher control over pacing and social order rules

OBJECT: focus of the episode

Indicator: teachers' use of linguistic and non-linguistic tools

Very low degree of specialization	**Low degree of specialization**	**High degree of specialization**	**Very high degree of specialization**
Skills-localized task engagement and conduct skills; contextualized, concrete and practical	Skills-localized; development of students' technical skills	Mostly universalistic/ school knowledge; **reinforcement** of students' content knowledge.	Development of students' understanding of specialized- concepts; abstract, decontextualized knowledge
1	2	3	4
Most of teacher's utterances (over 50 per cent) function to regulate students' actions in order to cover tasks	Most of teacher's utterances (over 50 per cent) function to transmit technical skills.	More than 50 per cent of teacher utterances (statements and questions) function predominantly to develop and reinforce students' content knowledge	Over 50 per cent of teachers utterances (statements and questions) function to explain mathematical content. More than 15 per cent of teacher talk takes the form of probing questions to develop students' metacognitive skills.

Outcome

Very low degree of specialization			Very high degree of specialization
1	2	3	4
Students' Conduct	Technically competent students	Mathematically literate students	Reflective students; mathematical competence

Level one			Restricted		Elaborated	
			1	2	3	4
Tools	Linguistic tools	Statements transmitting mathematical content				
		Questions transmitting mathematical content				
		Statements transmitting task skills				
	Non-linguistic tools	Blackboard: generative use				
		Blackboard: representational use				
		Computer: generative				
		Computer representational use				
		Other: generative use				
		Other: representational use				
Rules	**Instructional**	Evaluative	Evaluation of students' productions: explicit vs. implicit				
			Low teacher control		High teacher control	
		Pacing	Time on task				
	Social order	Order/ Discipline	Classroom management				
		Communication relations	Teacher-learner talk time				
			Teacher questioning				
			Questioning to promote interaction				

Appendix A

Object			Localized		Specialized	
		Focus of episode				
Level two			Symmetrical power		Asymmetrical power	
Division of labour	Non-linguistic	Strength of boundaries between teaching and learning spaces				
	Linguistic	Teacher student interaction: teacher roles				
		Teacher student interaction: student roles				
Outcome			1	2	3	4
		Type of object				

Appendix B

Training in the Pedagogical Model

Students who are registered for the Honours degree in Education can select to take a course in Teaching and Learning. This elective course runs over the course of a semester and four weeks of the course are dedicated to training students to use the novel pedagogical model discussed in this book. Each week students meet with the lecturer for 2.5 hours.

Week 1

In the first week of the course, students are introduced to Vygotsky's notion of mediation and to his core concepts such as scientific and everyday concepts; the general genetic law; 'germ cell', and the ZPD. They are also introduced to Hedegaard's double-move in a theoretical manner. Students are given three core readings to read for this lecture which is fairly didactic but allows for questions and interaction between student and lecturer. To create the motivation to learn, students are asked to write down their own theory of learning and hand this in before the lecture. During the lecture, the lecturer surfaces contradictions in the students' notions of learning and the theory they will be learning in this lecture series. For example, most students who did this course in 2021 indicated that their own school students learn through experience in school. This may sound intuitively correct, but the kind of knowledge one acquires through experience is everyday, concrete concepts, not abstract concepts. Experience will certainly enable the child to learn everyday concepts such as hot or cold, but abstractions such as boiling point need to be taught in school. To lead a discussion on germ cell analysis, students are asked to do a task that requires that they illustrate what the object of teaching/learning is in their classrooms. For most of my students, the answer is that the object is to develop school students' understanding of abstract concepts in specific subject domains. Students are then given a short video in which a teacher is teaching mathematics to grade 6 students. What is clear in the video is how the teacher tightly controls pace so that work is finished in the lesson. This simple example represents what I would call one of the main contradictions in education: the contradiction between curriculum coverage and developing understanding. the South Africa curriculum is extremely dense, and students are required to cover a large body of content knowledge, which at best leads to the acquisition of basic content facts (without any deep understanding) or at worst leads to teachers' teaching to tests.

Week 2

Having been introduced to the theoretical aspects of the course, students begin week 2's lecture with an interactive task that illustrates, practically, how one externalizes internal thinking processes. This is done by means of a task that is represented in Figure A.B1 below.

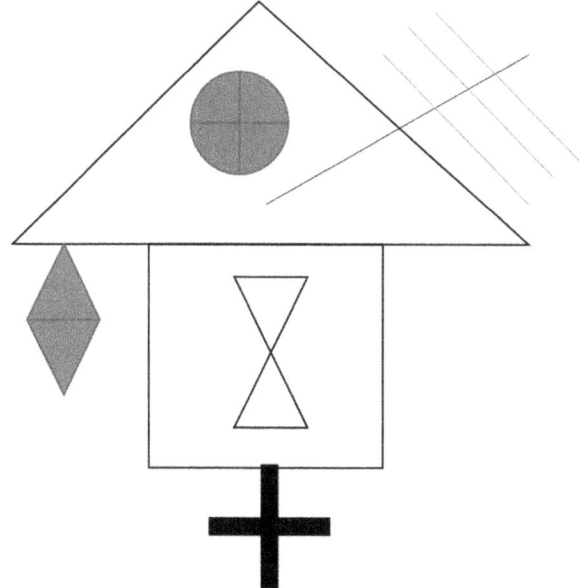

Figure A.B1 Hardman's conceptual figure.

Students are given 90 seconds to look at this figure. They are then required to reproduce it from memory on a piece of paper in 90 seconds. Once they have drawn their rendition of the figure, we compare what they have drawn with the actual figure in a bid to ascertain what concepts they utilize to solve this memory task. A normal human brain can hold around seven items in short-term memory at one time, making it impossible to remember every feature of this diagram merely using memory (Van den Berg et al, 2012). What is needed is cognitive tools to assist you to solve this task effectively and efficiently. My students are required to tell me what cognitive tools they use to solve this task. The most obvious tool used is shapes. Clearly this diagram consists of various shapes and to reproduce this diagram, you need to know, conceptually, what a shape is. But there is more that is needed to remember this accurately; one needs number concept. How many shapes are there? How many lines? Mathematical concepts like 'parallel lines' are also useful when reproducing this figure. However, one doesn't simply use abstract concepts as tools to remember this figure, one also uses everyday concepts. For example, the picture looks like a house. The diamond hanging off the triangle looks like an outside light one might have on a house. Remembering the cross requires that one draws on cultural knowledge, as this symbol is extremely well known not just to Christians but to a much wider audience. The meaning of this cross, however, for the person doing the remembering will depend on their cultural context. Finally, one needs to have the concept of 'colour' to reproduce the blue triangle and blue circle. Figure A.B1, then, illustrates how one mobilizes concepts, acquired throughout development through the process of mediation, as tools to aid in memorizing a diagram. Mediation, then, is not the scaffolding of skills but rather the acquisition of concepts and completing this task enables students to grasp this fact in a concrete manner. How this happens pedagogically is outlined by Chaiklin and Hedegaard (2005), who propose a radical local pedagogical model that is capable of operationalizing Vygotsky's work in classrooms, using the double-move in pedagogy, which students will have encountered in the first lecture.

The double-move requires that the teacher link the scientific/schooled concept with the everyday concepts the child brings to class. It does this to achieve cognitive development while also equipping students with the cognitive structures to alter their lived experiences. This 'move' then can be seen as double in two ways: first, there is the movement between the linking of the scientific and the everyday and then there is the movement from the child's 'head' to the engagement with the environment in ways that equip the child to transform their lived experiences. Pedagogically, the double-move enables the teacher to develop the child in the context of the classroom, while paying attention to dealing with authentic problems that the child faces in their everyday situation. In the current paper, the double-move operationalizes Vygotsky's (1986) notion of the necessity of linking everyday and scientific concepts. This pedagogical approach is particularly interesting in relation to teaching/learning in the developing world context, where children face various challenges in their lived experiences. Mediation in the ZPD is illustrated in Figure 2 below.

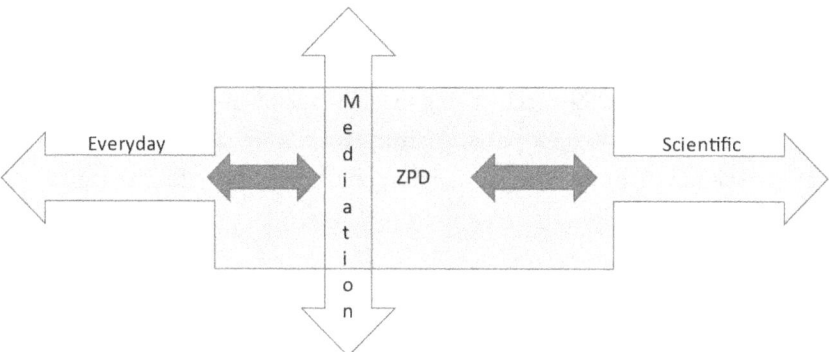

Figure A.B2 The double-move in pedagogy.

In order to illustrate how mediation happens between people, students are asked to sit in pairs. One member of the pair looks at a picture (Figure 3) represented on the whiteboard, while the other cannot see the picture. The 'mediator' is the person looking at the picture, and the novice is the person who is being required to represent the drawing exactly as it appears on the whiteboard under the guidance of the mediator. Mediators may use any language they like to get the 'novice' to represent the diagram exactly. They may not actually assist in drawing the diagram. This diagram is illustrated below.

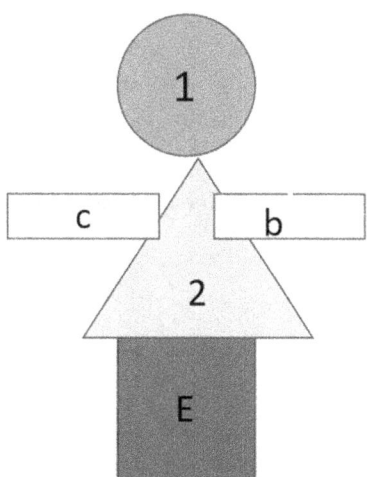

Figure A.B3 Diagram: The mediating interaction.

There are two broad ways to represent, verbally, what is depicted in this diagram; the one is to rely only on abstract knowledge saying things like, there are shapes in the diagram. There is a circle that sits on the apex of a triangle etc. Another way to describe this diagram fairly easily to the novice it to indicate that the figure looks like a woman drawn out of shapes, where the head is a circle, and the body is a triangle etc. Students are given 5 minutes to work on this activity. The lecturer walks around the hall listening to what type of language students use to mediate the diagram to their peers. After the mediating 'session' has ended, the lecturer spends 15 minutes explaining how one can mediate this diagram.

Week 3

In week 3, students return to the notion of a germ cell. They are each given a scientific concept (note, this refers to any abstract concept, and not necessarily to a concept drawn from the discipline of science) and are required to brainstorm in groups of four, to generate a picture of what the germ cell of this concept is. The germ cell is the foundational abstraction that generates the concept (the smallest unit illustrating all the relations of that system), and they are required to indicate how they would teach this concept to a child in a meaningful way. For Hedegaard (2020), in order to formulate a germ cell 'one must look for contradictions in the well-established subject area and then work backwards towards the origin of the subject area' (47). An example of a concept from grade 6 history is a plant called hoodia. This is unique to South Africa and, in fact, unique to the Western and Northern Cape areas of the country. Hoodia has a rare appetite suppressant property, known to the San who have used it for centuries. Interestingly, in terms of developing students' motivation to study the plant, it has a particularly awful smell, something like rotting fish. Bringing hoodia into a classroom is bound to elicit questions and spark interest. While hoodia is the concept here, the germ cell, the basic unit representing all inner relations, is something like the link between humans and nature.

Week 4

In week 4, students are introduced to Feuerstein's 3 MLE concepts, intentionality and reciprocity, mediation of meaning and mediation of transcendence. They are required, in this interactive lecture space, to develop a lesson plan in groups of 4, which illustrates all three MLE concepts. The product of the four-week lecture series is a lesson plan that illustrates the pedagogical model in practice. An example of such a plan is presented below with the student's permission.

Assignment: Lesson Plan

Lesson: Maths
Topic: Addition between 0 and 10
Grade: 1
You will need per child: ten pebbles; one blank page containing two circles with an addition sign between them, an equal sign after the second circle and a bigger circle drawn after the equal sign; laminated numerical symbols between 0 and 10.

MEDIATION	ACTIVITY	TIME
Intentionality and **reciprocity** are core parameters of the MLE interactionist model which highlight the importance of intentional, quality interaction. This parameter relies heavily on organization. The teacher is required to have clear intentions about what and how to teach. These intentions should be shared and made clear to the students, with the teacher being aware of the learner's response to their intentions (reciprocity) and if need be, altering their own for the needs of the student(s). Through such, mutual respect and understanding is instilled, and a working, reciprocal relationship is created. Consequently, an openness to learning among the students is formed.	I have prepared my classroom by placing the relevant material on each child's desk (before they come in from break). Following me lesson plan, I begin by explaining to the children that we will be learning about addition and this means putting things together. I ask the children if they like pebbles and if they want to count them with me and we count the 10 together. (Hopefully) with a positive response and a sense of excitement (and awe of the beautiful pebbles that they like), we begin our lesson.	5min
Mediation of **meaning** occurs when the relevance and significance of the learning experience or activity is made known to the students. In the mediator showing interest and involvement whilst highlighting the purpose behind knowing or doing such, greater interest behind the activity is instilled in the students. In adding value to the task or lesson and encouraging areas of personal relevance, teachers are able to motivate students to learn. Questions such as 'why are we learning/doing this?' and 'what is this for?' are asked.	While we are creating groups and moving the pebbles in addition, I talk about having to count how many more biscuits I have if I want to have friends over for tea. We pretend the pebbles are biscuits and I say for example, I have two left in a tin and three left in another, how many do I have altogether and therefore how many friends am I able to invite? We do this over with different related sweets/foods relevant to their lives. I tell them that if their mom has two sweets to give them and their friend has three sweets, how many sweets will they get? I ask if they ever have friends over and have to give biscuits/ treats and I ask if they think counting will be helpful in doing that, encouraging them to practice at home. I tell them to count their table-groups, counting girls then boys and when I know their number, I will give them each a sticker to keep.	15min

Mediation of **transcendence** occurs when the teacher or knowledgeable other links the concept being taught to other concepts. In this life-wide approach, learning takes place across various contexts and therefore enables the learners to see where else their knowledge can be used. In doing so, the acquisition of strategies and the development of a deeper understanding of the world is promoted and encouraged. Consequently, a curiosity about relationships between one topic and another across subjects, everyday life and time is instilled amongst the learners.	I tell the children that I want to know how many words they have written down in their word-bank book from Monday and Tuesday altogether and they count for me, building a sum with the pebbles. I tell them to count how many letters in the simple sentence we learnt yesterday ('Sam sat') by counting the first words' amount and then the second and adding them together. I tell them to count how many children are sitting at the one group-desk added to the other group-desk. I tell them to go home today and count how many girls/women and how many boys/men live in their house so that we know how many Christmas cards to make for their family in art class.	20min

Appendix C

The Practical Application: Lesson Plan

In this appendix, I outline a lesson plan, illustrating the content and pedagogical praxis involved in an actual classroom using the model developed in this book. In Chapter 7, I mentioned the San and their use of hoodia as a healing herb. In grade 5 in South African schools, children are taught about the San and are introduced to the hoodia herb in their textbooks. However, students are merely told what hoodia is and how it can be used as a medicinal plant or to curb your appetite. No more depth is given to this topic. In the lesson plan below, I develop a lesson, using my pedagogical model, to illustrate how one could teach about hoodia in a grade 5 lesson.

A lesson plan

Subject	History- Social Science *Hunter gatherers*
Grade	Grade 5
Duration	30 minutes
Lesson topic	Medicinal plants of the San-Hoodia
Learning Outcomes	By the end of the lesson(s), students will have developed their abilities to: • Investigate the medicinal properties of hoodia using appropriate internet searches • Describe hoodia using the appropriate terminology such as medicinal herb; appetite suppressant; indigenous flora. • Identify hoodia
Teaching Strategy/ Method	MLE – Intentionality and reciprocity. Begin the lesson by indicating *why* you are teaching about hoodia as part of the history of the San. Recruit students' interest by showing a short you-tube video on this. Remember to define the scientific concepts used such as *indigenous flora; ecosystem; appetite suppressant; herb.*

	MLE – mediating meaning. Link the topic to their everyday understanding of herbs. Does their parent cook using herbs? Why do they do this? Do they ever eat oranges and lemons when they are ill? Why would you do that? Because it has medicinal qualities, just as hoodia does. Use the double-move here where you link the abstract notion of medicinal herbs to their everyday understanding of using herbs and other foodstuffs to ward of illness (such as garlic for example). Ask them if their grandparents use any specific herbs or flowers when they are ill. How do they use them? Remember, you want to include their own voice but in such a way that it links to the abstract concept of medicinal plants.
	MLE – transcendence. Here you want to go beyond the classroom to their lived experience. How is hoodia useful to us outside of the classroom? • Environmentally useful; it is an indigenous plant and therefore, does not impact adversely on ecosystems. • Medically useful; it can be used for curbing a person's appetite, and this can help with the world crisis in obesity. Obesity is linked to many very dangerous outcomes, such as diabetes (define for the students). • Economically useful; it provides the San with much needed revenue as well as providing South Africa with revenue. • Scientifically useful; scientists are still studying its properties to find what other uses it has. Did you know that many of our medicines today come from plants or trees? Aspirin, for example, comes from the bark of a tree.
Selected technology and resources required	**Technology Selected:** Internet Connection; Computers (1 for 2 children); Access to YouTube **Resources Selected:** Video: https://www.youtube.com/watch?v=YIoDx3rMEuc Websites: https://www.timeslive.co.za/news/south-africa/2007-12-03-spotlight-on-hoodia/
Contextual considerations	The aims of this lesson focus on developing students' understanding of medicinal plants, using hoodia as an example. The use of YouTube and a website is appropriate for these aims as it allows for students to draw from online resources to develop these abilities. More importantly, their use substitutes the possible over-emphasis on the teacher in the lesson, allowing students to learn and develop their own understanding of the hoodia.

Lesson & Learning activity	Teachers actions	Students' actions	Time
	Introduce the lesson with the following YouTube clip https://www.youtube.com/watch?v=YIoDx3rMEuc	Students watch clip	5 min
	Ask questions about hoodia: What is it? What words do we use when we discuss it? What is a medicinal plant? Why should we know about this?	Students answer questions	5 min
	Now you must investigate hoodia yourself by (1) searching for information about it on the computer/tablet and (2) reading this link. https://www.timeslive.co.za/news/south-africa/2007-12-03-spotlight-on-hoodia/	Students visit the website.	20 min
	Homework: Ask your parent/carer about herbs, plants or fruits they use for medicinal purposes. Get them to show you how they use this. Explain to them what you have learnt about hoodia. As hoodia is indigenous, why not ask your parent/carer to buy a hoodia plant so that you can study it as it grows?		
Assessment	Assessment occurs twice in the lesson. The first is a brief formative assessment after the video to check the class's understanding and to help them with any unknown words. The second is in the homework assignment, where students will apply what they have learned to demonstrate their understanding.		

In Extract 1 we see the development of a lesson that accomplishes the linking of the scientific and everyday, enacting the double-move to develop the children cognitively but also to equip them with the cognitive resources to change their lived experiences. This lesson illustrates the central elements of the pedagogical model I propose:

1. The double move links the everyday concepts to the abstract, scientific concepts of medicinal plants.
2. This is accomplished using MLE. Intentionality and reciprocity engage and motivate the students to learn. The mediation of meaning is evident in the teacher's inclusion of the children's voices in the making of meaning in this context. Transcendence is mediated in the homework assignment where the teacher bridges the knowledge of medicinal plants in the classroom to what parents/care givers may use in the home to treat colds.

3. The focus on hoodia, an indigenous plant, brings indigenous knowledge into the Western cannon, thereby adding to the Western medicinal body of knowledge. In this sense, there is a moment of decolonizing the knowledge in this lesson through adding to the Western cannon.

Extract 1 illustrates how, practically, a teacher can use the high-level concepts covered in this book to teach in his/her lesson.

Notes

Chapter 2

1. It is easy, however, to see how Vygotsky's work can be interpreted as referring to properties of individual children especially in relation to the example of differential performance he gives in *Thought and Language* (1986: 186–7). Here he argues that two children who both have a mental age of eight (as determined on tests of actual development) perform differently when given assistance, with one child able to solve tasks four years above his mental age and the other able to solve tasks only one year above his mental age. Vygotsky (1986) states that 'The discrepancy between a child's actual mental age and the level he reaches in solving problems with assistance indicates the zone of his proximal development; in our example this zone is four for the first child and one for the second' (187). This is easily interpreted as a property of the individual child; however, it is more clearly Vygotskian to see the *zone* itself as social, not individual. The individual child brings certain maturation levels to bear on the social situation as well as a history of interactions from childhood; the child does not bring with it a ZPD; this is created in interaction.
2. Hedegaard (1998) refers to this as the upper level of the ZPD. On my reading, both Chaiklin and Hedegaard are referring to the same notion.
3. For Vygotsky, scientific concepts are specifically developed in schooling systems. This obviously calls into question the existence of these concepts outside of any formal schooling system. See Daniels (2001), however, for a counterargument to this.
4. It is in this sense of developing over time that mediation, rather than scaffolding, is the mechanism for conceptual development. Scaffolding is task specific, where mediation and the development of a true concept take place over development.
5. I am aware that this term is used in speech pathology in speaking deficits. The term is not used in this manner here. For my purposes, I use this term to refer to the degree that each co-constructor of meaning can make sense of what is under discussion in order to construct something that is meaningful to both parties involved.
6. For those unfamiliar with Sokal, he managed to get a nonsensical paper published in a postmodern journal by making use of vague, yet fashionable postmodern

terms. Post publication, he quickly indicated to the journal that they were publishing research that was, essentially, meaningless.
7   An ethics of care understands moral action as focused on interpersonal relationships with care and kindness viewed as a virtue.

Chapter 3

1   Based on the work of Calvin and his followers, these principles hold God as sovereign and see humans as depraved and in need of his salvation. Unlike Catholics who (at the same time as Calvin was writing in the sixteenth century) believed one could not approach God directly, Calvinists understand that one does not need a priest to intervene between an individual and God.
2   Performance, here, means what a child produces in the class. This is generally measured in tests and summative assessments. The point to note is that the child's performance tells us only what they already know, not what their potential to learn is.
3   Here the term 'asymmetrical' refers to asymmetry in power relations, with the teacher having the power to control the pacing, sequence and selection of content in the lesson.
4   I am not sure if this is Taylor's own understanding of learner-centredness or whether he is critiquing the government's understanding of the concept. He does not reference anyone when referring to this in the text I cite.
5   Learner centred here relates to a focus on the learner as an active cognizing agent, who co-constructs meaning together with a culturally more competent 'other' – in schooling, this person is generally the teacher.

Chapter 4

1   While fundamental pedagogy was the government-sanctioned pedagogy in South Africa under apartheid, this was not implemented without challenge. The 1976 student uprising that began in Soweto as a response to legislation requiring that Black students learn in Afrikaans saw the development of different pedagogies emerging in the 1980s as a response to fundamental pedagogy, National Christian Education and the consequent crisis in Black education. Based on Freire's understanding of educating oppressed people, a movement arose in South Africa driven by People's Education (for People's power) that indicated that 'each one teach one' (Hardman & Veary, 2021; Kruss, 1988). This was a response to school

closures under the emergency conditions set up by the apartheid government because of student unrest as well as to the grossly unfair apartheid education system. The basis of this pedagogy was that learning was a relationship between teacher and taught and that knowledge could be constructed between teacher and taught. Further, the acceptance that there was only one body of knowledge that could not be altered was also challenged. While People's Education was in many ways a central educational debate in the 1980s, no actual pedagogical praxis emerged from it largely, I would argue, because the movement was ultimately unable to re-examine the relationship between social forces and education systems (Kallaway, 2002).
2. John Watson is one of the founding fathers of Behaviourism, that field of psychology that sought to study only what could be observed; in the case of humans, behaviour.
3. The term academic here is used to refer to the fact that cognitive structures are necessarily taught in educational settings and are not simply discovered by children.
4. The separation of cognitive structures and emotions in this sentence should not lead one to assume that the Greeks believed one could exist without the other. Both are intricately entailed in each other.
5. Mahlangu, Dominic; July 2010; 'Outcomes-based Education to Be Scrapped' in https://www.timeslive.co.za/news/south-africa/2010-07-04-outcomes-based-education-to-be-scrapped/
6. This clash that occurs during the process of returning to an equilibrium echoes Vygotsky's dialectical logic. While clearly holding distinct theories, Piaget and Vygotsky are not as dissimilar as some authors claim.
7. I would argue that Piaget's theory is best viewed as he intended it: namely, a theory to discuss universal principles of learning and not as an instructional theory. Consequently, I feel that discovery-based learning of school concepts falls outside of the realm of his general theoretical plan.
8. Scientific concepts here are used in the Vygotskian sense as being abstract, general and systematic concepts that are necessarily taught.
9. While I agree that discovery-based learning can be useful for learning everyday concepts or for developing what Davidoff (1991) calls empirical learning, my argument is that it is not an effective way to develop theoretical learning.
10. I agree with Bidell (1992), though, that Piaget's constructivism certainly offers implicit support for such a contextualist approach; however, this is not well articulated, and hence, I would support the use of Piaget's cognitive constructivism together with Vygotsky's dialectical method (Daniels, 2001).
11. This is the final examination taken in South African schools at the end of schooling.

Chapter 5

1. For Vygotsky, scientific concepts are only acquired in school or a similar institutional context. Daniels (2001) suggests that this understanding of scientific concepts needs to be situated in the socio-historical context in which Vygotksy was writing. For Vygtosky's modernist project, the school held the promise of the 'good life' of 'progress' and served as an institution geared towards the development of advanced conceptual tools. In the first decade of the twenty-first century, we are arguably a long way from viewing schools as the only institutions capable of developing such concepts. However, while this might be so, there is still a very real sense in the Western world that schooling is precisely about induction into a specific mode of thought, which differs from what a child learns outside of the school.
2. I note, however, that the notion of 'active' that permeates the teachers' and students' texts appears to focus on practical activity and to ignore the fact that thinking is an active process. To this end, many practical 'activities' are set for the teacher to give to the students.

Chapter 6

1. In the textbook, the topic is 'farm' animals, but the underlying essential difference between farm and wild animals lies in the notion of domestication. As we shall see, Mrs Jenkins uses the word 'domestication' while Ms Naidoo sticks strictly to the textbook's use of 'farm' animal.
2. Not all schools charge fees in South Africa. Students can attend no-fee paying schools.

Chapter 7

1. This is a drill and practice type programme where children fill in answers to questions to progress to successive levels.
2. Reddy, Vijay (Date unknown) 25 years of TIMSS in South Africa: *Improved achievements but pace of improvement is slowing*, http://www.hsrc.ac.za/ 2022. Available at: http://www.hsrc.ac.za/en/review/hsrc-review-june-2021/25-years-of-timss-in-sa
3. The term Cultural Historical Activity Theory (CHAT) was coined in 1996 by Michael Cole and taken up by Yrjo Engestrom in a bid to situate Activity Theory more fully within the cultural historical school of thought.

4   I recognize that the use of racial categories is highly problematic in the twenty-first century, but these terms still have salience in post-apartheid South Africa.
5   Davis (2005) makes reference to evaluative events in his work. I define these events in different ways but my understanding of evaluation draws from Bernstein's work (1996).

Chapter 9

1   The San are hunter-gatherers in Southern Africa who inhabit largely arid regions.
2   Hoodia gordoni (Bushman's hat) is a succulent plant that grows in very arid regions of Southern Africa. It is a cactus with flowers that have a very distinctive, somewhat pungent smell.
3   I note here that Feuerstein does not refer to 'everyday' concepts but to students' understandings of the topics being discussed in the lesson.

Appendix A

1   This percentage of time is calculated using two stop-watches; one stop watch is used to calculate the time the teacher spends at the board and the other calculates the amount of time (in minutes) that the teacher spends away from the board.

References

Angeli, C., & Valanides, N. (2009). Epistemological and methodological issues for the conceptualization, development, and assessment of ICT–TPCK: Advances in technological pedagogical content knowledge (TPCK). *Computers & Education*, *52*(1), 154–68.

Anthony, A. B. (2011). Activity theory as a framework for investigating district-classroom system interactions and their influences on technology integration. *Journal of Research on Technology in Education*, *44*(4), 335–56.

Applebee, A. N., Langer, J. A., Nystrand, M., Gamoran, A. (2003). Discussion-based approaches to developing understanding: Classroom instruction and student performance in middle and high school English. *American Educational Research Journal*, *40*, 685–730.

Beeghley, L. (1983). Spencer's Theory of kinship evolution and the status of women: Some neglected considerations. *Sociological Perspectives*, *26*(3), 299–322. https://doi.org/10.2307/1389220.

Benjamin, W. (1920). Theses on the philosophy of history. In *Critical theory and society a reader* (pp. 255–63). UK: Routledge.

Bereiter, C. (1985). Toward a solution of the learning paradox. *Review of Educational Research*, *55*(2), 201–26. https://doi.org/10.3102/00346543055002201.

Bernstein, B. (1977). *Class, codes and control*. 2nd ed. (Vol. 3). London: Routledge and Kegan Paul.

Bernstein, B. (1990) *Class, codes and control, Volume 4: The Structuring of Pedagogic Discourse*. London: Routledge.

Bidell, T. R., & Fischer, K. W. (1992). Beyond the stage debate: Action, structure, and variability in Piagetian theory and research. Intellectual development, 100–140.

Boyd, M. P. (2015). Relations between teacher questioning and student talk in one elementary ELL classroom. *Journal of Literacy Research*, *47*(3), 370–404.

Bozalek, V., Zembylas, M., & Tronto, J. C. (Eds.), (2020). *Posthuman and political care ethics for reconfiguring higher education pedagogies*. London: Routledge.

Brown, P., Hesketh, A., & Wiliams, S. (2003). Employability in a knowledge-driven economy. *Journal of Education and Work*, *16*(2), 107–26.

Bruner, J. (1985). Models of the learner. *Educational Researcher*, *14*(6), 5–8.

Burbules, N. C. (1993). *Dialogue in teaching: Theory and practice*. New York, NY: Teachers College Press.

Carey, S., & Spelke, E. (1996). Science and core knowledge. *Philosophy of Science*, *63*(4), 515–33.

Cazden, C. B. (1986). Language in the classroom. *Annual Review of Applied Linguistics*, 7, 18–33.

Cazden, C. B. (2001a). The language of teaching and learning. *The language of teaching and learning*, 2.

Cazden, C. B. (2001b). *Classroom discourse: The language of teaching and learning* (2nd ed.). Portsmouth, NH: Heinemann.

Chaiklin, S. (2003). Analysis of learning and instruction. *Vygotsky's Educational Theory in Cultural Context*, 39.

Chaiklin, S., & Hedegard, M. (2005). *Radical-local teaching and learning*. ISD LLC.

Chaiklin, S. D., & Hedegaard, M. (2013). Cultural-historical theory and educational practice: some radical-local considerations. *Nuances: estudos sobre Educação*, 24(1), 30–44.

Chandra, S., & Patkar, V. (2007). ICTS: A catalyst for enriching the learning process and library services in India. *The International Information & Library Review*, 39(1), 1–11.

Chick, J. K. (1996). Safe-talk: Collusion in apartheid education. In H. Coleman (Ed.), *Society and the language classroom*. Cambridge: Cambridge University Press, 21–39.

Chikoko, V. (2021). Re-visiting the decolonising of south African higher education question: A systematic literature review. *South African Journal of Higher Education*, 35(1), 21–36.

Chisholm, L. (2005). The making of South Africa's national curriculum statement. *Journal of Curriculum Studies*, 37(2), 193–208.

Chisholm, L., Motala, S., & Vally, S. (2003). South African education policy review: 1993–2000.

Christie, P., & Collins, C. (1982). Bantu education: apartheid ideology or labour reproduction?. *Comparative Education*, 18(1), 59–75.

Cini, L. (2019). Disrupting the neoliberal university in South Africa: The# FeesMustFall movement in 2015. *Current Sociology*, 67(7), 942–59.

Cole, M., & Engeström, Y. (1993). A cultural-historical approach to distributed cognition. In *Distributed cognitions: Psychological and educational considerations*. Cambridge: Cambridge University Press, 1–46.

Cox, M., Webb, M., Abbott, C., Blakely, B., Beauchamp, T., & Rhodes, V. (2004). ICT and pedagogy: A review of the research literature: A report to the DfES.

Cross, M., Mungadi, R., & Rouhani, S. (2002). From policy to practice: Curriculum reform in South African education. *Comparative Education*, 38(2), 171–87.

Cultural Survival Quarterly Issue 26.1, The Kalahari San: Self-Determination in the Desert, 2002.

Dalby, D., & Swan, M. (2019). Using digital technology to enhance formative assessment in mathematics classrooms. *BJET*, 50, 832–45.

Daniels, H. (2001). *Vygotsky and Pedagogy*. London: RoutledgeFalmer.

Daniels, H. (2004). Activity theory, discourse and Bernstein. *Educational Review*, 56(2), 121–32.

Davids, M. N. (2018). Ideology critique as decolonising pedagogy: Urban forced removals as a case study. *Educational Research for Social Change*, 7(SPE), 16–30.

Davis, Z. (2005). Pleasure and pedagogic discourse in school mathematics: A case study of a problem-centred pedagogic modality (Doctoral dissertation, University of Cape Town).

Davydov, V. V. (1990). *Types of generalization in instruction: Logical and psychological problems in the structuring of school curricula. Soviet Studies in mathematics education.* Metlina L.S. (author). National Council of Teachers of Mathematics, Virginia, 121–132.

Denzin, N. K., & Lincoln, Y. S. (2008). Introduction: The discipline and practice of qualitative research. In N. K. Denzin & Y. S. Lincoln (Eds.), Strategies of qualitative inquiry (pp. 1–43). Sage Publications, Inc.

Denzin, N. K., & Lincoln, Y. S. (Eds.), (2011). *The Sage handbook of qualitative research.* sage.

Department of Basic Education (2001). Education white paper 6: Building and inclusive education and training system. DBE; Pretoria.

Department of Basic Education. (2011d). Report on the National Senior Certificate Examination 2011: Technical report. Available www.education.gov.za (accessed September 1, 2021).

Department of Education (1995). White Paper on Education and Training (Pretoria, Government Printers).

Department of Education (2002). *Education for all status report 2002 South Africa.* Pretoria: Department of Education.

Dewey, J. (1902). The school as social center. *The Elementary School Teacher*, 3(2), 73–86.

Dewey, J. (1963). *Liberalism and social action* (Vol. 74). New York: Capricorn Books.

Diaz. R. M., Neal, C. J., & Amaya-Williams, M. (1993). The social origins of self-regulation. In L. Moll (Ed.), *Vygotsky and education: Instructional implications and applications of sociohistorical psychology* (pp. 127–52). Cambridge: Cambridge University Press.

Dillon, J. T. (1982). The multidisciplinary study of questioning. *Journal of Educational Psychology*, 74(2), 147.

Dillon, J. T. (1982). The effect of questions in education and other enterprises. *Journal of Curriculum Studies*, 14, 127–152.

Donovan, L., & Green, T. (2013). *Making change: Creating a 21st century teaching and learning environment.* Teacher Created Materials.

Driver, R., Asoko, H., Leach, J., Scott, P., & Mortimer, E. (1994). Constructing scientific knowledge in the classroom. *Educational Researcher*, 23(7), 5–12.

Du Plessis, E., & Marais, P. (2015). Reflections on the NCS to NCS (CAPS): Foundation Phase teachers' experiences. *The Independent Journal of Teaching and Learning*, 10(1), 114–26.

Egan, K. (2002). *Getting it wrong from the beginning: Our progressive inheritance from Herbert Spencer*, John Dewey, and Jean Piaget. New Haven: Yale University Press.

Eiselen Report (1951). (Union of South Africa, Report of the Native Education Commission, 1949-51, UG53).

Elayyan, S. (2021). The future of education according to the fourth industrial revolution. *Journal of Educational Technology and Online Learning, 4*(1), 23-30.

Elliot, R., Fisher, C.T., & Rennie, D.L. (1999). Evolving guidelines for publication of qualitative research studies in psychology and related fields. *British Journal of Clinical Psychology, 38*, 215-29.

Engeström, Y. (1999). Activity theory and individual and social transformation. *Perspectives on Activity Theory, 19*(38), 19-30.

Engeström, Y., & Escalante, V. (1996). Mundane tool or object of affection? The rise and fall of the postal buddy. *Context and Consciousness: Activity Theory and Human-computer Interaction, 325-74.*

Ennis, R. H. (1996). Critical thinking dispositions: Their nature and assessability. *Informal Logic, 18*(2).

Falloon, G., Khoo, E. (2014). Exploring young students' talk in iPad-supported collaborative learning environments. *Computers & Education, 77*, 13-28.

Fataar, A. (2018). Placing students at the centre of the decolonizing education imperative: Engaging the (Mis)recognition struggles of students at the post apartheid university. *Educational Studies, 54*:6, 595-608.

Festinger, L. (1962). Cognitive dissonance. *Scientific American, 207*(4), 93-106.

Feuerstein, R., & Jensen, M. R. (1980, May). Instrumental enrichment: Theoretical basis, goals, and instruments. *The Educational Forum, 44*(4): 401-23).

Feuerstein, R., Rand, Y., & Hoffman, M. B. (1981). The dynamic assessment of retarded performers: The learning potential assessment device, theory, instruments and techniques. *International Journal of Rehabilitation Research, 4*(3), 465-66.

Fisher, B., Lucas, T., & Galstyan, A. (2013). The Role of iPads in constructing collaborative learning spaces. *Technology, Knowledge and Learning, 18*(3), 165-78.

Flanagan, J. C. (1954). The critical incident technique. *Psychological Bulletin, 51*(4), 3-27.

Fleer, M. (2010). *Early learning and development: Cultural-historical concepts in play*. New York: Cambridge University Press.

Fleer, M., & Hammer, M. (2013). Emotions in imaginative situations: The valued place of fairytales for supporting emotion regulation. *Mind, Culture, and Activity, 20*(3), 240-59.

Fleisch, B. (2008). *Primary education in crisis: Why South African schoolchildren underachieve in reading and mathematics*. Cape Town: Juta & Co.

Francis, S., & Hardman, J. (2018). Rhodesmustfall: Using social media to 'decolonise' learning spaces for South African higher education institutions: A cultural historical activity theory approach. *South African Journal of Higher Education, 32*(4), 66-80.

Freire, P., & Ramos, M. B. (1970). *Pedagogy of the oppressed*. New York: Continuum.

Gallimore, R., & Tharp, R. (1990). Teaching mind in society: Teaching, schooling, and literate discourse. In *Vygotsky and education: Instructional implications and applications of sociohistorical psychology* (pp. 175–205). Cambridge: Cambridge University Press.

Garrison, M. J., & Bromley, H. (2004). Social contexts, defensive pedagogies, and the (mis) uses of educational technology. *Educational Policy*, *18*(4), 589–613.

Geertz, C. (1973). *The interpretation of cultures*. New York: Basic Books.

Ginsberg, P., & Golbeck, S. L. (2004). Thoughts on the future of research on mathematics and science learning and education. *Early Childhood Research Quarterly*, *19*(1): 190–200.

Goetze, M. (2016). Five reasons why CAPS is harming our children. Retrieved from http://hookedonlearning.co.za.

Goodwin, P (Ed.). (2001). *The articulate classroom*. London: David Fulton.

Goos, S. (2020). 1:1 iPads and student achievement (Thesis, Concordia University, St. Paul). Retrieved from https://digitalcommons.csp.edu/teacher-education_masters/20.

Gumede, V., & Biyase, M. (2016). Educational reforms and curriculum transformation in post-apartheid South Africa. *Environmental Economics*, *7*(2), 69–76.

Gustafsson, M. (2019). *TIMSS, SACMEQ and PIRLS*. Cambridge: Cambridge University Press.

Halliday, M. A. (1993). Towards a language-based theory of learning. *Linguistics and Education*, *5*(2), 93–116.

Hamlin, J., & Fusaro, J. (2018). Contemporary strategies for creative and critical teaching in the 21st century. *Art Education*, *71*(2), 8–15.

Hardman, J. (2005). An exploratory case study of computer use in a primary school mathematics classroom: New technology, new pedagogy?: Research: Information and Communication Technologies. *Perspectives in Education*, *23*(1), 99–111.

Hardman, J. (2005a). An exploratory case study of computer use in a primary school mathematics classroom: New technology new pedagogy? *Perspectives in Education*, *23*(4), 1–13. ISSN0258-2236.

Hardman, J. (2005b). Activity Theory as a framework for understanding teachers' perceptions of computer usage at a primary school level in South Africa. *South African Journal of Education*, *25*(4), 258–65. ISSN 0256-0100.

Hardman. J. (2007a). Making sense of the meaning maker: Tracking the object of activity in a mathematics classroom using Activity Theory. *International Journal of Education and Development using ICT*, http://ijedict.dec.uwi.edu/viewissue.php ISSN 1814-0556.

Hardman. J. (2007b) Towards a methodology for using Activity Theory to explicate the pedagogical object in a primary school mathematics classroom. *Critical Social Studies*, (1), 53–69. ISSN 1904-0210.

Hardman. J. (2008). New technology, new pedagogy?: an activity theory analysis of pedagogical activity with computers. Cape Town: unpublished PhD thesis.

Hardman, J. (2008). Researching pedagogy: An activity theory approach. *Journal of Education, 45*(1), 65–95.
Hardman, J. (2012) Theories of development. In *Hardman, J.* (Ed.), *Child and adolescent development in South Africa: A socio-cultural perspective.* Cape Town: Oxford University Press. ISBN9780195999792.
Hardman, J. (2016). Learning theories and development. In Horstemkhe (Ed.), *Education studies: History, sociology, philosophy.* (pp. 528–49). Cape Town: Oxford University Press.
Hardman, J. (2019). Towards a pedagogical model of teaching with ICTs for mathematics attainment in primary school: A review of studies 2008–2018. *Heliyon, 5*(5), e01726.
Hardman, J. (2020). The folly of school assessment in a pandemic. *Mail and Guardian,* 13 September. https://mg.co.za/education/2020-09-13-folly-of-school-assessment-in-a-pandemic/.
Hardman, J. (2021). Towards a pedagogical model for teaching through rather than merely with technology: A cultural historical approach. *South African Journal of Higher Education, 35*(4), 104–15.
Hardman, J., & Ntlhoi. T. (2021). Online quizzes as mediating tools for teaching Information Communication Technology to first year students at a college of education in the developing context of Lesotho. *Asia Research Network Journal, 1*(2), 50–60.
Hardman, J., & Set, B. (2021). Investigating the Double-Move in pedagogy in a Grade 4 Namibian Science Classroom: A cultural historical analysis. *Creative Education, 12,* 1–17.
Hardman, J., & Teschmacher, N. (2019). Vygotsky's developmental pedagogy recontextualised as Hedegaard's double-move: Science teaching in grades 1 and 2 in a disadvantaged school in South Africa. In Cultural-historical approaches to studying learning and development (pp. 135–150). Springer, Singapore.
Hardman, J., & Veary, I. (2021). Each one teach one: Rethinking education in a pandemic. *Mail & Guardian.* Pg. 29. Cape Town. 26 January 2021.
Harley, K. and Parker, B. (1999). Integrating differences: Implications of an outcomes-based National Qualifications Framework for the roles and competencies of teachers. In J. Jansen and P. Christie (Eds.), *Changing curriculum: Studies on outcomes-based education in South Africa,* 13–27. Cape Town: Juta.
HarperCollins (2009). *Collins english disctionary and thesaurus.* London.
Harrison, G. 2011. Mediating self-regulation in a kindergarten class in South Africa: An exploratory case study. M.Ed. Thesis. University of Cape Town.
Hasan, R. (1992). Speech genre, semiotic mediation and the development of higher mental functions. *Language Sciences, 14*(4), 489–528.
Haßler, B., Major, L., & Hennessy, S. (2015). Tablet use in schools: A critical review of the evidence for learning outcomes. *Journal of Computer Assisted Learning, 32*(2), 139–56.
Haynes, J., & Murris, K. (2012). *Picturebook, pedagogy and philosophy.* New York: Routledge.

Hedegaard, M. (1998). Situated learning and cognition: Theoretical learning and cognition. *Mind, Culture and Activity*, 5(2), 114–26.

Hedegaard, M. (2020). Ascending from the abstract to the concrete in school teaching—the double move between theoretical concepts and children's concepts. *Psychological Science and Education*, 25(5), 44–57.

Hedegaard, M., & Chaiklin, S. (2005). Radical-local teaching and learning. In *Århus Universitetsforlag. Kapitel* (pp. 4–6). Denmark: Arhus University press.

Hennessy, S., Howe, C., Mercer, N., & Vrikki, M. (2020). Coding classroom dialogue: Methodological considerations for researchers. *Learning, Culture and Social Interaction*, 25, 100404.

Hennessy, S., Rojas-Drummond, S., Higham, R., Márquez, A. M., Maine, F., Ríos, R. M., ... & Barrera, M. J. (2016). Developing a coding scheme for analysing classroom dialogue across educational contexts. *Learning, Culture and Social Interaction*, 9, 16–44.

Hilton, A. (2018). Engaging primary school students in mathematics: Can iPads make a difference? *International Journal of Science and Mathematics Education*, 16, 145–65. DOI 10.1007/s10763-016-9771-5.

Hoadley, U. (2011). Knowledge, knowers and knowing: Curriculum reform in South Africa. *Curriculum in today's world: Configuring knowledge, identities, work and politics* (pp. 143–58).

Hoadley, U. (2015). Michael Young and the curriculum field in South Africa. *Journal of Curriculum Studies*, 47(6), 733–49.

Hoadley, U. (2017). *Pedagogy in poverty: Lessons from twenty years of curriculum reform in South Africa*. London: Routledge.

Hoadley, U., & Galant, J. (2019). What counts and who belongs?: Current debates in decolonising the curriculum. *Decolonisation in universities, the politics of knowledge* (pp. 100–14).

Hollinsworth, A., Raciti, M. & Carter, J. (2021) Indigenous students' identities in Australian higher education: found, denied, and reinforced, Race Ethnicity and Education, 24(1), 112–31. DOI: 10.1080/13613324.2020.1753681.

Howe, C., Hennessy, S., Mercer, N., Vrikki, M., & Wheatley, L. (2019). Teacher–student dialogue during classroom teaching: Does it really impact on student outcomes? *Journal of the Learning Sciences*, 28(4–5), 462–512.

Howie, S., Combrinck, C., Roux, K., Tshele, M., Mokoena, G., & Palane, N. M. (2017). PIRLS 2016. Pretoria: *Centre for Evaluation and Assessment*.

Howie, S. J., & Plomp, T. (Eds.), (2006). *Contexts of learning mathematics and science: Lessons learned from TIMSS*. London: Routledge.

Huitt, W. (1998). Critical thinking: An overview. *Educational Psychology Interactive*, 3(6), 34–50.

Ibrahim. A., Othman, T., Nurzatulshima, K., & Habibah, A.J. (2019). *The use of mobile application: Why play is important in teaching elementary mathematics?* In: 5th International Conference on Educational Research and Practice (ICERP) 2019, 22–23 October 2019, Palm Garden Hotel, Putrajaya, Malaysia; 249–57.

Jansen, J. D. (1999). Why outcomes-based education will fail: An elaboration. In J. D. Jansen and P. Christie (Eds.), *Changing curriculum: Studies on outcomes-based education in South Africa*, 145–156. Cape Town: Juta.

Jansen, J. (2017). Introduction-Part II. Decolonising the university curriculum given a dysfunctional school system?. *Journal of Education (University of KwaZulu-Natal)*, (68), 4–13.

Jerry, P. (1991). *Social purpose and schooling: Alternatives, agendas and issues* (1st ed.). London: Routledge. https://doi.org/10.4324/9781315225456.

Kain, D., & Wardle, E. (2014). Activity theory: An introduction for the writing classroom. *Wardle and Downs*, 273–83.

Kallaway, P. (Ed.). (2002). *The history of education under apartheid, 1948–1994: The doors of learning and culture shall be opened*. South Africa: Pearson.

Kaptelinin, V. (2005). The object of activity: Making sense of the sense-maker. *Mind, Culture, and Activity*, 12(1), 4–18.

Karpov, Y. V. (2003). Vygotsky's doctrine of scientific concepts. *Vygotsky's Educational Theory in Cultural Context*, 65–82.

Karpov, Y. (2005). *The neo-Vygotskian approach to child development*. New York: Cambridge University Press.

Kiger, D., Herro, D., & Ponty, D. (2012). Examining the influence of a mobile learning intervention on third grade math achievement. *JRTE*, 45(1), 61–82.

King, D., & Hansen, R. (1999). Experts at work: State autonomy, social learning and eugenic sterilization in 1930s britain. *British Journal of Political Science*, 29(1), 77–107.

King, P. M., & Kitchener, K. S. (2004). Judgment model: Twenty years of research on epistemic cognition. *Personal Epistemology: The Psychology of Beliefs about Knowledge and Knowing*, 37.

Kirkpatrick, L., Brown, H. M., Searle, M., Smyth, R. E., Ready, E. A., & Kennedy, K. (2018). Impact of a one-to-one iPad initiative on grade 7 Students' achievement in language arts, mathematics, and learning skills. *Computers in the Schools*, 35(3), 171. DOI: 10.1080/07380569.2018.1491771

Kitchener, K. S., & King, P. M. (1981). Reflective judgment: Concepts of justification and their relationship to age and education. *Journal of Applied Developmental Psychology*, 2(2), 89–116.

Klinck, K. (2013). Education for unsuccessful school leavers in South Africa – a proposal to prevent exclusion of the majority of South Africa's learners from further education and training. Presentation at 2 nd National Qualifications Framework (NQF) research conference: Building articulation and integration. 4th–6th March 2013. Available http://www.saqa.org.za/docs/events/2013/nqf_conf/presentations/klinck_k.pdf.

Kozulin, A. (2003). Psychological tools and mediated learning. *Vygotsky's Educational Theory in Cultural Context*, 4(6), 15–38.

Kozulin, A., & Presseisen, B. (2001). *Mediated learning experience and cultural diversity*. ICELP, Jerusalem, Israel.

Kruss, G. (1988). People's Education. An Examination of the Concept. People's Education Research Project: No. 1. Centre for Adult and Continuing Education, University of the Western Cape, Private Bag X17, Bellville 7535, South Africa.

Lee, M., Yun, J. J., Pyka, A., Won, D., Kodama, F., Schiuma, G., … & Zhao, X. (2018). How to respond to the fourth industrial revolution, or the second information technology revolution? Dynamic new combinations between technology, market, and society through open innovation. *Journal of Open Innovation: Technology, Market, and Complexity, 4*(3), 21.

Lefebvre, H., & Nicholson-Smith, D. (1991). *The production of space* (Vol. 142). Blackwell: Oxford.

Leontiev, A. N. (1978). *Activity, consciousness and personality*. New Jersey: Prentice Hall.

Leontiev, A. (1981). The problem of activity in psychology. In J.V. Wertsch (Ed.), *The concept of activity in soviet psychology*, 156–163. Armonk, NY: M.E. Sharpe.

Li, Q., & Ma, X. (2010). A meta-analysis of the effects of computer technology on school students' mathematics learning. *Educational Psychology Review, 22*(3), 215–43.

Littleton, K., Mercer, N., Dawes, L., Wegerif, R., Rowe, D., & Sams, C. (2005). Talking and thinking together at key stage 1. *Early Years, 25*(2), 167–82.

Long, W. (2018). Decolonising higher education: Postcolonial theory and the invisible hand of student politics. *New Agenda: South African Journal of Social and Economic Policy, 2018*(69), 20–5.

Luria, A. R. (1976). *The neuropsychology of memory*. (Trans. B. Haigh). New York: VH Winston & Sons.

Luria, A. R. (1976). *Cognitive development: Its cultural and social foundations*. Boston: Harvard University Press.

Mann, C. R. (1917). *The teaching of physics for purposes of general education* (reprint ed.). New York: Macmillan.

Manuguerra, M., & Petocz, P. (2011). Promoting student engagement by integrating new technology into tertiary education: The role of the iPad. *Asian Social Science, 7*(11), 61–5. https://doi.org/10.5539/ass.v7n11p61.

Marx, K. (1857). The method of political economy. In M. Nicolaus, (Trans.), *The Grundrisse* (pp. 100–11). London: Penguin.

Marx, K. (1923). England and materialist philosophy. In Max Beer (Eds., and Trans.), *Further Selection from the Literary Remains of Karl Marx*. Labour Monthly, 105–13.

Mbembe, A. (2001). *On the postcolony*. California: University of California Press.

McFeetors, P., & Palfy, K (2018). Educative experiences in a games context: Supporting emerging reasoning in elementary school mathematics. *The Journal of Mathematical Behavior, 50*, 103–25.

McKinney, C., Carrim, H., Marshall, A., Latyon, L. (2015). What counts as language in South African schooling?: Monoglossic ideologies and children's participation. *AILA Review, 28*(1), 103–26.

Mehan, H. (1979). "What time is it, Denise?": Asking known information questions in classroom discourse. *Theory into Practice, 18*(4), 285–94.

Mercer, N. (2000a). How is language used as a medium for classroom education? In B. Moon, S. Brown & M. Ben-Perez (Eds.), *The Routledge international companion to education* (pp. 69–82). London: Routledge.

Mercer, N. (2000b). *Words and minds: How we use language to think together.* London: Routledge.

Mercer, N. (2005a). How is language used as a medium for classroom education? In *Teaching, learning and the curriculum in secondary schools* (pp. 189–208). London: Routledge.

Mercer, N. (2005b). Sociocultural discourse analysis: Analysing classroom talk as a social mode of thinking. *Journal of Applied Linguistics, 1*(2), 137–68.

Mercer, N. (2010). The analysis of classroom talk: Methods and methodologies. *British Journal of Educational Psychology, 80*(1), 1–14.

Mercer, N. (2012). What has the study of classroom talk told us that can improve the quality of education. Retrieved from http://www.slideshare.net/margarubiosoto/exploratory-talk-in-professor-neil-mercer.

Mercer, N., Dawes, L., & Staarman, J. K. (2009). Dialogic teaching in the primary science classroom, *Language and Education, 23*(4), 353–69. DOI: 10.1080/09500780902954273.

Mercer, N., & Fisher, E. (1997a). Scaffolding through talk. In R. Wegerif & P. Scrimshaw (Eds.), *Computers and talk in the primary classroom* (pp. 196–211). Clevedon: Multilingual Matters.

Mercer, N., & Fisher, E. (1997b). The importance of talk. In R. Wegerif & P. Scrimshaw (Eds.), *Computers and talk in the primary classroom.* (pp. 13–22). Clevedon: Multilingual Matters.

Mercer, N., & Kleine Staarman, J. (2005). *Dialogue and activity: A methodological gap that needs to be filled.* Presented at the 1st International ISCAR conference, September 20–25, Seville, Spain.

Mercer, N., & Littleton, K. (2007). *Dialogue and the development of children's thinking: A sociocultural approach.* London: Routledge.

Mercer, N., & Wegerif, R. (1998). Is 'exploratory talk' productive talk? In K. Littleton & P. Light (Eds.), *Learning with computers: Analysing productive interactions* (pp. 79–101). London: Routledge.

Mercer, N., Wegerif, R., & Dawes, L. (1999). Children's talk and the development of reasoning in the classroom. *British Educational Research Journal, 25*(1), 95–111.

Mignolo, W. (2001). Coloniality of power and subalternity. In Saldivar-Hull, S & Guhar, R. USA (Eds.) *The Latin American subaltern studies reader* (pp. 424–44). Duke University Press.

Mignolo, W. D. (2005). On subalterns and other agencies. *Postcolonial Studies, 8*(4), 381–407.

Mignolo, W. D. (2021). *The politics of decolonial investigations*. North Carolina: Duke University Press.

Mishra, P., & Koehler, M. J. (2006). Technological pedagogical content knowledge: A framework for teacher knowledge. *Teachers College Record*, *108*(6), 1017–54.

Mohr, K. A. J., Mohr, E. S. (2007). Extending English-language learners' classroom interactions using the response protocol. *The Reading Teacher*, *60*, 440–50.

Moll, L. C., & Greenberg, J. B. (1990). Creating zones of possibilities: Combining social contexts for instruction. In L. C. Moll (Ed.), *Vygotsky and education: Instructional implications and applications of sociohistorical psychology* (pp. 319–48). New York: Cambridge University Press.

Moodley, D. E. (2021). Towards education for 21st century democratic citizenry—Philosophical Enquiry Advancing Cosmopolitan Engagement (PEACE) curriculum: An intentional critique. *Analytic Teaching and Philosophical Praxis*, *41*(2), 92–105.

Morais, A., Neves, I., & Pires, D. (2004). The what and the how of teaching and learning: Going deeper into sociological analysis and intervention. In *Reading Bernstein, researching Bernstein* (pp. 93–108). London: Routledge.

Morris, A., Hardman, J., & Jacklin, H. (2016). School Science for six ear olds: A neo-Vygotskian approach to curriculum analysis. *Journal of Education*, *64*, 1–26.

Morris, C. W. (1992). *Academic press dictionary of science and technology* (Vol. 10). Boston: Gulf Professional Publishing.

Motshekga, A. (2009) We've signed OBE's death certificate: Statement by Minister of Basic Education, Angie Motshekga, on curriculum review process. National Assembly 5 November 2009. Online. Available HTTP: http://www.politicsweb.co.za/politicsweb/view/politicsweb/en/page71656?oid=150055&sn=Detail (accessed 3 2 November 2021).

Msimanga, A., Lelliot, A. D., (2012). Making sense of science: Argumentation for meaning-making in a teacher-led whole class discussion. *African Journal of Research in Mathematics, Science and Technology Education*, *16*(2), 192–206.

Muller, J. (2000) *Reclaiming knowledge: Social theory, curriculum and education policy*. London: Routledge Falmer.

Muller, J. (2009). Forms of knowledge and curriculum coherence. *Journal of Education and Work*, *22*(3), 205–26.

Myhill, D. (2006). Talk, talk, talk: Teaching and learning in whole class discourse. *Research Papers in Education*, *21*, 19–41.

Myhill, D., & Dunkin, F. (2005). Questioning learning. *Language and Education*, *19*(5), 415–27.

Myhill, D., & Warren, P. (2005). Scaffolds or straitjackets? Critical moments in classroom discourse. *Educational Review*, *57*(1), 55–69.

Namkung, J. M., Peng, P., & Lin, X. (2019). The relation between mathematics anxiety and mathematics performance among school-aged students: A meta-analysis. *Review of Educational Research*, *89*(3). https://doi.org/10.3102/0034654319843494.

Nussbaumer, D. (2012). An overview of cultural historical activity theory (CHAT) use in classroom research 2000 to 2009. *Educational Review*, *64*(1), 37–55.

Nystrand, M. (2006). Research on the role of classroom discourse as it affects reading comprehension. *Research in the Teaching of English*, *40*, 392–412.

Nystrand, M., Wu, L. L., Gamoran, A., Zeiser, S., & Long, D. A. (2003). Questions in time: Investigating the structure and dynamics of unfolding classroom discourse. *Discourse Processes*, *35*, 135–98.

O-Saki, K., & Agu. A. (2002). A study of classroom interaction in primary schools in the united republic of tanzania. *Prospects*, *32*(1), 103–16. DOI: 10.1023/A:1019713014049.

Papadakis, S., Kalogiannakis. M., & Zaranis. N (2016). Developing fundamental programming concepts and computational thinking with ScratchJr in preschool education: A case study. *International Journal of Mobile Learning and Organisation*, *10*(3), 187–202.

Papert, S. (1980a). *Teaching children to be mathematicians us. Teaching about mathematics* (No. 249). memo.

Papert, S. (1980b). "Mindstorms" children. *Computers and Powerful Ideas*.

Piaget, J. (1964). Cognitive development in children: Piaget development and learning. *Journal, of Research in Science Teaching*, *2*, 176–86.

Piaget, J. (1970). *Genetic epistemology*. New York: Columbia University Press.

Piaget, J. (1976). Piaget's theory. In Inhelder, B., Chipman, H. H., & Zwingmann, C. (Eds.). *Piaget and his school* (pp. 11–23). Berlin, Heidelberg: Springer.

Piaget, J. (1977). *The development of thought: Equilibration of cognitive structures*. (Trans. A. Rosin). New York: Viking.

Piaget, J. (1995). *Sociological studies*. (Trans. L. Smith, et al. and Ed. L. Smith). London: Routledge.

Pinard, A. (1986). 'Prise de conscience' and taking charge of one's own cognitive functioning. *Human Development*, *29*(6), 341–54.

Pinker, S. (2019). *Enlightenment now*. New York: Penguin Books.

Presseisen, B. Z., & Kozulin, A. (1992). Mediated Learning–the contributions of Vygotsky and Feuerstein in theory and practice. Paper presented at the Annual Meeting of the American Educational Research Association (San Francisco, CA, April 20–24, 1992).

Rachel R. Harari, Rose K. Vukovic & Sean P. Bailey (2013). Mathematics anxiety in young children: An exploratory study. *The Journal of Experimental Education*, *81*(4), 538–55.

Ratele, K. (2019). *The world looks like this from here: Thoughts on African psychology*. Johannesburg: Wits University Press.

Reddy, V., Prinsloo, C., Arends, F., Visser, M., Winnaar, L., Feza, N., … & Maja, M. (2012). Highlights from TIMSS 2011: The South African perspective.

Reddy, V., Zuze, T. L., Visser, M., Winnaar, L., Juan, A., Prinsloo, C. H., & Rogers, S. (2015). *Beyond benchmarks*. Pretoria: HSRC Press.

Reeves, Cheryl, & Muller, J. (2005). Picking up the pace: Variation in the structure and organization of learning school mathematics. *Journal of Education, 37*(1), 103–30.

Rieber, R. W., & Robinson, D. K. (Eds.), (2013). *The essential Vygotsky*. London: Springer Science & Business Media.

Rorty, R. (1991). Solidarity or objectivity. *Objectivity, Relativism, and Truth, 1*, 21–34.

Rorty, R. (1996). Who are we? Moral universalism and economic triage. *Diogenes, 44*(173), 5–15.

Rosen, Y., & Salomon, G. (2007). The differential learning achievements of constructivist technology-intensive learning environments as compared with traditional ones: A meta-analysis. *Journal of Educational Computing Research, 36*(1), 1–14.

Roth, W. M., & Jornet, A. (2017). Understanding educational psychology. In *A late Vygotskian, Spinozist approach* (pp. 35–47). Switzerland: Springer International Publishing.

Roth, W. M., & Lee, Y. J. (2007). 'Vygotsky's neglected legacy': Cultural-historical activity theory. *Review of Educational Research, 77*(2), 186–232.

Rusznyak, L., Hlatshwayo, M. N., Fataar, A., & Blackie, M. (2021). Knowledge-building and knowers in educational practices. *Journal of Education (University of KwaZulu-Natal)*, (83), 1–12.

Ryff, C. D. (2014). Psychological well-being revisited: Advances in the science and practice of eudaimonia. *Psychotherapy and Psychosomatics, 83*(1), 10–28.

Saljo, R. (1999). Learning with interactive graphical representations. *Learning and Instruction, 9*(4), 303–425.

Sameroff, A. (2010). A unified theory of development: A dialectic integration of nature and nurture. *Child Development, 81*(1), 6–22.

Sarbu, I., Matei, C., Benea, V., & Georgescu, S. R. (2014). Brief history of syphilis. *Journal of Medicine and Life, 7*(1), 4.

Schollar, E. (2001). A review of two evaluations of the application of the READ primary schools program in the Eastern Cape Province of South Africa. *International Journal of Educational Research, 35*(2), 205–16.

Seligman, M. E. (2002). *Authentic happiness: Using the new positive psychology to realize your potential for lasting fulfillment*. UK: Simon and Schuster.

Sharoom, A. A. & Hussin, N. (2018). Industrial revolution 4.0 and education. *International Journal of Academic Research in Business and Social Sciences, 8*, (9).

Shayer, M. (2003). Not just Piaget; not just Vygotsky, and certainly not Vygotsky as alternative to Piaget. *Learning and Instruction, 13*(5), 465–85.

Shklovsky, V. (1917). Art as technique. *Literary Theory: An Anthology, 3*.

Sinclair J, Coulthard, M. (1975) *Toward an analysis of discourse: The English used by teachers and pupils*. Oxford: Oxford University Press.

Siraj-Blatchford, I. (1999). Early childhood pedagogy: Practice, principles and research. *Understanding Pedagogy and Its Impact on Learning*, 20–45.

Smagorinsky, P. (1995). The social construction of data: Methodological problems of investigating learning in the zone of proximal development. *Review of Educational Research, 65*(3), 191–212.

Smagorinsky, P., Cook, L., & Johnson, T. (2003). The twisting path of concept development in learning to teach. *Teachers College Record, 105*(8), 1399–436.

Song, Y., Chen, X., Hao, T., Liu, Z., & Lan, Z. (2019). Exploring two decades of research on classroom dialogue by using bibliometric analysis. *Computers & Education, 137,* 12–31.

South African Department of Education (1995). *curriculum framework for general and further education document.* Pretoria: South African Department of Education.

South African Department of Education (2000a) *A South African curriculum for the twenty first century: Report of the review committee on curriculum 2005,* presented to the Minister of Education, Professor Kader Asmal, Pretoria: South African Department of Education.

Spaull, N. (2013). Poverty & privilege: Primary school inequality in South Africa. *International Journal of Educational Development, 33*(5), 436–47.

Spaull, N. (2013). South Africa's education crisis: The quality of education in South Africa 1994-2011. *Johannesburg: Centre for Development and Enterprise, 21*(1), 1–65.

Spelke, E. S. (2013). Where perceiving ends and thinking begins: The apprehension of objects in infancy. In *Perceptual development in infancy* (pp. 209–46). London: Psychology Press.

Spencer-Smith, G., & Hardman, J. (2014). The impact of computer and mathematics software usage on performance of school leavers in the Western Cape Province of South Africa: A comparative analysis. *International Journal of Education and Development Using ICT, 10*(1), 22–40.

Spreen, C. A., & Vally, S. (2010). Outcomes-based education and its (dis) contents: Learner-centred pedagogy and the education crisis in South Africa. *Southern African Review of Education with Education with Production, 16*(1), 39–58.

Stake, R. E. (2013). *Multiple case study analysis.* New York: Guilford Press.

Stetsenko, A. (2021). Scholarship in the context of a historic socioeconomic and political turmoil: Reassessing and taking stock of CHAT. Commentary on Y. Engeström and A. Sannino 'from mediated actions to heterogenous coalitions: Four generations of activity-theoretical studies of work and learning'. *Mind, Culture, and Activity, 28*(1), 32–43.

Sylva, K., Melhuish, E., Sammons, P., Siraj-Blatchford, I., & Taggart, B. (2004). *The effective provision of pre-school education (EPPE) project: Final report. A longitudinal study funded by the DfES 1997–2004.* London: Institute of Education, University of London.

Talyzina, N. F. (1981). *The psychology of learning: Theories of learning and programmed instruction.* Moscow: Progress Publishers.

Tama, M. C. (1989). *Critical thinking: Promoting it in the classroom.* Washington: ERIC Clearinghouse.

Tamim, R. M., Bernard, R. M., Borokhovski, E., Abrami, P. C., Schmid, R. F. (2011). What forty years of research says about the impact of technology on learning: A second order meta-analysis and validation study. *Revue of Educational Research, 81*(1), 4–28.

Tay, C. (2020). Comparison of the impact of information and communication technology between bilateral trade in goods and services. *Journal of System and Management Sciences*, *10*(1), 1–31.

Tay, H. Y., (2016). Longitudinal study on impact of iPad use on teaching and learning. *Cogent Education*, *3*(1). DOI: 10.1080/2331186X.2015.1127308.

Taylor C. (1989). *Sources of the self: The making of the modern identity*. Cambridge, MA: Harvard University Press.

Taylor, N. (2007). Equity, efficiency and the development of South African schools. In Townsend, T. (ed.) *International handbook of school effectiveness and improvement* (pp. 523–40). Dordrecht: Springer.

Taylor, N. (2008). What's wrong with South African schools. In *What's Working in school development conference, JET education services*, Cape Town.

Taylor, N., & Vinjevold, P. (1999). *Getting learning right*. Johannesburg: Joint Education Trust.

Teo, T., Unwin, S., Scherer, R., & Gardiner, V. (2021). Initial teacher training for twenty-first century skills in the Fourth Industrial Revolution (IR 4.0): A scoping review. *Computers & Education*, 104223.

Tharp, R. (1993). Institutional and social context of educational practice and reform. *Contexts for Learning: Sociocultural Dynamics in Children's Development*, 269–82.

Tharp, R. G., & Gallimore, R. (1988). *Rousing minds to life: Schooling in social context*. New York: Cambridge University Press.

Thorvaldsen, S., Vavrik, L. & Salomon, G., (2012). The use of ICT Tools in mathematics: A Case-control study of best practice in 9th grade classrooms. *Scandanavian Journal of Educational Research*, *56*(2), 213–28.

Tlostanova, M., & Mignolo, W. (2009). Global coloniality and the decolonial option. *Kult*, *6*(Special Issue), 130–47.

Tudge, J. R., & Winterhoff, P. A. (1993). Vygotsky, Piaget, and Bandura: Perspectives on the relations between the social world and cognitive development. *Human Development*, *36*(2), 61–81.

Twining, P. (2017). Some guidance on conducting and reporting qualitative studies. *Computers & Education*, *106*, A1–A9

Valley, S., & Spreen, C. (1998). Education policy and implementation developments, Februay to May 1998. *Epuu Quarterly Review of Education and Training in SouthAfrica*, *5*(3).

Vally, S., & Spreen, C. A. (2009). Learning from and for community: Participatory action research and post-apartheid education. *International Journal of Learning*, *15*(11), 125–137.

Valsiner, J. (Ed.). (1988). *Child development within culturally structured environments: Parental cognition and adult-child interaction*. New York: Ablex Publishing.

Valsiner, J. (1998). The development of the concept of development: Historical and epistemological perspectives.

Van den Berg, R., Shin, H., Chou, W. C., George, R., & Ma, W. J. (2012). Variability in encoding precision accounts for visual short-term memory limitations. *Proceedings of the National Academy of Sciences*, *109*(22), 8780–5.

Van der Veer, R., & Valsiner, J. (1991). *Understanding Vygotsky: A quest for synthesis*. Blackwell Publishing. Oxford.

Venkat, H., & Spaull, N. (2015). What do we know about primary teachers' mathematical content knowledge in South Africa? An analysis of SACMEQ 2007. *International Journal of Educational Development*, *41*, 121–30.

Verspoor, A. (2006). Effective Schools in Sub-Saharan Africa. Paper presented at the Association for the Development of Education in Africa. Gabon 27–31 March 2006.

Von Glasersfeld, E. (1984). An introduction to radical constructivism. *The Invented Reality*, *1740*, 28.

Voogt, J., Fisser, P., Pareja Roblin, N., Tondeur, J., & van Braak, J. (2013). Technological pedagogical content knowledge–a review of the literature. *Journal of Computer Assisted Learning*, *29*(2), 109–21.

Vygotsky, L. (1930/1997). The instrumental method in Psychology. In *The Collected Works of L. S. Vygotsky*, Volume 3 (pp. 85–90). New York: Plenum Press.

Vygotsky, L. (1934/1987). Thinking and speech. In *The Collected Works of L. S. Vygotsky*, Volume 1 (pp. 39–288). New York: Plenum Press.

Vygotsky, L. S. (1962). *Thought and language*. (Trans. and Eds. E. Hanfmann & G. Vakar). Cambridge, MA: MIT Press. (Original work published 1934).

Vygotsky, L. S. (1978). *Mind in society. The development of higher psychological processes*. (Trans. and Ed. M. Cole, V. John-Steiner, S. Scribner, & E. Souberman Cambridge, MA: Harvard University Press.

Vygotsky, L. S. (1986). *Thought and language*. (Trans. and Eds. E. Hanfmann & G. Vakar). Cambridge, MA: MIT Press.

Vygotsky, L. S. (1987). *The collected works of LS Vygotsky: The fundamentals of defectology* (Vol. 2). Springer Science & Business Media.

Vygotsky, L. S. (1987). *The collected works of L. S. Vygotsky, Vol. 1: Problems of general psychology*. R. W. Rieber and A. S. Carton (Eds.), N. Minick, (Trans.) New York: Plenum Press.

Vygotsky, L. S. (1997a). *The collected works of L. S. Vygotsky: Problems of the theory and history of psychology* (Vol. 3). Springer Science & Business Media.

Vygotsky, L. S. (1997b). *Educational psychology*. Boca Ratan: St Lucie Press.

Vygotsky, L. S. (1998). The problem of age (Trans. M. Hall). In R. W. Rieber (Ed.), *The collected works of L. S. Vygotsky: Vol. 5. Child psychology* (pp. 187–205). New York: Plenum Press.

Vygotsky, L. S. V. (2002). *Fantasi och kreativitet i barndomen*. Sweden: Daidalos.

Vygotsky, L. S. (2012). *Thought and language*. Cambridge, Massachusetts: MIT Press.

Waghid, Z., & Hibbert, L. (2018). Advancing border thinking through defamiliarisation in uncovering the darker side of coloniality and modernity in South African higher education. *South African Journal of Higher Education*, *32*(4), 263–83.

Walton, E. (2018). Decolonising (through) inclusive education? *Educational Research for Social Change, 7* (SPE), 31–45.

Ward, C. L., & Benson, S. K. (2010). Developing new schemas for online teaching and learning: TPACK. *MERLOT Journal of Online Learning and Teaching, 6*(2), 482–90.

Wardekker, W. L. (1998). Scientific concepts and reflection. *Mind, Culture, and Activity, 5*(2), 143–53.

Webb, M., & Cox, M. (2004). A review of pedagogy related to information and communications technology. *Technology, Pedagogy and Education, 13*(3), 235–86.

Wedin, A. (2010). A restricted curriculum for second language learners – A self-fulfilling teacher strategy. *Language and Education, 24*(3), 171–83. DOI: 10.1080/09500780903026352.

Wegerif, R. (1997a). Children's talk and computer software: A response to Fisher. In R. Wegerif & P. Scrimshaw (Eds.), *Computers and talk in the primary classroom* (pp. 99–113). Clevedon: Multilingual Matters.

Wegerif, R. (1997b). Factors affecting the quality of children's talk at computers. In R. Wegerif & P. Scrimshaw (Eds.), *Computers and talk in the primary classroom* (pp. 177–89). Clevedon: Multilingual Matters.

Wegerif, R., & Dawes, L. (1997a). Computers and exploratory talk: An intervention study. In R. Wegerif & P. Scrimshaw (Eds.), *Computers and talk in the primary classroom* (pp. 226–38). Clevedon: Multilingual Matters.

Wegerif, R., & Mercer, N. (1997b). Using computer-based analysis to integrate quantitative and qualitative methods in the investigation of collaborative learning. *Language and Education, 11*(4), 271–86.

Wegerif, R., & Mercer, N. (1997c). A dialogical framework for investigating talk. In R. Wegerif & P. Scrimshaw (Eds.), *Computers and talk in the primary classroom* (pp. 49–65). Clevedon: Multilingual Matters.

Wegerif, R. and Scrimshaw, P. (1997d). Introduction: Computers, talk and learning. In R. Wegerif and P. Scrimshaw (Eds.), *Computers and talk in the primary classroom* (pp. 1–13). Clevedon: Multilingual Matters.

Wells, G. (1993). Reevaluating the IRF sequence: A proposal for the articulation of theories of activity and discourse for the analysis of teaching and learning in the classroom. *Linguistics and Education, 5*(1), 1–37.

Wells, G. (1999). *Dialogic inquiry* (pp. 137–41). Cambridge: Cambridge University Press.

Wells, G. (2001). The case for dialogic inquiry. In Wells, G. (Ed.), *Action, talk, and text: Learning and teaching through inquiry* (pp. 171–94). New York, NY: Teachers College Press.

Wertsch, J. V. (Ed.). (1986). *Culture, communication, and cognition: Vygotskian perspectives*. CUP Archive.

Wertsch, J. V. (1991). A sociocultural approach to socially shared cognition. In L. B. Resnick, J. M. Levine, & S. D. Teasley (Eds.), Perspectives on socially shared cognition (pp. 85–100). American Psychological Association. New York.

Western Education Department (2001). Cape schools prepare for 'electronic education'. WCED Cape Town.

Wink, J., & Putney, L. A. (2002). The zone of proximal development (ZPD). *A Vision of Vygotsky*, 85–116.

Wink, J. & Putney, L. G. (2002). A vision of Vygotsky. In J. Wink & L. G. Putney (Eds.), Boston, MA: Allyn and Bacon. http://www.worldcat.org/oclc/834114661.

Winkler-Rhoades, N., Carey, S.C. and Spelke, E.S. (2013). Two-year-old children interpret abstract, purely geometric maps. *Developmental Science*, 16(3), 365–76.

Wood, D. (1992). Teaching talk: How modes of teacher talk affect pupil participation. In Norman, K., (Ed.), (1992) *Thinking voices: The work of the National Oracy Project* (pp. 203–14). London: Hodder & Stoughton.

Wood, D., Bruner, J. S., & Ross, G. (1976). The role of tutoring in problem solving. *Journal of Child Psychology and Psychiatry*, 17, 89–100.

Wragg, E (2001). *Assessment and learning in the primary school*. New York: Routledge.

Yin, R. K. (1981). The case study as a serious research strategy. *Knowledge*, 3(1), 97–114.

Yin, R. K. (1992). The case study method as a tool for doing evaluation. *Current Sociology*, 40(1), 121–37.

Young, M. (2012). Education, globalization and the 'voice of knowledge'. In *The knowledge economy and lifelong learning* (pp. 335–47). Netherlands: Brill.

Young, M. (2013). Powerful knowledge: An analytically useful concept or just a 'sexy sounding term'? A response to John Beck's 'Powerful knowledge, esoteric knowledge, curriculum knowledge'. *Cambridge Journal of Education*, 43(2), 195–8.

Young, M. (2014). What is a curriculum and what can it do? *Curriculum Journal*, 25(1), 7–13.

Zavala, M. (2016). Decolonial methodologies in education. *Encyclopedia of Educational Philosophy and Theory*, 361–6.

Zurita, G. & Nussbaum, M. (2004). Computer supported collaborative learning using wirelessly interconnected mobile computers. *Computers & Education* 42(3), 289–314. DOI: 10.1016/j.compedu.2003.08.005.

Index

abstract concepts. *See* scientific/abstract concepts
accommodation 30, 63
acquisition pedagogy 41, 57, 74, 81, 83, 139–40, 157, 182
active cognizing agents 30, 57, 63, 85, 116, 132, 134, 156, 192 n.5
active learner 47–8, 69
activity system 117–19, 122–3
apartheid education system 7–8, 42–3, 58–9, 71, 155–6, 168, 192 n.1. *See also* fundamental pedagogics; outcomes-based education (OBE)
    to democratic education 8, 42–3, 54–5, 74 (*see also* decolonial education)
    distinct schooling 37–8
    to progressive pedagogy 43–4, 57–8, 60–7 (*see also* progressive pedagogics)
artefacts 39, 78, 118–19, 126, 128

Bantu education system 37–9, 46–7, 58–9, 156
behaviourism 59–60, 156–7, 193 n.3
benchmarking tests 1, 77, 115
Bereiter, C. 65
Bernstein, B. 25, 40, 49, 52–3
binary logic 9, 28, 45
Bruner, J. S. 13, 22–3

CAMI maths software 115, 131, 149, 152, 166
categorical thinking 82–3
Centre for Education Policy Development (CEPD) 43
Chaiklin, S. D. 12–14, 22, 81–2, 97, 159–60, 162, 164, 168–9, 182, 191 n.2
Christian National Education 39, 42, 67
classification 52–3

climate change 86
cognitive ability/skills 23, 30, 167
cognitive constructivism 30, 48
cognitive development 9–10, 23, 27, 61, 63–6, 79, 84
    computer-based lessons 115–16
    double-move 159, 182
    language 134
    in ZPD 163
Cole, M. 65, 194 n.3
collaborative pedagogy 126–9, 130, 132, 166
competence model curriculum 11–12, 40, 67
complexes 17–18
computational thinking 30–1
computer-based pedagogy 123, 166
    with ICTs (*see* information and communication technologies (ICTs))
    software and mathematics 115–18, 130–1, 137, 144, 152, 166
    talk in classrooms 135–7 (*see also* peer talk, computer-based/iPad lessons)
concepts, development 17–19, 99–100. *See also* everyday concepts; scientific/abstract concepts
Congress of South African Trade Unions (COSATU) 43
consciousness 28, 33, 63–7
constructivism 30–1, 47, 49, 62, 85, 134, 157, 193 n.10
constructivist pedagogy 41, 66, 71, 131–2, 134
content knowledge 46–8, 84, 94–5, 98–9, 124–5
critical thinking 30
cultural historical activity theory (CHAT) 116–17, 194 n.3
    activity system 117–18
    case study 120–1

Index 215

collaborative pedagogy 126–8, 166
data collection 121–3
defensive pedagogy 129–31
evaluative episodes 121–2
expansive learning 119
Likert scale 122
mathematical content questions 122–3
reinforcement pedagogy 123–5
cultural-historical theory 8, 30, 48.
    See also computer-based pedagogy; peer talk, computer-based/iPad lessons; talk
consciousness 63–7
qualitative research approach 137–8
culturally more competent other 9–12, 45, 52, 78, 135, 157, 163
cumulative talk 136
curriculum 85, 100–1, 161. *See also* progressive pedagogics
    Bantu education system 37–8, 46–7
    content and assessment 49–50
    models of 40
    performance and competencies in relation to 40
    as signs 39
    as tools 39–42
    transformation in 44–5, 66–73
    for white and Black children 37–40, 156
Curriculum 2005 (C2005)
    failure of 45–6, 156
    outcomes-based education 43–4
    in post-apartheid South Africa 46–7
Curriculum Assessment Policy Statement (CAPS) 49–50, 53–5, 83, 85, 93–4, 100, 156
Curriculum Model for South Africa (CUMSA) 42

Davydov, V. V. 18–20, 51, 84
decolonial education xi, 2, 8, 51, 161–4
    and cognitive development 27
    colonial epistemologies and 26–7
    modernity and colonialism 28–9, 161
    as social justice project 24–6
decolonialism 2, 27, 162
decolonial knowledge 51, 161. *See also* knowledge
decolonial pedagogy 2, 26–9, 34–5, 55, 161–4, 167–9

defamiliarization pedagogy 27
defensive pedagogy 129–31
democratic discourse in education 42–3, 57–8, 66–7, 74. *See also* progressive pedagogics
Department of Basic Education (DBE) textbook 83, 100
Department of National Education (DNE) 42
Dewey, J. 15, 58
dialectical education 2, 8–9
dialectical logic 9, 28, 32, 40, 45
dialogical pedagogy 20, 24, 135–7
dialogue 11, 20, 135–6, 144–6, 157
disciplinary norms 172
discovery-based learning 48, 64, 157, 193 n.9
disequilibrium 63
disputational talk 136
distinct schooling 37
    for Black and white children 37–40
    funding for 38
    progression 38
division of labour 118–19, 121–3, 173–9
double-move 21–2, 31, 33–4, 81
    analysis 101
    in authentic problems 110–11, 159
    case study
        talk, coding framework 101–4
        wild and farm/domesticated animals 101–7
    developing concepts 99
    everyday and scientific concepts 101, 110–12, 159–60, 163, 167, 182–3, 189
    Initiate Respond Evaluate sequence 103–4
    in pedagogy 106–7, 159–60, 182–3
    in real-life lived experiences 110–11, 159
    schooled concept (*see* scientific/abstract concepts)
    textbook as resource 107–10
Driver, R. 18–19

education 1, 57. *See also* decolonial education; dialectical education; knowledge; outcomes-based education (OBE); pedagogy(ies)
    democratic discourse in 42–3

social justice in 10, 24–6, 28, 33, 44
transmission of knowledge 58
Educational Renewal Strategy (ERS) 42
Education Research for Social Change journal 27
Eiselen commission of 1951 37
Eleyyan, W. 29
empirical knowledge 51, 99
empirical learning 19–21, 193 n.9. *See also* discovery-based learning
empty signifier 25, 161
Engeström, Y. 117–19
evaluation criteria 53
evaluative episodes 121–2
   collaborative pedagogy 126–8
   defensive pedagogy 129–31
   directive pedagogy 128–9
   reinforcement pedagogy 123–5
everyday concepts 15–22, 83, 87, 99–100. *See also* scientific/abstract concepts
   to abstraction 41, 47–8, 54, 71, 81, 86, 96, 100, 106, 135, 157, 163–5, 180
   in double-move 22
evolutionary learning 119
executive functioning 23. *See also* higher cognitive functions (HCF)
expansive learning 119
exploratory talk 136–7

#feesmustfall movement 8, 24–6, 50, 161
Feuerstein, R.
   and mediated learning experiences 23–4, 162–4, 184–5
   mediation in ZPD 22–3, 28, 106
Flanagan, J. C. 122
fourth industrial revolution, competencies 2, 29
framing 52–3
Freedom Charter (1955) 1, 60
Freire, P. 20, 24, 162–3, 192 n.1
fundamental pedagogics 39–40, 43–8, 53, 58–9, 66–7, 156, 192 n.1. *See also* progressive pedagogics

Gagne 64–5
general genetic law 9, 23, 28, 65, 78, 130, 180

germ cell, developmental method 22, 78–9, 180, 184
Goetze, M. 50
Goodwin, P. 122
group promoting learning 45–6

Halliday, M. A. 78
Hardman, J. 86
Hardman's conceptual figure 158–9, 181
Hedegaard, M. 81–2, 159, 163
   double-move in pedagogy 21–2, 31, 33–4, 97–112
   on scientific and everyday concepts 20, 28, 81–2, 84
Hibbert, L. 27
higher cognitive functions (HCF) 10, 15, 23, 30, 41, 47, 78, 98, 157–8
   content knowledge 98–9
   semiotic mediation in 82
   social interaction 64
   using ICTs 133–4
   word meaning 79
Hilton, A. 133
Hoadley, U. 66

imitation of child 11, 14
information and communication technologies (ICTs) 116–17. *See also* computer-based pedagogy; talk
   coding framework 101–4
   language 134
   as mediating tools 133–4
Initiate, Respond, Evaluate (IRE) sequence 58, 70–1, 103, 125, 135–6
   reinforcement pedagogy episode 123
internalization in development 23, 65
International Mathematics and Science Study (TIMSS) 1

Jacklin, H. 86
Jansen, J. D. 45, 51

Karpov, Y. V. 64
Khanya project 115–16, 120
knowledge. *See also* content knowledge; empirical knowledge
   classification and framing concept 52–3
   decolonial 51

empirical and theoretical 51–2
pedagogic device 52–3
powerful 98

language 134–7
learner-centred pedagogy, 40–1, 45–6, 57–8, 61–2, 192 n.5
learning 2, 12, 19–20, 40–1. *See also* empirical learning; teaching/learning; theoretical learning
learning paradox 65
Lefebvre, H. 27
Leontiev, A. N. 118
lesson plan 187–90
Long, W. 25, 161
Luria, A. R. 82–3

Mann, C. R. 80–1, 94
Marx, K. 26–9, 78
material tools 124, 135, 171
mathematical concepts 115, 130–1, 159
mediated learning experiences (MLE) 23–4, 163–4
mediation 9, 78, 119. *See also* semiotic mediation
　as developmental process 23, 157–8
　of intentionality and reciprocity 24
　learning and creating through 29–30
　of meaning 24
　of transcendence 24
　in zone of proximal development 9–12, 22–3, 157, 160, 162–4
Mercer, N. 79, 137
Mignolo, W. 26, 161
missionary education system 37–8
Morris, A. 86, 91

National Christian Education 45, 58–9
National Curriculum Statement (NCS) 46, 49
National Education Policy Investigation (NEPI) reports 42–3
National Training Board (NTB) 43
National Training Strategy Initiative policy document 43
neo-Vygotskian work 2, 31, 33, 134–5, 160–1
neuroplasticity 23

objective zone of ZPD 13–16
object of activity 39, 50, 62–3, 80, 117–18, 177
obuchenie (teaching/learning) 8–9. *See also* teaching/learning
outcomes-based education (OBE) 43–4, 48, 53, 60–3, 156

pacing 53, 66, 71, 125–6, 172
pedagogy(ies). *See also* curriculum; *specific pedagogies*
　changes from 1994 to 2021 68–74
　classification and framing in 52–3
　definition of 57
　double-move in (*see* double-move)
　fourth IR, competencies 2, 29
　with ICTs 134–5 (*see also* computer-based pedagogy)
　model and training 180–6
　political weapon xi, 168
　in South Africa 7–8
　teacher- *vs.* learner-centred 40–1
　transmission mode of 39, 57, 66–7
peer talk, computer-based/iPad lessons 136–8. *See also* talk
　conceptual acquisition framework 140
　data collection 140–2, 166
　NVIVO and coding analysis 138–9, 142–5
　quantitative/qualitative analysis 138–9
　as teaching tools 133–4
　triangulation and interpretations 138
perceptions of intelligibility 20
perezhivanie 9
performance model curriculum 40–1, 192 n.2
Piaget, J.
　accommodation 30, 63
　on cognitive development 63–4, 84
　concrete operational stage 95
　constructivism, notion of 30–1, 47–9
　disequilibrium 63
　on scientific concepts 15
potential scientific concepts 87–8
powerful knowledge 20, 98
procedural knowledge in concept 18
Progress in International Reading Literacy Study (PIRLS) 1, 77

progressive pedagogics 41
   Curriculum 2005 43–4
   discovery-based learning 48–9, 64, 157, 193 n.9
   fundamental pedagogics to 45, 60–7, 135–7
   group works 45–6
   learner-centred approach 44
   in South Africa 49–50, 60–7
   theoretical foundations of 48
   transformation in curriculum 44–5
Promotion of Bantu Self-Government Act, 1959 38
pseudo-concepts 17
psychological developmental tools 39

radical behaviourism 60
radical constructivism 85
radical-local pedagogy 21–2, 81, 97, 159, 160
Ratele, K. 28, 34
reasoning 16, 30. *See also* critical thinking
reinforcement pedagogy 123–5
relativism 34
#Rhodesmustfall movement 24–5
Ross, G. 22–3
rote learning 58, 69
rules 119, 171–3, 178

Sameroff, A. 8
scaffolding 22–3, 157, 164, 191 n.4
schooled concepts. *See* scientific/abstract concepts
scientific/abstract concepts 16–17, 97, 99–100, 163, 194 n.1. *See also* simple scientific concepts; zone of proximal development (ZPD)
   analytical indicators 86–8
   everyday concepts and 17–18, 25, 41–2, 47–8, 54, 80–4, 155, 159–60, 163–7
      CAPS document 93–4
      wild/farm animals topic, case study 85–95, 99–107
   findings and discussion on topics 89–93
   powerful knowledge 20–1, 52–4
   procedural knowledge 18–19
   as school-based concepts 18–19, 81–4, 98, 159, 182

subject content knowledge 15
teaching content 16, 66, 86
textbook analysis, science concepts 85–95
as theoretical and empirical learning 19–21
verbalism 20
selection 53
semiotic mediation 78
   cognitive outcomes of variation in 82–5
sequencing 53, 71, 118
Shklovskij, V. 27
signifier xi, 25. *See also* empty signifier
signs 39, 119
simple scientific concepts 84–5, 87, 91–3, 95–6, 109
   rating scale for 87–8
social justice in education 10, 24–6, 28, 33, 44
social/psychological space. *See* zone of proximal development (ZPD)
Socio Cultural Discourse Analysis 137
socio-cultural theory 63–7. *See also* cultural-historical theory
South Africa
   Curriculum 2005 46–7
   curriculum reform in 43–8
   educational transformation in 67, 156–7 (*see also* apartheid education system)
   mathematical skill 77, 115–16
   pedagogical transitions in 1, 7–8, 66–73, 155–6
   progressive pedagogy in 49–50, 60–7
   teaching/learning 47–8, 65–6, 160–1
South African Schools Act (1996) 44
spontaneous concepts. *See* everyday concepts
subjective zone of ZPD 13–16
subject of activity 83, 104, 117–19

talk 79, 82–3. *See also* peer talk
   case study design 137–8
   exploratory talk 136–7
   qualitative analysis of 146–52
   timing and concepts 129, 143, 173
   traditional to dialogic pedagogy 135–7
Taylor, N. 40–1
teacher-centred pedagogy 40–1, 57–8

teaching/learning 8–9. *See also* computer-based pedagogy
  analytical framework for 119
  cognitive development 65–6
  computational thinking development 30–1
  cultural historical factors in 66–7
  ICTs for 133–4
  South African context 47–8, 66–7
theoretical knowledge/learning 19–21, 51
third generation activity theory. *See* cultural historical activity theory (CHAT)
Tlostanova, M. 26
tools 39, 53, 78, 178, 116, 119
  computer technology as 116–17, 120–30
  information communication technology 133–4
  language as 134
  linguistic 122–5, 170
  material 124, 135, 171
traditional pedagogy. *See also* fundamental pedagogy
  to dialogic pedagogy 135–7
  language in 135
transformation 7, 31–5, 44
  from fundamental to progressive pedagogy 66–7
transmission-based pedagogy 41, 57, 69
true concepts. *See* scientific/abstract concepts
twenty-first-century pedagogy 29–31
  abstract concepts 95
  African psychology 32
  Black children's education 37
  computer-based lessons (*see* computer-based pedagogy)
  content 31–5
  decolonizing the curriculum 8, 26, 33–5
  double-move in 31–3
  modernity 34
  relativism 34
  Western psychology 32

ubuntu 28, 32–3, 162

verbalism 20, 97
vertical and horizontal discourses 25
Vygotsky, L. S. 1–2
  on cognitive development 63–4, 78–9, 97, 164
  constructivism (*see* constructivism)
  cultural-historical theory 8, 30, 63–7
  everyday and scientific concepts of (*see* everyday concepts; scientific/abstract concepts)
  higher cognitive functions 10, 47, 64, 78–9
  language as tool 134–5
  mediation (*see* mediation)
  obuchenie (teaching/learning) 8–9
  perezhivanie 9
  powerful knowledge 98
  psychological tools 39
  zone of proximal development 9–16, 79–80

Waghid, Z. 27
Walton, E. 26
Watson, John 59–60, 193 n.2
  climate change 86
Wood, D. 22–3
Wragg, E. 122

Young, M. 20–1, 98

Zavala, M. 161
Zippin 3, 25
zone of proximal development (ZPD)
  computer software and mathematics 116
  decolonial pedagogy and 27–8
  double-move in 160
  imitation 11, 14
  instruction 80
  mediation in 9–12, 22–3, 31, 79, 134–5, 157, 160, 163
  objective and subjective zones of 13–16
  as scaffolding tool 33
  scientific concepts in 15–17, 81, 112, 133, 139–40

www.ingramcontent.com/pod-product-compliance
Lightning Source LLC
Chambersburg PA
CBHW062218300426
44115CB00012BA/2125